THE WORLD TEXTILE INDUSTRY

In recent years, the textiles and clothing sector has seen intense competition as a result of increasing globalization. Competitive advantage has become more difficult to sustain in this rapidly changing environment.

The World Textile Industry examines a vital part of the global economy. It focuses on the sources of competitive advantage in textiles and clothing, and considers in detail such factors as input costs, demand conditions, company strategy, organizational structure, chance, and government policy. Applying Michael Porter's framework for analysing the determinants of competitive advantage, John Singleton generates a new framework with which to assess the forces influencing the development of the textiles and clothing sector in the long term.

Providing a fascinating insight into one of the major industries of the world, this volume will be of interest to students and researchers of industrial economics, business and international trade, as well as those interested in the textiles and clothing sector.

John Singleton is Senior Lecturer in Economic History at the Victoria University of Wellington in New Zealand.

ROUTLEDGE COMPETITIVE ADVANTAGE IN WORLD INDUSTRY

Series editor: Maurice Kirby

THE WORLD
TEXTILE INDUSTRY

John Singleton

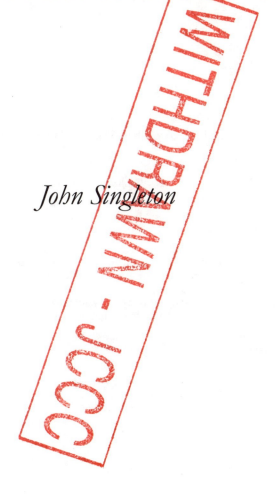

London and New York

First published 1997
by Routledge
11 New Fetter Lane, London EC4P 4EE

Simultaneously published in the USA and Canada
by Routledge
29 West 35th Street, New York, NY 10001

© 1997 John Singleton

Typeset in Garamond by RefineCatch Limited, Bungay, Suffolk
Printed and bound in Great Britain by
Biddles Ltd, Guildford and King's Lynn

British Library Cataloguing in Publication Data
A catalogue record for this book is available from the British Library

Library of Congress Cataloguing in Publication Data
Singleton, John, 1960–
The world textile industry / John Singleton.
p.   cm.   (Routledge competitive advantage in world industry)
Includes bibliographical references and index.
1. Textile industry.   2. Clothing trade.   I. Series.
HD9850.5.S56   1997
338.4'7677–dc20   96–31745
CIP

ISBN 0–415–10767–9 (hbk)

CONTENTS

TABLES

ACKNOWLEDGEMENTS

I would like to thank Maurice Kirby for suggesting that I write this book. Douglas Farnie read and commented upon all of the draft chapters in some detail, for which I am very grateful. Paul Robertson kindly commented upon most of the chapters and I also received helpful advice at various stages from Takeshi Abe, Gordon Boyce and Kent Deng. Wools of New Zealand allowed me to use their library. Tables 1.1 (p. 14) and 1.2 (p. 15) are taken from UNIDO (1993), *Handbook of Industrial Statistics 1992*, Aldershot: Edward Elgar, pp. 62–3, and are reprinted by permission of Edward Elgar and UNIDO. Tables 1.3 (p. 16) and 1.4 (p. 17) are taken from GATT (1994), *International Trade: Trends and Statistics 1994*, Geneva: GATT, p. 80, and are reprinted by permission of the World Trade Organization. Table 2.1 (p. 27) is taken from G. Clark (1987) 'Why isn't the whole world developed?', *Journal of Economic History* 47, 1, p. 150, and is reprinted by permission of Cambridge University Press. Table 2.2 (p. 30) is taken from Fred Deyo, *Beneath the Miracle: Labor Subordination in the New Asian Industrialism*, p. 184. © 1989 The Regents of the University of California. Reprinted by permission. Table 2.3 (p. 47) is taken from Richard R. Nelson (ed.), *National Innovation Systems: A Comparative Analysis*, pp. 238–9. © 1993 Oxford University Press, Inc. Reprinted by permission. Table 3.1 (p. 55) is taken from J. Coker (1993) 'World textile and clothing consumption: forecasts to 2002', *Textile Outlook International*. Permission requested from the publishers. Table 5.1 (p. 104) is taken from M. Lücke (1993) 'The diffusion of process innovations in industrialized and developing countries: a case study of the world textile and steel industries', *World Development* 21, 7, pp. 1232–5, and is reprinted with kind permission from Elsevier Science Ltd, The Boulevard, Langford Lane, Kidlington OX5 1GB, UK. Table 6.1 (p. 125) is taken from A. D. Chandler (1986) 'The evolution of modern global competition', in M. E. Porter (ed.) *Competition in Global Industries*, and is reprinted by permission of Harvard Business School Press. Table 8.1 (p. 179) is taken from W. R. Cline (1990), *The Future of World Trade in Textiles and Apparel*, revised edition, p. 163, reprinted by permission of the Institute for International Economics.

1
COMPETITIVE ADVANTAGE IN TEXTILES

International trade in textiles and clothing is conducted on an immense scale. Textile and clothing producers were responsible for 9.3 per cent of world exports of manufactures in 1993 (GATT 1994: 79, 83). Barriers to entry for new firms and exporters are low, and consequently the degree of international competition is intense. Competitive advantage is very difficult to sustain for long periods of time. Successful exporters of basic products are speedily challenged by newcomers, and they must redirect their activities towards the production of higher value-added textiles and clothing in order to survive and prosper. Many businesses are ephemeral, but this hardly matters because there has never been a shortage of new firms bidding to replace them. Recent decades have witnessed an increase in the globalization of the textile and apparel industries, in so far as production units in several countries may cooperate in the manufacture of a given item. For example, wool could be grown in New Zealand, then spun and woven in Germany, made into a jumper in Morocco and sold to a consumer in Holland. The German firm may either own or have a cooperation agreement with the Moroccan garment maker, and it may also have close ties with the Dutch retailer. In many other cases, international transactions in intermediate textile products are conducted in an impersonal manner through the market. The textile and apparel sector has many facets and these are constantly changing. The rapidity of change adds to the interest of investigating this segment of world industry.

Competitive advantage in textiles and clothing is the theme of this volume. What factors are likely to give the textile and clothing industries of a certain region a competitive advantage in the international market? Are these factors constant or do they vary according to such circumstances as the overall level of economic development of the region in question? What causes some regions to lose their competitive advantage? What can be done to create a competitive advantage where it does not yet exist? All of these questions are important and each deserves a thoughtful answer. In attempting to provide answers, this book makes use of a framework developed by Michael Porter for analysing the determinants of competitive advantage. For

1

the sake of convenience, this will be referred to as the 'diamond framework'. As we shall see, the diamond framework is a useful organizational tool. It draws together, in a simple form, a great deal of wisdom about the causes of industrial success.

This introductory chapter proceeds by outlining and discussing the diamond framework in the context of some other approaches to understanding the dynamics of competitive advantage. A brief account is given of the evolution of the textile and clothing industries, and an overview is provided of the competitive environment in which they operate in the 1990s. Finally, an attempt is made to explain the main forces influencing the long-run development of the textile sector. The results of this exercise indicate that the diamond framework must be imagined and applied in an evolutionary manner. This accords with Porter's own explanation of the unfolding of competitive advantage. The following chapters employ the categories of the diamond framework to analyse the textile and clothing sector in more detail.

THE GEOMETRY OF COMPETITIVE ADVANTAGE

In *The Competitive Advantage of Nations* (1990) Michael Porter develops a framework to illustrate the factors which influence the competitive advantage of industries. This approach builds on his earlier work in closely related areas (Porter 1980; 1985). Competitive advantage is defined in terms of a country's ability to gain a significant share of world export markets in a certain product. Porter uses the diamond framework to organize his analysis of the performance of the industrial sectors of eight countries up to, and including, 1985. The diamond consists of four elements: factor conditions, demand conditions, related and supporting industries, and firm strategy, structure and rivalry. Competitive advantage is affected by the state of these four elements and by the interaction between them. However, competitive advantage is also influenced by two further sets of forces which hover outside the diamond, namely, government policy and chance. It could be argued that a hexagonal framework would have been more appropriate. But Porter separates government policy and chance from the diamond because these are largely exogenous forces whereas, in many respects, factor conditions, demand conditions, related and supporting industries, and firm strategy, structure and rivalry are determined endogenously.

Each element of the diamond framework can be broken down into subcategories. For instance, factor conditions refers to the quantity and the quality of various inputs. A detailed consideration of factor conditions would involve the analysis of each important input. Firm strategy, structure and rivalry is a category with such a rich content that it has been given two chapters in this book, one focusing on strategy and the other on structure. Thus, Porter's diamond has been transformed, first into a hexagon, and now into a heptagon. I make no claim (other than that of convenience) for

2

Singleton's heptagon, and will continue to refer to the diamond throughout this book.

The diamond is a taxonomy rather than a theory. It assists the investigator to arrange the evidence, but it does not supply a ready-made theory of what determines competitive advantage. The inclusiveness of the diamond framework does, however, militate against the adoption of monocausal explanations. Attention is drawn to interactions between the elements of the diamond. Each component receives a different weight, according to which industry, in which country, is under discussion. This apparent looseness has both advantages and disadvantages. Porter (1994: 428–9) argues that the diamond framework encourages researchers to be more flexible, enabling them to attain greater realism. There is no temptation to twist evidence to fit preconceived theories when using the diamond framework. Although Porter is critical of standard economic methodology, he concedes that formal statistical techniques may be of value in checking the conclusions derived from the use of the diamond framework. The danger with the diamond is that it could foster too much flexibility, leading to prevarication and *ad-hocery*. So many forces are at work in the diamond that it may be difficult to identify the most important ones. While such pitfalls must be guarded against, those who are experienced in the techniques of economic history should welcome the freedom offered by the diamond.

As the titles of Porter's books suggest, competition is the spirit activating the diamond and preventing it from becoming a collection of empty boxes. Firms must compete in order to survive. They compete in one of two ways (or a mixture of the two): through cost minimization or through the manufacture of differentiated products of higher value. A competitive advantage due to low costs, such as cheap labour, is difficult to sustain, because success leads to the bidding-up of input costs relative to those faced by emerging competitors in other countries. But a competitive advantage based on product differentiation and high quality is less vulnerable to rapid erosion. Continual upgrading is necessary to maintain this competitive advantage, however. Each firm must choose which path to take in the quest for competitive advantage. Indeed, each business must make a series of choices relating to strategy during its lifespan. Early choices may constrain the firm's options later on. The ability of a firm's leaders to make consistently good choices in a shifting environment is likely to be an important factor in its success (ibid.: 430, 434). Although the overall condition of the industry affects the prospects of individual firms, their future is at least partly in their own hands. Lazonick (1993: 2–9) hints that Porter's treatment of competition may be contradictory. Porter stresses strong domestic rivalry, but he also produces evidence of cooperation among firms within regional clusters in such activities as the training of personnel, the collection and dissemination of information and the establishment of standards. This is a false dichotomy. There is nothing to stop firms from competing in some activities and

3

cooperating in others. Such cooperation may assist the region as a whole to overcome competition from outsiders.

Firms build and sustain competitive advantage in world markets by establishing a strong home base and by continually improving the quality of their inputs, processes, products and distribution networks. Such upgrading adds greater amounts of value at each stage of the value chain, extending from the provision of inputs to final delivery to the consumer. Firms, their suppliers (including workers) and their customers share in the benefits of upgrading. All firms have some freedom to upgrade themselves, but in some respects they are at the mercy of exogenous forces. The quality of the school system, and the transport and communications networks, affect the firm's ability to upgrade and generate more value. In many cases these activities are under the control of the government. Unless the government upgrades the areas of the business environment which it controls, the plans of industrialists may be frustrated. Similarly, unexpected events, such as the outbreak of war, may affect the capacity of firms to develop their competitive advantage. There is a strong element of circularity in Porter's argument. The diamond framework summarizes the firm's environment at a given moment, and this constrains the choices open to its decision-makers. The firm's choice of strategy then reacts upon the features of the diamond, and so on. Although this circularity could be regarded as a weakness, it merely reflects the practical difficulty of separating cause and effect over intervals of time. Success or failure in the struggle to upgrade in one round affects the composition of the diamond which confronts the firm at the beginning of the next round of the competitive process. This suggests that there is a tendency for both success and failure to be cumulative, barring unexpected developments in the environment (such as an invention) or a revolution in the firm's business strategy. A faltering enterprise would seem to have a strong incentive to develop a new strategy, although its leaders may become so blinkered or despondent that they fail to identify the correct antidote to decline. An enterprise with a record of success in the recent past may become complacent and neglect further opportunities, unconsciously falling into a downward spiral.

Regions occupy an important place in Porter's analysis. For individual industries, it is likely that a region within a nation will be the setting of the diamond framework. Of course, entities such as Hong Kong and Singapore are too small to contain regions, but this does not detract from the overall value of this approach. Clusters of related industries gather in successful regions and provide each other with support and a spur to further achievement. Within these clusters, external economies are generated, and firms in related trades cooperate for mutual gain. For example, textile machinery makers and weavers could work together to perfect a new type of loom. In the textile sector, clustering may not be necessary for the initial attainment of competitive advantage, which frequently stems from low labour costs, but the development of a resilient cluster of supporting industries may be essential for the maintenance of competitive advantage in the long run, once labour costs have risen. Even those firms which compete on a global level, owning several foreign subsidiaries and coordinating production and sales according to a world strategy, can derive substantial benefits from the presence of strong clusters of supporting industries in their home regions. Porter fundamentally disagrees with Reich (1991), who argues that home regions no longer matter to the increasingly footloose global organizations of the late twentieth century. According to Reich, these corporations purchase expertise and other inputs wherever in the world they can be found in the right quality at the right price. We need not make an inflexible choice between these alternatives. In practice, we would expect to observe a range of behaviour among firms. Some will be more footloose, others less so. The more detailed and accurate the information flowing into the firm from around the world, the more disposable its home base is likely to be.

Towards the end of *The Competitive Advantage of Nations*, Porter (1990: 683–734) offers prescriptions to each of the eight nations in his care. Although the details of this advice vary from patient to patient, the underlying message is broadly the same: firms and governments should give a higher priority to upgrading those parts of the diamond for which they are responsible. This involves the creation of more effective systems of education, curbs on the waste of taxpayers' money in unproductive areas, rising investment, a greater commitment to R&D, and so on. Porter explains that these strategies are followed in Japan as a matter of course. Other countries should try to be more like Japan, regardless of how difficult this may be in the short and medium terms. Such conclusions place *The Competitive Advantage of Nations* firmly in the mainstream of late twentieth-century academic advice to government and business.

How are we to assess the diamond framework as a contribution to the analysis of competitive advantage? *The Competitive Advantage of Nations* is already a historical document. It describes the world in 1985. As such, it will be an invaluable resource for future economic historians. Those who are interested in the world in 1996, 2006 or 1896 must take care to distinguish between the diamond framework itself and Porter's use of the diamond to discuss the situation prevailing in eight countries in the mid-1980s. The diamond framework ought to be of considerable assistance in the analysis of the development of particular industries and regions. The main purpose of this book is to employ the diamond to aid our understanding of long-run growth and change in the textile complexes of the world. Before proceeding, we shall discuss some of Porter's forerunners and competitors in this quest, so that the diamond can be put into context.

One of the characteristics of the diamond framework is that it makes an explicit link between microeconomic and macroeconomic factors. When the diamond framework is used to investigate long-run industrial change, it is necessary to consider the interaction between the business history of particular firms and the economic history of the nation. This approach has a long history. Karl Marx (1970), in the first volume of *Capital*, gave a detailed account of the strategies of firms in the Lancashire cotton industry during the mid-nineteenth century, and explained how their behaviour was both a cause and an effect of the rapid growth of the national economy. Marx portrayed economic growth in capitalist societies as a process driven by competition between firms, and he treated the cotton mills as the representative modern businesses. But the dominant tendency, in the late nineteenth century, was for economists to enter increasingly narrow specialisms, and the study of individual firms and industries was allocated a separate and distant compartment from the study of economic development. During the twentieth century, the introduction of the terms 'microeconomics' and 'macroeconomics' gave sanction to this process of disintegration. Economic and business historians were less hampered by these doctrinal issues and, as we shall discover, their work continued to give credit to individual businesses, and more often industries, for bringing about wider economic changes. Since the apparent failure of macroeconomic management in the 1970s, mainstream economists have taken a greater interest in the search for the microeconomic origins of national prosperity, and it is against this background that Porter's synthesis has emerged. It could be said that Porter was moving into territory which was already partially occupied by business and economic historians.

Alfred Chandler (1962; 1977; 1990), the leading figure in the development of business history, focuses on the detailed analysis of the strategy and organizational structure of individual businesses. This marks a significant departure from the strictly narrative approach of most company history. Chandler argues that changes in the strategy and structure of the firm could have a powerful effect on the development of the national economy. Writing from an American perspective, Chandler concludes that the economic strength of a nation depends upon the emergence of vast multidivisional business corporations, such as Du Pont and General Motors, managed by professionally trained executives. These corporations become vertically integrated, in order to insulate themselves from the worst uncertainties of the market, and develop aggressive long-term strategies instead of merely reacting to short-term shifts in demand. Many major American business corporations originated in the late nineteenth and early twentieth centuries, in industries which, for technological reasons, required lavish investments in fixed capital and high levels of throughput in order to minimize unit fixed costs. They enjoyed large economies of scale in production and distribution. As they widened their product ranges and diversified into related areas, these firms introduced a multidivisional management structure. While a head office concentrated on dealing with strategic and financial issues, operational decisions, including questions of output and price, rested in the hands of the managers of the product divisions. The Chandlerian blueprint inevitably calls into question the rationality of other forms of business organization, especially the seemingly amateur family firm, which remained a prominent feature of the industrial scene in Britain, much of continental Europe and Asia. Chandler's latest book, *Scale and Scope* (1990), compares American, British and German businesses, and their management structures, between the mid-nineteenth and mid-twentieth centuries. His conclusions are much to the detriment of the British. The Germans occupy an intermediate position between the modernistic Americans and the nepotistic Britons. It should be pointed out that Chandler makes no attempt to apply his blueprint to the Asian economies. Also, Chandler stresses that the large corporation has fewer advantages in those industries, such as textiles and apparel, served by technologies that do not generate large economies of scale (ibid.: 22). Chandler's approach is much narrower than that of Porter. Sustained competitive advantage is an attribute of the multidivisional corporation, according to Chandler. But Porter confines strategy and structure to one corner of the diamond framework.

Lazonick (1990; 1991; 1992; Mass and Lazonick 1991; Lazonick and West 1995) modifies the Chandlerian framework by paying greater attention to the role of labour and the work process, and by applying the resulting synthesis to the economic histories of the UK, USA and Japan. The goal of Lazonick is to explain how industrial leadership passed from Britain to the USA in the late nineteenth century, and then from the USA to Japan in the late twentieth century. Rather curiously, in the light of Chandler's scepticism about the need for large corporations in textiles and the fact that the textile industry has been in relative decline in Japan since 1945, Lazonick chooses this sector as one of his most important case studies. Lazonick compares the typical labour regimes of British, US and Japanese firms across a variety of industries. Craft workers in British family firms possessed considerable authority on the shopfloor, and cooperated with managers in the exploitation of unskilled labour. When British firms encountered severe competition from abroad, owners and craftsmen simply increased the workloads of the unskilled operatives. For a time the British could attain higher levels of efficiency by these means, without the expense of investing in new technology. Britain was locked into this pattern of behaviour, partly by the opposition of craft unions to any loss of status and partly by the unwillingness of family firms to combine into stronger corporations along American lines. Chandlerian corporations, in the USA, adopted what are now called Fordist methods on the shopfloor. Although labour was paid high wages, the corporations attacked the privileges of skilled craftsmen and turned American workers into mindless automatons chained to assembly lines. This transformation gave the USA a competitive advantage over the UK and other European countries in most industries. But the American system proved vulnerable in the long run. American corporations used advanced technology, but they failed to win the willing cooperation of their workers, who harboured an understandable resentment against their dictatorial employers. American firms faced a new challenge from Japan in the 1960s and 1970s. Since they lacked flexibility and the goodwill of their employees, many American firms were unable to respond in a positive way to this foreign threat. The post-war success of Japanese capitalism, argues Lazonick, is the result of a combination of the professionally managed corporation with a more humane attitude towards labour relations. Japanese workers were made to feel that they counted. They were encouraged to retain their skills and to employ them for the good of the company. Skilful and well-disposed workers were a great asset. Their presence made it easier for managers to modify their production plans in the light of changing market conditions. Lazonick certainly paints a glowing picture of factory life in Japan. By contrast, US corporations were locked into inflexible planning schedules, due to the monolithic nature of their organizational structures and the absence of skills and motivation on the shopfloor. Both Britain and the USA experienced a remarkable degree of success until they had the misfortune to meet a competitor possessing superior organizational structures.

Like Chandler, Lazonick focuses on just one corner of the diamond framework. In view of East Asia's growing role in the world economy, it is important to find out how far Japanese business systems are replicated in other parts of this region. Hong Kong is a society of smallish family firms, in many ways reminiscent of early Victorian Britain. South Korea possesses some major corporations, the *chaebol*, which are superficially similar to large Japanese businesses. But the *chaebol* also have a reputation for violent labour repression, unlike Lazonick's idealized Japanese firms. Taiwanese business structures exhibit traits which combine elements of the Hong Kong and South Korean systems. At a time when a group of Asian countries, deploying a variety of business strategies and structures, are entering the ranks of the developed world, the relevance of a framework which reaches its apotheosis in the Japan of the 1980s may be short-lived.

A strong current of thought emphasizes the links between innovation and competitive advantage. A study of leading US, European and Asian corporations in a number of industries, between 1960 and 1986, concludes that R&D spending as a share of revenue was a key determinant of changes in these firms' shares of world markets (Franko 1989). Innovation may have an effect upon all four corners of the diamond. Technical innovation is likely to have most impact on the textile and clothing sector through the acquisition of new machinery, and this involves two elements of the diamond, namely, factor inputs, and related and supporting industries. Firms in the textile sector rarely manufacture their own equipment. Innovation could influence demand factors, if the introduction of a new product or style were to stimulate a response from consumers. Firm strategy and structure may affect the propensity of businesses to generate innovations and to remain open to the adoption of those originating elsewhere. Innovation is the driving force of economic development in the work of Joseph Schumpeter. His definition of innovations or 'new combinations' is a broad one, including new products, processes, markets, raw materials and structures (Heertje 1977: 97–8). Schumpeter changed his mind about the connection between firm strategy and structure and innovativeness. The early Schumpeter stressed that pioneering individual entrepreneurs were responsible for searching out and implementing new concepts (Schumpeter 1961: 57–94). Later in his career, he put forward the opposite view that large corporations were the greatest innovators because they could devote more resources to the quest for new products and processes. As a result of the development of modern capitalism, the scale of business activity had increased, and major corporations replaced entrepreneurs as the leading innovators (Schumpeter 1950: 131–42).

Utterback (1994) argues that organizational sophistication and innovative success may not be closely related, especially in the early stages of the development of a radically new process or product. Utterback suggests that the most important innovations are likely to come from unexpected quarters. Current market leaders tend to confine their research to well-worn paths, partly because they wish to minimize disruption to their operations, whereas newcomers have fewer sunk costs in old technology and are in a better position to engage in lateral thinking. For instance, firms which had invested in equipment to cut up icebergs and transport blocks of ice across the oceans, failed to take advantage of the appearance of refrigerators at the end of the nineteenth century. It may take some time for a dominant design of a new product or process to appear. Once a dominant design has emerged, but not before, there are opportunities for firms to experiment with mass production and travel along the Chandlerian trajectory of increasing scale and scope. Process innovations tend to be more common than product innovations in textiles and other non-assembled product industries. For Utterback, the key to the creation of competitive advantage is the early capture of the dominant design. Richard Arkwright achieved this objective, at least for a while, with his water frame in cotton spinning in the late eighteenth century, as did Courtaulds with rayon in the early twentieth century.

Ultimately, the differences between those scholars, such as Chandler and Lazonick, who stress that organization is the foundation of competitive advantage, and those, including Schumpeter and Utterback, who claim that innovation should be given priority, are ones of nuance. Technology and organization are closely related. Use of the diamond framework enables the interactions between these two factors, and their relationships with other factors, to be analysed without resort to preconceived notions about the strength and direction of causation.

The writers discussed above take a rather narrow view of the determinants of competitive advantage. We now examine work which, because of its

9

more comprehensive nature, has closer parallels with the contribution of Porter. Alfred Marshall (1921) considered in depth the various factors responsible for the development of industry and trade in the UK, France, Germany and the USA, over the longer term. Like Porter, Marshall recognized the importance of clusters of related industries at the regional level (ibid.: 599). The spinning and weaving industries of northern England attracted textile engineering companies and marketing firms to this region during the nineteenth century. Consequently, this textile complex was strengthened, at least in the period before the First World War. Prominence is given to differences in national culture, in Marshall's explanation of the timing and nature of industrialization in the leading Western nations. English determination and initiative helped this nation to become an industrial pioneer (ibid.: 32–85). The French were a more artistic nation, and their industries were differentiated from those of Britain by an emphasis on design and craftsmanship (ibid.: 107–20). The Germans, respected for their thoroughness, made science the foundation of their industrial success (ibid.: 121–39). And, in America, the dynamism of the entrepreneur, combined with a huge domestic market, led to the emergence of mass production (ibid.: 140–62). Marshall did not dwell upon Japan, although he was very optimistic about its prospects of becoming a major industrial power (ibid.: 161). While rivalry between these nations was intense, each had a distinctive competitive advantage, and therefore each found a substantial niche in the world economy. Porter (1990: 109) does not share Marshall's strong interest in the industrial consequences of national culture, while admitting that it plays some part in determining company strategy. Since Marshall lacks a diamond, *Industry and Trade* has a less sharply focused structure than *The Competitive Advantage of Nations*. But Marshall's systematic analysis of the elements of competitive advantage in four major economies bears obvious comparisons with Porter's study of competitive advantage in eight countries.

Among more recent authors, Landes provides an extensive historical analysis of many of the factors discussed in the diamond framework. In *The Unbound Prometheus* (1969), Landes explains the evolution of competitive advantage in a range of major European industries between 1750 and the 1960s. Landes demonstrates how significant differences emerged in the ability of certain countries to upgrade their industries and to introduce more advanced products and processes. According to Landes, the UK was starting to become an industrial laggard by the end of the Victorian era. A similar conclusion is reached by Porter in his brief account of Britain's woes (1990: 481–507). Landes, the author of an ambitious comparative industrial history, could hardly fail to examine demand conditions, the supply of inputs, related and supporting industries, the strategy, structure and rivalry of firms, government policy, and chance. In a sense, the composition of the diamond is so obvious, and all-embracing, that it must be implicit in earlier work on competitive advantage. Porter's achievement is to make an implicit framework explicit. This has obvious presentational advantages. Whether this exercise in repackaging results in a fundamental improvement in our understanding of competitive advantage is more questionable.

We have already noted that it is difficult to find an approach to the analysis of business which can be applied with equal facility throughout the world. A recent collection of essays on East Asia (Fitzgerald 1994) casts some doubt on the usefulness of the diamond framework in the context of Asia. Suzuki (1994) claims that Porter goes overboard in his eulogy of the Japanese economic system. By choosing 1985 as the year for his cross-sectional study, Porter catches the Japanese economy at a particularly favourable moment. Clusters of industries which appear invulnerable, on the basis of 1985 figures, are less robust when viewed from a longer-term perspective, argues Suzuki. Japanese industries do not always succeed in their attempts to upgrade and add value. High costs of production are a real disadvantage, and other Asian countries are able to undercut Japan in a large number of industries. Consequently, Japan's position in the world economy is far from impregnable. An examination of the industrial development of Hong Kong since 1945 concludes that the colony prospered in spite of its lack of a favourable constellation of diamond factors. Hong Kong businesses did not enjoy access to a sophisticated domestic market. Many of the more complex inputs for its industries had to be imported. Its manufacturing sector was dominated by networks of modestly sized family firms, as opposed to large Western- or Japanese-style corporations. Furthermore, chance played a vital role in the growth of Hong Kong. One need only refer to the influx of the Shanghainese entrepreneurs in the late 1940s and early 1950s, the colony's survival during the period of tension between the West and China, and the economic reforms on the mainland since 1978 to illustrate the importance of exogenous factors in Hong Kong's success. Perhaps chance should be given an equal role in Hong Kong's diamond (or pentagon), instead of being viewed as a vague influence floating above it (Redding 1994). South Korea is examined by Cho (1994), who finds one diamond inadequate, and therefore employs two diamonds to analyse the growth of Korean industry. The first diamond comprises endowed resources, the business environment, related and supporting industries, and domestic demand. The second diamond consists of human factors, namely, workers, politicians and bureaucrats, entrepreneurs, and professional managers and engineers. At successive stages in the expansion of the Korean economy, the human diamond was dominated by different groups of people. As an underdeveloped economy, in the 1950s, South Korea had few human assets except cheap labour, and unskilled workers formed the crucial element of the human diamond in this period. Next, the intervention of politicians and bureaucrats was required to stimulate the development process. Thirdly, an entrepreneurial class emerged to take advantage of the new opportunities arising from the beginnings of growth. Finally, as the Korean economy approached maturity, modern business corporations took over from individual entrepreneurs. Like Porter, Cho makes room for chance as a significant exogenous factor. This double diamond is another interesting geometrical development in the study of competitive advantage. Its principal merit is that it explicitly incorporates time into the diamond framework. Although Suzuki, Redding and Cho do not conclude that Porter's diamond framework should be abandoned, they argue that it may require substantial modification to take account of diverse environments. Given the inherent flexibility of the diamond, this does not present a grave problem.

The diamond framework has both strengths and weaknesses. On the positive side, the diamond provides a means of integrating microeconomic and macroeconomic influences, it emphasizes clustering and firm strategy and structure, it is extremely comprehensive and it is highly flexible, to the extent that it is possible to alter the geometry without undermining its underlying purpose. On the negative side, it could be argued that the diamond framework is so flexible that it provides the researcher with little guidance. But a framework is neither a model nor a theory; it is similar to the scaffolding on a building site. The scaffolding is a network of poles and planks which exists for the convenience and safety of the builders, but it does not dictate the quality or appearance of the finished building. Seen in this light, the diamond may be of considerable value, and it is in such a spirit that it is used in this book.

THE TEXTILES AND CLOTHING SECTOR

Unlike the manufacture of items such as aircraft and computers, the production of textiles and clothing has been carried on for many thousands of years. Garments are a necessity. Without access to clothing, human beings would find it much more difficult to survive, not least because of their vulnerability to the elements. Textiles have also been required for many other purposes, including sails for ships and bandages for wounds. The production of a garment usually involves a number of distinct activities. First, the fibre must be grown and harvested. Second, the fibre is cleaned and prepared for use. Third, the fibre is spun into long, thin strands called yarn. Fourth, vertical (warp) and horizontal (weft) lengths of yarn are woven into a fabric. Knitting is an alternative at this stage. Fifth, the fabric is bleached, dyed or printed, and possibly treated in other ways to improve its qualities (in some cases dyeing occurs before weaving). Sixth, the fabric is made up into a garment. Transport and marketing services are utilized at several intermediate stages. Until quite recently, even in developed countries, the manufacture of clothing often took place within the household. As late as the 1960s and 1970s, many women spent a significant proportion of their time in the sewing and knitting of garments for family members. Herodotus (1972: 142), writing in the fifth century BC, claimed that in Egypt the sexual division of labour was the opposite of that prevailing in most societies. Egyptian women went out to trade in the market while their husbands stayed at home spinning and weaving. The trend away from the domestic manufacture of clothing is mainly due to the rising opportunity cost of devoting time to this activity.

I can give only a summary account of the evolution of the world textile and clothing sector. Suffice it to say that fibres and cloth have long been an important component of regional and international trade. For instance, raw silk was exported by caravan from China to the Mediterranean in the third century BC (L. Casson 1984: 256) and Dalmatian underwear was imported by Roman-occupied Palestine (Safrai 1994: 389). By the thirteenth century, there was a thriving export trade in woollen cloth, of varying quality, from Flanders and northern France to the Mediterranean (Chorley 1987). England established itself as an important exporter of woollen cloth to continental Europe in the fifteenth century (Power 1942; Coleman 1977: 49). Exotic silks and cottons were imported by Europe from Asia. Textiles tended to be produced by cottage workers, although in China there were large imperial silk factories before the sixteenth century. A complex network of merchants, middlemen and carriers was needed to organize the distribution of inputs and outputs at each stage of the production process, and to supply working capital to lubricate this system. The mechanisms by which merchants arranged the activities of rural and urban outworkers were quite similar in China and northern England (Wadsworth and Mann 1931; L. M. Li 1981: 37–61). The textile sector commenced its transformation from a traditional cottage industry, powered by human muscles, into a modern factory industry, powered by water and steam, in the eighteenth century. This revolution was due to a favourable conjuncture between rising demand and a quickening pace of technical development (Chapman 1987). Britain took the lead in the mechanization of textile production and, in the first half of the nineteenth century, a similar path was trod by continental Europe and the USA. Japan and India commenced the process of mechanization in the second half of the nineteenth century. The twentieth century saw the introduction of man-made fibres, most notably rayon and nylon. In the 1950s, the USA was the largest manufacturer of textiles in the capitalist world, producing a higher output than the combined totals of its two nearest rivals, the UK and Japan. But it is important to note that, although the American textile industry was the biggest in the world, it did not possess a strong competitive advantage. Britain, Japan and France each exported more textiles than the USA in 1955 (Maizels 1963: 341–2). Asia has built a new competitive advantage in world textiles during the twentieth century. Japan, India and China were joined by Hong Kong, South Korea, Taiwan, Indonesia, Malaysia and others, as major producers during the 1950s and subsequent decades. Since the commencement of economic reform, in 1978, China has established a formidable presence in world export markets for textiles and clothing. China has the potential, given its low wages and huge labour force, to sweep aside much of the competition in low-grade textiles and garments. During the twentieth century, the textile and clothing mills of developed countries have been forced to upgrade (or retreat) into niche markets, and to press for protection, in order to survive. Asia was a net exporter of textiles to Britain and Western Europe, until the Industrial Revolution, so perhaps we are merely witnessing the restoration of an earlier pattern of trade.

Tables 1.1 and 1.2 display the shares of the fifteen leading textile and apparel producers in world value added in 1980 and 1990. Naturally, large economies appear towards the top of each table. Selling at home is easier than exporting, due to transport costs, differences in taste and the effects of tariffs and quotas. A better idea of a country's competitive advantage is given by its share of world exports, and this is the indicator favoured by Porter. Table 1.3 shows the world market shares of the leading exporters of textiles. It may seem surprising that a high-income country such as Germany occupies a strong position. In accounting for Germany's leadership, and for the respectable standing of other wealthy European countries and the USA, it is necessary to point out that trade in textiles and clothing has been riddled with controls, including the Multi Fibre Arrangement (MFA). The MFA

Table 1.1 Share of fifteen leading producers in world textile production, 1980, 1990

Country	1980 (%)	Country	1990 (%)
United States	15.9	United States	17.0
Japan	11.0	Italy	9.5
Italy	9.0	Japan	9.3
Germany (FR)	6.4	Germany (FR)	5.8
France	6.0	India	5.8
India	4.9	France	4.4
United Kingdom	4.2	United Kingdom	3.7
Brazil	3.7	Turkey	3.7
Spain	3.3	Spain	3.2
Mexico	2.8	Brazil	3.0
Argentina	1.9	Korea (Rep. of)	2.7
Taiwan Province	1.8	Mexico	2.5
Korea (Rep. of)	1.7	Taiwan Province	1.9
Turkey	1.7	Argentina	1.6
Yugoslavia	1.6	Canada	1.6
Sum of above	75.9	Sum of above	75.7

Source: UNIDO (1993: 62)
Note: Percentage share in world total value added excluding Eastern Europe, the USSR and China, at constant 1980 prices

permits economically advanced countries to moderate the growth of imports from the developing nations. These controls encourage the substitution of trade between the developed countries for trade between developed and developing countries. Members of the European Union (EU) discriminate in favour of textiles and apparel supplied by other member states. Germany, for example, has won orders in the EU which could otherwise have gone to South Korea or Hong Kong. Even this is no mean achievement. It shows that the German textile industry has secured a competitive advantage over those of other advanced European states, such as the UK and France. Germany has achieved this success, partly by upgrading its products and processes and partly by subcontracting the more labour-intensive parts of textile production to poorer countries in Eastern Europe, the Mediterranean and Asia (Spinanger and Piatti 1994). The performance of Japan is perhaps more impressive than the figures in Table 1.3 would suggest, since Japan has been one of the countries discriminated against under the MFA and other restrictive measures. In a world of complete free trade, the newly industrializing Asian countries would attain a considerably higher share of global textile markets. Between 1980 and 1993, the countries showing the most marked increases in world market share were South Korea, China, Taiwan, Pakistan and Indonesia. Their relative advance was at the expense of the

Table 1.2 Share of fifteen leading producers in world wearing apparel production, 1980, 1990

Country	1980 (%)	Country	1990 (%)
United States	24.2	United States	25.8
Italy	11.2	Italy	10.8
Germany (FR)	8.3	Japan	6.3
France	6.6	Germany (FR)	6.0
Japan	6.5	United Kingdom	5.3
United Kingdom	4.6	France	5.2
Spain	4.2	Hong Kong	4.0
Hong Kong	2.6	India	3.9
India	2.4	Spain	3.5
Canada	2.3	Korea (Rep. of)	2.4
Brazil	1.9	Canada	2.3
Mexico	1.9	Yugoslavia	2.0
Yugoslavia	1.5	Mexico	1.9
Switzerland	1.4	Brazil	1.5
Belgium	1.3	Belgium	1.4
Sum of above	80.9	Sum of above	82.3

Source: UNIDO (1993: 63)
Note: Percentage share in world total value added excluding Eastern Europe, the USSR and China, at constant 1980 prices

15

Table 1.3 Fifteen leading exporters of textiles, 1993

Country	Value (US$bn)	Share in world exports (%)		Average annual change (%)	Share of textiles in economy's merchandise exports (%)	
	1993	1980	1993	1980–93	1980	1993
Germany	11.9	11.4	10.3	5	3.3	3.1
Hong Kong	11.2	—	—	15	8.7	8.3
domestic exports	2.1	1.7	1.8	7	6.6	7.3
re-exports	9.1	—	—	20	13.0	8.6
Italy	10.0	7.6	8.7	7	5.3	5.6
Korea (Rep. of)	9.0	4.0	7.8	11	12.6	10.9
China[a]	8.7	4.6	7.5	10	14.0	9.5
Chinese Taipei (Taiwan)	8.2	3.2	7.1	12	9.0	9.7
Japan	6.7	9.3	5.8	2	3.9	1.9
Belgium–Luxembourg[b]	6.5	6.5	5.5	5	5.5	5.2
United States	6.0	6.8	5.2	4	1.7	1.3
France	5.4	6.2	4.7	4	3.0	2.6
United Kingdom	4.1	5.7	3.5	2	2.8	2.3
Pakistan	3.5	1.6	3.0	11	33.5	52.4
India[b]	2.9	2.1	2.5	8	13.3	15.0
The Netherlands	2.6	4.1	2.3	1	3.1	1.9
Indonesia	2.6	0.1	2.3	37	0.2	7.2
Above 15	90.2	74.9	78.1	—	—	—

Source: GATT (1994: 80)
Notes: a Includes trade through processing zones
      b 1992

economically more advanced nations, and Japan in particular suffered a large cut in market share. Table 1.4 paints a similar picture for global clothing exports. The five leading textile exporters of 1993 also dominated exports of apparel. Portugal's entry into the EU in 1986 strengthened its position as a supplier of cheap clothing to the more advanced economies of Western Europe (Corado and Gomes 1995). Japan's absence from the apparel export table serves to emphasize the importance of labour costs in garment manufacturing. High wages and a strong yen have rendered it difficult for Japan to remain a major apparel exporter. Western cultural leadership means that Japanese producers are also at a comparative disadvantage in the fashion trade.

A number of countries appear in both Tables 1.3 and 1.4. Germany, South Korea, Taiwan, the USA, France, the UK and The Netherlands all have higher exports of textiles than of clothing. Hong Kong, Italy, China, Indonesia and India all have larger exports of clothing than of textiles. Since textile production is more capital-intensive than apparel production, it is only

Table 1.4 Fifteen leading exporters of clothing, 1993

Country	Value (US$bn)	Share in world exports (%)	(%)	Average annual change (%)	Share of clothing in economy's merchandise exports (%)	(%)
	1993	1980	1993	1980–93	1980	1993
Hong Kong	21.0	—	—	12	24.5	15.5
domestic exports	9.3	11.5	7.0	5	34.1	32.2
re-exports	11.7	—	—	32	4.7	11.0
China[a]	18.4	4.0	13.9	21	8.9	20.1
Italy	11.8	11.3	8.9	8	5.9	6.6
Germany	6.7	7.1	5.1	6	1.5	1.8
Korea (Rep. of)	6.2	7.3	4.6	6	16.8	7.5
United States	5.0	3.1	3.7	11	0.6	1.1
France	4.6	5.7	3.4	5	2.0	2.2
Turkey	4.3	0.3	3.3	31	4.5	28.3
Thailand	4.2	0.7	3.1	24	4.1	11.4
Portugal[b]	4.0	1.6	3.1	17	13.6	21.9
Chinese Taipei (Taiwan)	3.7	6.0	2.8	3	12.3	4.4
India	3.6	1.5	2.7	15	6.9	16.5
Indonesia	3.5	0.2	2.6	32	0.4	9.5
United Kingdom	3.4	4.6	2.6	5	1.7	1.9
The Netherlands	2.5	2.2	1.9	8	1.2	1.8
Above 15	91.2	66.9	68.7	—	—	—

Source: GATT (1994: 84)
Notes: a Includes trade through processing zones
     b 1992

to be expected that Germany, the USA, France and the UK should be found in the first group, and the developing economies in the second group. Italy's membership of the second group is an indication of its comparative advantage in fashion goods, and does not indicate any particular weakness in textiles.

Another approach to the measurement of competitive advantage involves the calculation of the revealed comparative advantage (RCA) of each country in each product group. RCA can be estimated in a variety of ways. Essentially, it is a measure of the export performance of a given country in a given product group relative to a benchmark, such as the country's export performance across all industries or the share of this product group in the exports of all countries. A major advantage of the RCA approach is that it makes a correction for the size of the economy. A large country with a moderate comparative advantage does not overshadow a small country with a high comparative advantage. Studies of RCA in the textile and clothing sector, covering a wide range of countries and using different techniques, may be found in UNIDO (1986: 212, 220) for the 1970s and UNIDO (1993: 318–60) for the 1980s. The findings of the latter UNIDO study are summarized in Table 1.5. Countries have been split into three groups, representing high, intermediate and low RCA. Italy had the highest RCA, in both textiles and clothing, of the major industrial countries in 1990. But even Italy lagged a long way behind the more successful developing countries. Pakistan had the highest RCA in textiles, while Tunisia led in wearing apparel, but too much weight should not be given to the rankings of individual countries,

Table 1.5 Revealed comparative advantage in textiles and clothing, 1990

Textiles		*Clothing*	
RCA ≥ 2		*RCA ≥ 2*	
Greece	Hong Kong	Colombia	Morocco
India	Indonesia	Cyprus	Pakistan[a]
Korea (South)	Morocco	Greece	Philippines[b]
Pakistan[a]	Portugal	Hong Kong	Portugal
Turkey		India	Thailand
		Indonesia	Tunisia
		Italy	Turkey
		Korea (South)	Uruguay
2 > RCA ≥ 1		*2 > RCA ≥ 1*	
Austria	Switzerland	Hungary	Singapore
Belgium	Thailand	Israel	Yugoslavia
Colombia	Tunisia	Malaysia[b]	
Germany (FR)	Uruguay		
Italy	Yugoslavia		
1 > RCA		*1 > RCA*	
Argentina	Japan	Argentina	Ireland
Australia	Malaysia[b]	Australia	Japan
Brazil[a]	Mexico	Austria	Mexico
Canada	The Netherlands	Belgium	The Netherlands
Chile	New Zealand	Brazil	New Zealand
Cyprus	Norway	Canada	Norway
Denmark	Philippines[b]	Chile	Spain
Finland	Singapore	Denmark	Sweden
France	Spain	Finland	Switzerland
Hungary	Sweden	France	United Kingdom
Ireland	United Kingdom	Germany (FR)	United States
Israel	United States		

Source: UNIDO (1993: 318–60)
Notes: RCA is the share of the product group in the total manufactured exports of the named country divided by the product group's share in the total exports of all the countries in the study. Unfortunately, figures were unavailable for China
a 1989
b 1988

since these may fluctuate from year to year. The general picture is much more important, and this establishes the superior competitiveness of the developing countries, broadly defined. Some of the smaller Mediterranean and Asian economies, such as Morocco and Hong Kong, attained high RCA rankings. Portugal and Greece show up rather well, partly as a result of their privileged position in the EU. Most of the large developed economies, especially the USA, Japan, France and Britain, exhibit low RCAs. This need not be a matter for lamentation, since it is impossible for any country to have a comparative advantage in all industries. Low RCA scores in textiles and clothing should be balanced by better scores in other sectors.

THE EVOLUTION OF COMPETITIVE ADVANTAGE

We now turn to the more difficult task of accounting for the evolution of competitive advantage in the textile and clothing industries. This exercise absorbs the remainder of this book, but in this section we examine a number of general interpretations of textile history and try to relate them to the diamond framework. In other words, the diamond should now be imagined as revolving and travelling through time. The industrial revolution originated in textiles and, in consequence, this industry has attracted considerable interest from economists and historians. Cyclical patterns play an important role in this analysis. First, we consider the relationship between the development of the textile sector and that of the national economy. Second, we consider the internal dynamics of textile history.

Hoffmann (1958) suggested that consumer goods industries, such as textiles, were usually the first to undergo mechanization, because of their comparatively simple technology, their economical use of capital and the ease with which they drew upon existing pools of craft labour. As economic development proceeded, the share of the consumer goods industries in national output began to fall, relative to the share of the capital goods industries. The rise of the capital goods industries reflected the diminishing scarcity of capital and the growth in demand for more sophisticated products. Other studies confirm the existence of this general pattern of industrial development. Moreover, as an economy increases in maturity, there appears to be a shift in emphasis from the manufacture of products with a high income elasticity of demand at low incomes, to products with a high income elasticity of demand at high incomes (L. G. Reynolds 1985: 59–60; Chenery, Robinson and Syrquin 1986). Akamatsu advances a 'flying geese' pattern of industrial development, in which industries take off and fly, one after another, in a long line. Textiles is normally the first industry to become airborne because it requires only modest amounts of skill and capital. Heavier and more sophisticated industries follow in series. During the course of the flight, latecomers assume the leadership of the flock of geese, so that the textile industry falls further and further back in the group (Korhonen 1994:

19

49–63). There seems to be general agreement that, while textile production is likely to grow in relative importance during the early stages of industrialization, its share in industrial output cannot be maintained over the very long run. For instance, in Japan, textiles accounted for 35 per cent of the rise in the real output of the manufacturing sector between 1878 and 1900. But the contribution of textiles to the growth of manufacturing output declined throughout the twentieth century, reaching a nadir of −0.1 per cent in 1971–87 (Minami 1994: 100).

Rather more dramatically, Rostow (1978) argues that cotton textiles often acts as a 'leading sector' in the early stages of a nation's industrialization. The creation of a mechanized textile industry requires relatively modest investments in fixed and human capital. Entrepreneurs in developing countries are attracted to textiles because they are generally short of capital, and there is always a ready market for necessities. According to Rostow's stages of growth framework, the rapid expansion of the textile industry generates demand for the output of other industries, such as engineering, coal, transport and construction, thereby stimulating the rapid development of these sectors. As the process of development unfolds, capital-intensive industries replace cotton as the leading sectors. Rostow regards the cotton industry as a leading sector in the take-off (or industrial revolution) of a number of countries, and most clearly in the cases of the UK, USA, Japan and Taiwan (Rostow 1978: 379, 393, 422, 546). It would seem that Rostow greatly exaggerates the role of textiles as the locomotive of national economic development. Later research on British industrialization suggests that the cotton industry remained an island of modernity, in a slowly growing economy, for many decades (Crafts 1985). At the regional level, however, such as Lancashire in cotton, and West Yorkshire in wool, the transmission mechanism linking dynamic textile concentrations to other industries was far more powerful (Pollard 1981: 3–41; Berg and Hudson 1992: 38–9). During early industrialization, textile industries become the centres of strong regional clusters, which extend beyond the activities of direct relevance to the support of textile and clothing manufacture. Lowell, Bombay, Osaka and Hong Kong were, in various ways, copies of Manchester, and other towns and cities are queueing to take their place.

A cyclical framework also helps us to understand the internal development of the textile and clothing industries. Flows of technology make a large contribution to the cycles which affect the textile sector. Britain, the original industrializer, established a lead in cotton textile technology in the late eighteenth century. Lancashire exploited its competitive advantage and imperial connections and built up large export markets for cotton textiles. British technical knowledge gradually seeped abroad, firstly to the USA and continental Europe, then to Japan and finally to the rest of the world. As this technology was assimilated by a wide range of countries, there was a tendency for low labour costs to become the key to competitive advantage, especially in the case of basic textile products. But the migration of competitive advantage from the technically advanced centres towards Asia, Latin America and Africa was not a smooth process. Countervailing processes worked for the restoration of the technological supremacy of the mature Western economies. New generations of textile machinery, and eventually man-made fibres and microelectronics, were developed in the West. These technologies served to restore the gap in knowledge between the developed nations and their followers. To reiterate, waves of new textile-related technology emanated from the mature countries. As these waves travelled further from their source, the competitive advantage which they conferred on the developed countries was increasingly eroded. New technical breakthroughs were required in order to rebuild the competitiveness of the advanced nations. The persistence of protectionism, in the form of the MFA, and the permanent crisis in the textile industry of the developed world suggest that the rate of innovation may have fallen behind the rate of diffusion (although it cannot be assumed that this situation will persist). To exacerbate matters, developing countries are able to obtain a competitive advantage by using second-hand machinery, which would be considered obsolete in Europe, Japan or the USA, in combination with cheap labour (Pack 1977).

Yamazawa (1990: 74–5) applies the cyclical framework to the history of the Japanese cotton industry. His 'catch-up product cycle' is a variant of Akamatsu's flying geese approach. Yamazawa divides the development of the textile industry in Japan into a number of phases. First, between 1883 and 1895, the cotton spinning industry assimilated Western technology and engaged in import substitution. Second, between 1895 and 1914, the large spinners started to export yarn and began to install modern looms, so that they could drive imported cloth from the domestic market. Third, the 1920s and 1930s saw a decline in yarn exports, as spinning mills were opened in former overseas yarn markets, but a dramatic expansion in the export of cloth. Fourth, after 1945, the cotton industry failed to regain its competitive advantage. It faced increasing competition from developing countries. Japanese firms adopted more capital-intensive techniques and invested in new factories abroad. Imports of cotton textiles by Japan began to rise in the 1970s, as the industry entered its final phase. The Japanese cotton industry followed a path which is familiar to students of the British cotton industry. Import substitution in the eighteenth century (Inikori 1989) was followed by a century of booming exports, first of yarn, and then of cloth, in the late eighteenth and nineteenth centuries (Farnie 1979). The cotton industry faltered after 1918 (Sandberg 1974), and finally collapsed after the Second World War (Singleton 1991).

Generalizing from these examples, we can advance a typical industrial life cycle for textiles. At first, the country in question is a net importer of textiles. Then it either invents or imports a better technology, and enters a period of import substitution (with or without the assistance of tariffs). Next, if all goes well, it becomes a successful exporter. Sooner or later its costs start to rise, and countries further down the development ladder undermine its export markets. Finally, the country's home market becomes vulnerable to cheap imports. Toyne *et al.* (1984: 20–1) produce a similar stages framework for the textile sector. Their labels for these epochs are 'embryonic', the 'golden age', 'maturity' and 'decline'. Their content should be self-explanatory.

Dickerson (1995: 129–43) develops the stages framework of Toyne *et al.*, emphasizing the options available to those countries which are on the brink of decline. Mature textile industries can choose between three possible strategies: moving their labour-intensive processes to poorer countries, investing in more advanced equipment or seeking government aid and protection. Naturally, it would be possible to select a mixture of these strategies. Irreversible decline can be avoided, it would seem, if firms in mature economies are prepared to operate on an international level. Porter (1987) states that configuration and coordination are crucial aspects of international strategy. Configuration refers to the geographical location of activities. A firm could open facilities in other countries for a number of reasons – the one which concerns us here is the minimization of costs. Coordination refers to the extent to which the firm's business around the world is conducted according to an overall plan. Japanese textile producers opening weaving mills in Malaysia, or German textile producers subcontracting the assembly of garments to allied firms in North Africa, are adopting an international (or global) strategy. Internationalization allows cooperative links to be forged between textile and apparel firms and industries which occupy different positions on the industrial life cycle. Mature textile complexes in Europe, the USA and Japan seek to preserve themselves by sacrificing the least profitable aspects of their domestic production base. Whether or not this strategy merely delays the ultimate collapse of established firms in mature economies is a question which time alone can answer.

It would be misleading to think of the textile and clothing sector as a single entity. Different parts of the sector are likely to pass through the various stages of growth and decline at different times. K. Anderson (1992: 2–14) suggests that, in the first place, the typical nation is an exporter of natural fibres; for instance, in the Middle Ages England was an exporter of raw wool before it developed into an internationally competitive exporter of woollen cloth. Since most underdeveloped countries have a surfeit of labour, and a dearth of capital and technical knowledge, the apparel industry is usually the first segment of the textiles and clothing sector to become competitive in world markets. Yarn and cloth, which are less labour-intensive than apparel, rise to prominence as exports somewhat later. When clothing and textile exports begin to run out of steam, possibly as a result of rising relative costs, the sector as a whole may receive a final boost from increasing exports of synthetic fibres. Anderson's account of sequential shifts in competitive advantage is less applicable to earlier periods in history, when clothing exports were rare and synthetic fibre exports were non-existent, but this framework does make sense in the context of the last four decades. Moreover, there are exceptions to Anderson's pattern of development. Lloyd (1992) shows that Australia and New Zealand, despite their high income levels, remain strong in natural fibre exports, and deficient in other areas of the textile cluster, as a result of their distinctive resource endowments, namely, plenty of land and sheep but relatively few human beings.

The availability of impoverished labour is not a sufficient condition for the launching of an industrial cycle in textiles and apparel. African countries have been less successful than either Asian or Latin American states in the production and export of textiles and clothing. A country must possess a reasonable pool of entrepreneurial talent, a work-force with a smattering of skills and education, moderately efficient capital markets and a sound institutional framework, as well as low wages, before it can expect to attain a competitive advantage, even in apparel manufacturing. Schmid and Phillips (1980) found that the most successful textile exporting countries, between 1968 and 1974, were those such as Brazil, Colombia, Greece and South Korea, which were already sufficiently developed to be able to use capital efficiently. Firms in these countries paid high wages, in comparison with those in most developing countries, but they also reached respectable levels of labour productivity, so that their unit labour costs were very low.

These industrial life cycle frameworks have some points of contact with the product life cycle model (Vernon 1966; 1979; Taylor 1986). Vernon's theory is that new products are developed in the most advanced economy. Over a period of time, other countries learn how to make the product. Once knowledge about the product is commonplace, it is cheaper to manufacture it in countries with low wages. Companies from the most advanced country establish subsidiaries abroad to take advantage of these low costs. New products are developed in the leader country and the cycle begins again. Although textiles were not a new product during the Industrial Revolution, mechanized textile production was gradually diffused throughout the world in the manner suggested by Vernon. However, until comparatively recently, this diffusion was accomplished with minimal assistance from textile multinationals. Furthermore, in textiles, the initial technological leader failed to maintain its supremacy. Other nations succeeded in catching up with, and in most areas surpassing, the products of the British textile machinery industry. A product life cycle may be observed at the more ephemeral level of fashion goods. The ideas of the leading Paris or London designers are rapidly emulated by less famous designers, until cheap versions reach the racks of the clothing multiples. The product cycle takes a design from Milan to Middlesbrough in a few months.

Several cyclical frameworks have been discussed in the preceding paragraphs. One cycle is concerned with the contribution of textiles to national economic development. A second cycle deals with the evolving competitive advantage of a nation's textile industry within the context of international trade and technology. A third cycle involves the brief career of individual fashion designs. At any moment, an individual firm or industry will be at different points of several cycles. Cyclical theories of industrial growth are compatible with the orthodox view that comparative costs, based upon factor endowments, determine the pattern of international competitiveness. Comparative advantage and factor endowment are cross-sectional concepts, whereas the cycles run through time. Relative factor endowments and comparative costs are likely to change, as nations increase the stock and improve the quality of their factors of production, at varying rates.

A revolving and evolving diamond framework has no difficulty incorporating the elements of the industrial life cycle. The industrial life cycle merely adds the third dimension of time to the two-dimensional geometry of the diamond framework. Porter is not looking for industrial life cycles. He is interested in formulating recommendations which will enable industries (and nations) to avoid, or at least to delay, the descent phase of their trajectory. Perhaps it is possible to extend the lifespan of a mature industry for decades, or even longer, by the adoption of such strategies as globalization. When viewed from a historical perspective, however, the life cycle possesses a great deal of descriptive and explanatory force.

CONCLUSION

Porter's diamond framework is a convenient way of packaging a number of widely accepted views about the determinants of competitive advantage. The fact that Porter has chosen a four-cornered framework is of little significance. Five, six, seven or eight cornered figures would have been equally appropriate. Factor conditions, demand conditions, related and supporting industries, and firm strategy, structure and rivalry are, beyond question, important aspects of the industrial situation. The stress placed on clustering, strategy and structure, and the interplay between microeconomic and macroeconomic factors, is fully justified. The diamond framework can be adapted to fit almost any set of circumstances. It is fully compatible with the industrial life cycle framework which explains many of the historical processes at work in the textile and clothing sectors.

The evolution of competitive advantage in textiles and clothing is strongly influenced by cyclical factors. Textile industries rise and fall, both in relation to other sectors in their home countries, and in relation to their foreign competitors. Mature economies attempt to compete in textiles and clothing by moving into niche markets, adopting new generations of technology or subcontracting labour-intensive processes to less developed countries. Poorer countries compete on the basis of lower costs, particularly of labour. The ease of entry of new countries into the more labour-intensive branches of the textile and clothing sector ensures that it is in a constant state of flux. Since the Second World War, the life cycle in this sector has actually accelerated.

2

FACTOR CONDITIONS

A nation's factor endowments exert a strong influence over its competitive advantage in the production of goods and services: Sweden, for instance, would be uncompetitive in the supply of bananas due to its cold climate, but the West Indies are ideal for the cultivation of tropical fruits. Introductory economics textbooks stress the importance of relative factor endowments in the determination of competitive advantage. But their approach is a static one in which the distribution of factors is given. The real world is far more complicated. While some factors of production, such as climate, terrain and mineral deposits are inherited from prehistoric times, many others are created and improved by human activity. Human capital, industrial plant and machinery, physical and social infrastructure, and technical knowledge are all manufactured by human beings (Porter 1990: 74–5). The respective rates at which factors are created, improved and modified to suit the needs of particular industries affect the development of competitive advantage. Porter (ibid.: 81–5) goes further and suggests that even selective factor disadvantages could be beneficial, if they stimulate endeavours to overcome them. A good example would be Japan. Despite its limited natural resources, Japan has succeeded in becoming a leading industrial power. This concept of selective factor disadvantages is similar to Toynbee's notion of challenge and response in history (Tomlin 1978: 20–3). Although this approach can be illuminating, it is difficult to understand why people respond positively to constraints in some situations, but fail to do so in others.

Factors which have undergone little modification are described as 'basic', while those which have been manufactured (for instance highly qualified personnel) are termed 'advanced'. Porter considers the advanced factors to be decisive because of their relative scarcity, the difficulty of importing them and their role in the upgrading of industries. He distinguishes between generalized factors, which cannot sustain competitive advantage over the long term, and specialized factors, which are expensive to create but harder for others to copy (Porter 1990: 77–9). The competitive advantage of a given industry in a given country is affected by its ability to mould the factors

26

available to it, and to find substitutes for factors which are either very scarce or completely absent.

A plentiful labour supply has often been regarded as the critical factor in determining competitive advantage in textiles and clothing, although there has been a reaction against this viewpoint in recent times (Mass and Lazonick 1991). A competitive advantage which relies on cheap labour, rather than on the performance of more sophisticated factors, is difficult to sustain. If a region wishes to build an enduring competitive advantage in textiles and clothing, it must upgrade its factors of production in order to reduce its exposure to competition from firms in emerging industrial countries, where labour is cheaper. This task is not an easy one. Established regions may find it difficult to upgrade their factor inputs with sufficient rapidity to stay ahead of competition from countries with apparently inexhaustible supplies of standard labour.

LABOUR

The most basic human resource, a large supply of inexpensive, unskilled or semi-skilled labour, is of great value during the early development of mechanized textile and clothing industries. Low-wage labour, even though it may not be particularly efficient, helps emerging textile industries to compete with their more sophisticated rivals.

A demonstration of the significance of low wages was given by Clark (1987). He examined manufacturing costs in the cotton weaving industries of Britain and a number of other countries, in 1910 (see Table 2.1). The countries with the lowest wages, Japan, India and China, were competitive in costs with the UK, despite the fact that their factories employed fewer

Table 2.1 International costs in cotton weaving, *c.* 1910

	Weekly wage rate (US$)	Machinery per worker (loom-equivalent)	Corrected yearly labour cost (US$)	Manufacturing cost (England = 1.00)
New England	8.8	2.97	6.04	1.25
USA (South)	6.5	2.65	5.00	1.12
England	5.0	2.04	5.00	1.00
Spain	2.7	0.91	6.05	1.32
Mexico	2.6	1.15	4.61	1.19
Italy	2.4	0.88	5.56	1.20
Japan	0.80	0.53	3.08	1.01
India	0.78	0.50	3.18	0.91
China	0.54	0.48	2.30	0.75

Source: Clark (1987: 150)

machines per worker than the English mills. The number of looms per worker was higher in the USA than it was in the UK. But the American mills remained uncompetitive: even higher loom complements would have been necessary to compensate US firms for their workers' relatively generous wage levels. Spain and Mexico, two semi-developed countries, experienced wage and productivity levels which were in between those of England and the three Asian countries, and they were unable to compete with either the English or the Asian mills. Looked at from one perspective, lower wages enabled the Japanese mills to offset the higher productivity of English workers. Seen from the opposite vantage point, higher loom complements made it possible for English mills to offset lower Japanese wages. Clark concluded that the low ratios of looms to operatives, in developing regions, was due to the hold of traditional cultures which were unconducive to hard work. This assessment provoked some strong reactions, and was rather rash. Loom complements in developing countries could have been affected by several alternative factors, including management practices and a rational decision to substitute plentiful labour for scarce capital (Wilkins 1987; Clark 1988; Hanson 1988; Mass and Lazonick 1991: 19–20, 31–8).

With regard to standard grades of labour, it should be emphasized that all human beings possess some skills or industrially useful attributes, regardless of formal training. Even child labourers have some advantages over more experienced employees. Child labour was popular during the Industrial Revolution in England, partly because it was cheap, but also because children were small and nimble and therefore capable of working underneath and in between running machinery (Rose 1989). The first skill learned by new adult factory operatives in many societies was how to work at a constant pace for fixed hours. Prior to industrialization in the UK, most labourers were accustomed to the seasonal and flexible working patterns of agriculture and cottage industry, and it was difficult for them to conform to the unfamiliar work discipline of the mill (Pollard 1965: 181–92; Thompson 1991: 352–403). Child labour and family group labour, whereby an adult male supervised the work of his wife and children, provided temporary answers to these disciplinary problems. Measures to control adults sometimes took extreme forms. Before the First World War, private detectives were employed at the Amoskeag mills in New Hampshire to spy on workers and report their plans to managers (Harevan and Langenbach 1978: 78). Severe exploitation was especially common in the apparel industries during the nineteenth and early twentieth centuries. Clothing production in Britain, the USA and elsewhere was generally carried on in small establishments or else put out to homeworkers. Such workers had no bargaining power and minimal protection from the law (Walkley 1981; Scranton 1994).

Labour control was at its most rigid in the Japanese dormitory system, which existed from the late nineteenth century until after the Second World War. Young female workers were held under virtually military conditions in factory compounds owned by the large spinning companies. These young women worked to supplement the incomes of their families, who lived in the countryside, or to save up for a dowry (Tsurumi 1984). Similar methods were used in parts of New England, in the early nineteenth century, where young women boarded away from home in houses owned by the cotton mills (Dalzell 1987: 32–4). Japanese dormitory workers were not devoid of skill, although their skills were not of a high order. Statistical research suggests that labour productivity in the Japanese spinning factories between 1891 and 1935 was positively related to the level of schooling of the operatives in such basic subjects as reading and writing. Although there was a high turnover rate of dormitory girls, those workers who stayed in the mills for a number of years became increasingly productive as a result of their experience (Saxonhouse 1977; Otsuka, Ranis and Saxonhouse 1988: 196–8). On-the-job training significantly improved the quality of the labour force in other industrializing regions, including the Lancashire cotton districts in the first half of the nineteenth century (Boot 1995). The failure of young female spinners to resist changes in work practices in the 1920s and 1930s, when new labour-saving machinery was installed, assisted the Japanese textile industry to gain a decisive competitive advantage over its Indian rival. Mills in India were unable to employ young women, largely for cultural reasons, and adult male workers offered sturdy opposition to labour reforms which increased their workloads and threatened their jobs (Wolcott 1994). Textile employers around the world were united in thinking that docile workers were more profitable to employ than independently minded workers of a similar competency.

The early labour practices of textile and clothing producers in Britain, the USA and Japan were emulated in the developing countries of East Asia after 1945. Rising manufacturing sectors in the newly industrializing countries drew their labour supplies from overstocked rural areas. Textile and clothing employers were particularly eager to hire young women. These women were kept on short-term contracts, subjected to authoritarian discipline and paid very low wages. As in previous generations, young factory girls sold their labour power in order to earn enough money for a dowry. Parents collaborated with employers to instil obedience into their daughters. If independent unions arose, among either female or male workers, they were beaten down by the bosses in conjunction with the paramilitary forces of the state (Diamond 1979; Deyo 1989). The dormitory system was prevalent in Hong Kong during the period of rapid post-war development. Hong Kong employers gave the traditional Japanese rationalization for this practice, namely, that the provision of supervised accommodation was necessary for the moral welfare of young girls in a big city (Wong 1988: 70–2). Discipline was tight, even in workshops that did not use the dormitory system. Young women working in the Hong Kong garment industry in the early 1970s complained of hard driving by the overlookers and the weeding out of older women who could not keep up with the pace. Workers retaliated by failing to report faulty work. When urgent deadlines had to be met, women were locked in the factories to make them work overtime. Their only recourse was to quit, which they did at an increasing rate as jobs in the colony became more plentiful (Salaff 1981: 70–117). Hong Kong's labour laws were weak and laxly enforced, since the colonial government was keen to comply with the requests of the business community. Although it was illegal for children aged under fourteen to work in establishments employing ten or more people, these laws were regularly flouted by textile and apparel firms, such as the Texwood jeans factory, where twelve-year-olds were discovered working late into the evening on several occasions in 1969. The use of children as outworkers was unregulated. One study estimated that 12,500 children under the legal working age were employed in textiles in Hong Kong in 1971 (R. Porter 1975). Uncompromising labour policies were retained for many years, even in the more capital-intensive branches of the textile industry. At the Melon Polyester Company, which was a joint venture between the Thai Blanket Industry, the Bangkok Bank and Rhone Poulenc, popularly known as the 'Kingdom of Fear', two labour leaders were mysteriously murdered in 1975 (Frenkel 1993: 99–100).

Table 2.2 confirms the importance of women workers, most of whom possessed low levels of skill, in the textile and apparel sectors of Asia. A strategy of relying on low-wage female labour assisted newly industrializing areas to compete with textile producers in more advanced economies. This was possible because East Asian workers also managed to attain reasonable levels of efficiency. The wages of South Korean spinning operatives, for example, were only 40 per cent of those of similar Japanese workers in 1965. But labour productivity in South Korean mills was about 60 per cent of the Japanese level. The result was that the wage cost of spinning a bale of cotton was US$9 in Korea, compared to US$13 in Japan (K. D. Woo 1978: 191–4). Conditions of work in Asia, in the 1960s and 1970s, were comparable with those in Lancashire or New England in the early nineteenth century. However unpleasant life was for the workers, the regime was a source of competi-

Table 2.2 Females as a percentage of all workers in textiles and apparel and footwear in the Asian NICs in the 1980s

	South Korea (1980)	Singapore[a] (1985)	Hong Kong (1981)	Taiwan (1986)
Textiles	69	73	49	63
Apparel and footwear	78	93	68	74

Source: Deyo (1989: 184)
Notes: a Excludes managerial workers

30

tive advantage to the newly industrializing countries for several decades. Similar conditions were found in the clothing and textile industries of other developing countries (Hadjicostandi 1990; Tiano 1990). The Asian tigers' tactic of competing on the basis of low labour costs has been undermined in recent years. Wages have risen in the wake of the elimination of labour surpluses and a new challenge has been issued by such countries as China, Indonesia and Pakistan, where pay is much lower (Khanna 1993).

Labour subcontracting systems abound in the small-scale textile and garment industries of Asia. Employers delegate to self-employed foremen the tasks of hiring, driving and paying the wages of unskilled female and child workers. Such arrangements are, for instance, a feature of the network of apparel firms which has emerged around Tiruppur in India (Cawthorne 1995). Practices in Tiruppur are reminiscent of those in cotton spinning during industrialization in Britain, whereby adult males in the spinning mills acted as labour subcontractors, hiring their wives and children as assistants (Mason 1987). Primitive labour conditions have not been eradicated in the most advanced OECD countries, where substantial pockets of sweatshop production and outworking remain. The Japanese government estimated that there were about 700,000 homeworkers in the garment and textile industries in 1981, mostly engaged on piecework for small firms, which were in turn subcontractors for larger businesses (Chalmers 1989: 91). There is always an underclass of workers who, for various reasons, including the demands of child-rearing, seek part-time or casual jobs. Clothing manufacturers are in an ideal position to take advantage of them (Weiner and Green 1984; Mitter 1986).

Skilled manual labour has been rather less important in textiles and clothing than it has in certain other industries, such as shipbuilding or aircraft production. Technicians and overseers are the most highly skilled workers in textile mills, whilst in apparel workshops those who prepare the designs and patterns are the most valuable operatives. But the minding of most textile and sewing machines requires comparatively little technical knowledge. The craft status of the Victorian mule spinners was due to their role as labour subcontractors rather than their technical skills (Fowler and Wyke 1987; Lazonick 1990: 78–114). On-the-job training was the norm in the textile sectors of the developing regions of Asia in the 1980s, and this method was sufficient for most firms' needs. Many firms resisted attempts by their governments to force them to contribute to the cost of training schemes. A training centre for textile workers was closed in Singapore in 1985, apparently due to lack of demand (Salome and Charmes 1988: 44–7, 66–8). In 1990, a survey of textile establishments in the Philippines found that 55 per cent of them gave their workers no formal training. This proportion was typical of Philippine industry as a whole. Those firms that provided some training concentrated on inducting new recruits, rather than on upgrading the skills of existing employees (Standing 1992). Under the conditions ruling in most developing countries, it does not benefit employers to invest in the training of operatives. The work-force is disposable and transitory. South Korean companies with textile plants in China in the late 1980s complained about the poor quality of the labour force, but this drawback was outweighed by their low wages (Hong, Yim and Park 1991: 73).

When an industry is under pressure to upgrade, in order to meet competition from states occupying a lower rung on the development ladder, it has a greater incentive to invest in the skills of its shopfloor personnel. But the difficulty of inducing a large number of small- and medium-sized firms to cooperate in the provision of training facilities means that it often falls on the government to take the initiative. Hong Kong, for example, introduced a state-sponsored Vocational Training Council in 1982. By 1986–7, this organization was running full-time courses for weavers (eight weeks) and knitting mechanics (six months), as well as a part-time course in the maintenance of computerized knitting machines. There were other schemes for textile workers in Hong Kong, including day-release and evening classes. Help for apparel workers was provided by the Clothing Industry Training Authority (Sit and Wong 1989: 63–5). The training of technicians, as opposed to machine operatives, is of much greater importance in developing countries, if modern machinery is installed in the mills. Where such training is defective, as it is in Thailand, it may not be possible for firms to run their expensive machinery properly (Limqueco, McFarlane and Odhnoff 1989: 45).

Textile businesses in developed countries may find it difficult to recruit shopfloor workers of a quality commensurate with their high wages in relation to those in developing countries. Standards of secondary (or high school) achievement are quite low in the English-speaking countries. Textile and clothing factories offer unattractive wages and prospects in comparison with other industries, and therefore tend to employ the least capable school-leavers. Remedial action is necessary to bring the reading and writing skills of many operatives up to scratch. For instance, in 1992, Milliken & Co. was reported to be taking part in a drive, initiated by the governor of South Carolina, to improve the basic skills of the state's industrial work-force. Classes at Milliken covered reading and writing as well as mathematics and technical subjects (Cole 1992). This state of affairs marked a return to nineteenth-century practice. In early English cotton mills, child workers were given lessons in the factory schoolrooms. Mills in late nineteenth-century Japan taught many of their teenage workers how to read and write (Levine and Kawada 1980: 231–3). The efficiency of the school system needs to be taken into account when assessing a region's factor conditions, because it is advantageous for firms to employ literate and numerate, rather than ill-educated, recruits. In Japan, the quality of schooling is excellent and pupils are several years ahead of British children in mathematics (Prais 1987). Better education and training gave German apparel firms, in the 1980s, an advantage over their British rivals (Steedman and Wagner 1989). Employee training adds further layers of human capital. The Milliken subsidiary in Europe made substantial investments in worker and management training in the 1980s and 1990s, as the firm strove to upgrade (Caulkin 1994: 32). Collins & Aikman revitalized its training programmes in the 1990s, providing its workers with classes in the use of computers and software (Anon 1993b).

Improvements in the quality of the labour force in high-income nations are unlikely to offset the low wages enjoyed by developing countries in the production of undifferentiated textiles and clothing. However, the availability of better-quality labour should assist firms in the wealthier countries to move into more defensible niche areas. Low wages generate a competitive advantage in low-quality textiles and garments, but skilled labour sustains competitive advantage in higher-quality segments of the market. Over long periods of time, successful low-wage producers, such as Hong Kong, gravitate towards the more differentiated end of the spectrum.

ENTREPRENEURSHIP

Entrepreneurship, or creative personal leadership, and management, or collective leadership and oversight, constitute the other key human resources. Entrepreneurs are far less homogeneous than workers. Their role is to make judgements which affect the future of their businesses in an ever-changing environment. Schumpeter (1961: 57–94) emphasized the importance of entrepreneurs, whom he defined as people who can transform industries through the introduction of new products and processes. Lazonick (1992: 78–82) picks up this theme, and explains that one of the foremost duties of an entrepreneur in a mature textile industry is to amalgamate small firms and forge them into modern business corporations. Thus, the entrepreneur should facilitate the transfer of power from personal to team leadership. He regrets that, in the British case, this process did not happen quickly enough. Generally speaking, the entrepreneur in the consumer goods industries is required to solve problems which are less complicated than those in most other industries (M. Casson 1993: 52–3). It is easier for a clothing workshop to change the cut of a dress than it is for a motor vehicle manufacturer to redesign a truck. But this does not mean that most textile and garment entrepreneurs have an untroubled life. Entrepreneurs in light consumer goods industries, such as textiles, must respond with alacrity to quite small variations in tastes and market opportunities. Unless they have long-term contracts with retail chains, textile and clothing entrepreneurs must learn how to cope with conditions of great uncertainty. In this section we shall consider the nature of entrepreneurship in young textile industries. It is assumed that wherever opportunities exist, there will be an adequate number of entrepreneurs with the ability to make the most of them. Lack of development does not imply the absence of entrepreneurial skill. Rather, it suggests that entrepreneurs are being stifled by their environment (E. L. Jones 1988).

Entrepreneurship is a matter of possessing the appropriate skills for use in a particular environment. The attributes required of textile entrepreneurs in young firms have many similarities across cultural and historical boundaries. A capacity for hard work and good judgement are of universal relevance. But one major difference between the entrepreneurs of the late eighteenth century and those in developing countries after 1945 is that the former did not have access to a stable technology. Richard Arkwright of Preston had to develop his own machine, the water frame, before he could enter into large-scale cotton yarn production (Fitton 1989). As an inventor–manufacturer, Arkwright was exceptional, but even his more mundane contemporaries needed the skill to choose between several comparatively untried techniques. The backgrounds of Lancashire's early cotton masters are interesting because they were repeated in other textile sectors around the world. Honeyman (1982: 62) identifies the previous occupations of seventy-five Lancashire textile mill owners in 1787. An impressive sixty-five of these early capitalists hailed from other parts of the textile and clothing trades, where they had been either merchants or small-scale manufacturers, and in two cases employees. The remaining ten capitalists included a former banker, two brewers, two landowners, a lawyer, a metal manufacturer and three mechanics. Very few cotton masters originated among the lowest classes. The mechanized textile industry evolved out of the existing textile trade. Mill-building entrepreneurs were responding to various stimuli: the emergence of the new spinning technology, rising home demand for cottons, protection against Indian imports and an increase in the productivity of the handloom which raised the demand for yarn (Chapman 1967).

A direct link was forged between the early factory entrepreneurs in England and those in the USA. Samuel Slater was an apprentice of Jedediah Strutt, a partner of Arkwright. Slater owed his position to the fact that the Slaters and the Strutts were neighbours. Slater was instructed by Strutt in textile engineering and the rudiments of mill management. After completing his apprenticeship, Slater broke the British emigration laws and left for New England, where he became the founder of the mechanized cotton industry. Slater's plan in the USA was to exploit his knowledge of the new textile technology. He joined up with local interests in Rhode Island and opened a spinning mill there in 1790 (White 1967; Tucker 1981). If not quite an Arkwright, Slater was beyond question a very adventurous pioneer. Other early American textile mill entrepreneurs were prepared to take large risks, including the Boston merchant, Francis Cabot Lowell, who visited Manchester on a mission of industrial espionage in 1810 (Dalzell 1987: 5). An entrepreneur planning to open a textile factory in South Korea in the 1950s would not have required the innovative brilliance of Arkwright, or even the technical knowledge of Samuel Slater, but he would have needed similar organizational, risk-taking and decision-making skills.

Pioneering textile entrepreneurs in Meiji Japan encountered severe difficulties, especially in the assimilation of unfamiliar Western technology. Yasumuro (1993) stresses that Japanese entrepreneurs relied heavily upon the advice of their engineers. Eiichi Shibusawa, the first president of the First National Bank, and promoter of the Osaka Boseki spinning company, in 1882, could not have proceeded without the assistance of a trained engineer, Takeo Yamanobe, who had studied in London and worked in a Blackburn cotton mill. This mutually beneficial alliance between an entrepreneur and an engineer proved to be an enduring feature of Japanese business. By contrast, most of the merchants and financiers who founded the Indian cotton industry had no access to reliable engineering advice, and this seems to have resulted in a poor choice of technology (Kiyokawa 1983). Moreover, many Indian entrepreneurs were willing to delegate the management of their enterprises to managing agencies. This behaviour suggests a lack of entrepreneurial drive on the part of some Indian capitalists. In the eighteenth and nineteenth centuries, successful entrepreneurs needed ready access to knowledge about what was, by the standard of the times, a highly sophisticated technology. By the mid-twentieth century, however, the basic types of textile machinery were quite standardized and textiles could no longer be regarded as a high-technology industry. The mechanization of textile production in South Korea and Indonesia involved a much less dramatic leap forward in organizational and technical know-how than that which was needed in Meiji Japan.

In many parts of the world, political influence has superseded privileged access to technical knowledge as the main weapon in the armoury of the pioneering textile entrepreneur. Large numbers of leading textile and clothing entrepreneurs in Asian countries have found it advantageous to form close and highly dependent alliances with local political elites. For business moguls in South Korea and Taiwan, participation in the textile industry was an important step on the road to more grandiose projects. Take the case of Lee Byung Chull, who founded Samsung in 1939. In its early days, Samsung was involved in trucking, property, trading and food processing. A sugar refinery with monopoly powers was opened in 1953. Profits from this venture were invested in the new Cheil Wool Company in 1954. Cheil Wool became the most important element of the Samsung empire until the 1970s. Lee also acquired large holdings in banks and insurance companies. When President Park came to power in 1961, Lee and other prominent entrepreneurs were convicted in show trials of bribing politicians and evading taxes. The extent to which the government's allegations were justified is uncertain, but there were very close ties between the private and public sectors in the 1950s. To obtain release from jail, Lee agreed to donate most of his wealth to the state and to act as one of Park's principal business collaborators, becoming the first head of the Federation of Korean Industries. Despite further crises, Samsung was encouraged by the government to enter the electronics industry, and subsequently a range of other sectors including shipbuilding (Jones and Sakong 1980: 350–4; Clifford 1994: 316–27). Founders of large Korean enterprises tended to begin their careers as merchants. They gravitated towards work on government and army contracts, and soon fell in with important politicians. Then they moved into textile production, in the 1950s, in order to benefit from protective duties. Generals and ministers invariably gained a stranglehold over these business leaders. It is fair to say that the textile industry was regarded by the state as a nursery for entrepreneurs. Obedient and talented textile bosses were selected by ministers to spearhead the country's drive into more glamorous industries, such as engineering, motor vehicles and electronics in the 1960s and 1970s. These were invitations which could not be refused. Similar tales could be told about large Taiwanese business groups (Numazaki 1986; 1993). Of course, these large-scale entrepreneurs were far from typical. Most textile and clothing firms remained small, and their owners never entered the world of high politics (Jones and Sakong 1980: 316–19). It is not suggested that corporatism was essential for the growth of large South Korean firms in either textiles or any other industry. But the pathway to growth, and the skills required by entrepreneurs, were different in South Korea than they were in, say, Hong Kong.

Yoshihara (1988) writes of the phenomenon of 'ersatz capitalism' in the second wave of industrializing Asian countries, such as Thailand, Indonesia, Malaysia and the Philippines. As elsewhere, the skilful cultivation of political leaders, rather than business competence, was the key to success for textile entrepreneurs. But there were added complications in these countries. Official corruption was much more deeply ingrained than it was in South Korea and Taiwan. Moreover, racial tensions led to the introduction of disruptive policies of discrimination against some groups of entrepreneurs, especially the Chinese. Western technology was never fully assimilated, due to acute shortages of technicians. In such an environment, it was difficult to distinguish between businessmen, politicians and gangsters. Under Indonesia's Benteng policy in the 1950s, Chinese textile traders were discriminated against in the allocation of import licences, and a clique of indigenous capitalists, who were lucky enough to have friends in the government, was able to dominate the textile industry (Robison 1986: 40–59). Nevertheless, many businessmen of Chinese origin were able to survive the period of discrimination. The growth of the Thai Blanket Industry group was facilitated by close ties between its founder, a Chinese fabric salesman called Sukree Photiratanangkun, and Field Marshal Phibun and government ministers during the 1950s and 1960s. Sukree was quite open about the reasons for his prosperity. Links with the nation's rulers enabled his firm to take over the army's troubled textile mill and win a monopoly contract to supply the military with blankets (Doner and Ramsay 1993: 694–7). Entrepreneurs in such states were even more insecure than those in South Korea and Taiwan,

36

and this was reflected in their often reckless behaviour. For instance, Dewey Dee, a leading Chinese textile entrepreneur and speculator, absconded from the Philippines in 1981 after running up huge debts through gambling and speculation (Yoshihara 1988: 80, 186).

No doubt the path trod by Asian entrepreneurs was determined by circumstances beyond their control. Hong Kong, where markets were free and the authorities Cobdenite, provides an example of classic entrepreneurship. The Shanghai textile capitalists who escaped to Hong Kong in the late 1940s and 1950s were hardly novices. Their new spinning mills in Hong Kong were far more successful than those they had left behind on the mainland. First-born sons of textile mill bosses were prominent among these migrants. They were well educated: 80 per cent of Hong Kong's leading spinning entrepreneurs in 1978 possessed university degrees, usually in a technical or business discipline (Wong 1988: 35, 62–3). Hong Kong entrepreneurs' stress on education was rather exceptional. Almost 75 per cent of the productive capacity of Pakistan's cotton industry in 1958 was controlled by industrialists who lacked a university or equivalent education (Papanek 1971: 240). A study of smaller Hong Kong textile and clothing businesses found that the most common occupation of the owner's father was that of merchant. This transition from selling to producing mirrored that in eighteenth-century Lancashire (Sit and Wong 1989: 141). Overseas Chinese were particularly successful entrepreneurs. Their energy could have been the product of a number of factors, including their sense of insecurity, their commitment to improving the status of the family and, in some countries, their desire to overcome the discrimination and hostility of the majority population (Redding 1993). Recent economic reforms in China suggest that there is no shortage of entrepreneurial talent on the Chinese mainland.

Successful entrepreneurs adapt their businesses to their environment, and pursue strategies which modify their environment so that higher profits can be made. They must be ready to take their chances. These enduring principles applied in eighteenth-century England, Meiji Japan, post-colonial Indonesia and post-war Hong Kong. While entrepreneurship may give a competitive advantage to some firms, it is unlikely to be an enduring one. Once the founder dies or retires, many firms lose their dynamism, since there is no guarantee that entrepreneurial qualities will be inherited by the next generation.

MANAGEMENT

At the level of the small firm, textile management is not separable from entrepreneurship. Specialist textile managers were a product of the development of multi-unit businesses. It was not until the end of the nineteenth century that managers received a systematic training. In the textile combine run by the Peel family in England in about 1800, the day-to-day management of individual mills was entrusted to loyal employees, drawn from the artisan class, some of whom rose to the status of junior partner in the firm (Chapman and Chassagne 1981: 70–7). But the Peels were exceptional, and most early textile businesses were small enough to be managed by the owner or partners. With the establishment of joint stock textile companies in the USA, after 1815, the formal separation of ownership from everyday control became more pronounced. Mill treasurers were chosen from among the relatives and friends of leading investors because it was felt that they would be more trustworthy than outsiders. They dealt with financial and strategic matters in Boston. The actual factories, in outlying townships, were managed by mill agents who were of a lower social status (Chandler 1977: 67–72; Gross 1993: 5–6, 104–8). Although much has been written about the rise of professional management in the USA, between 1850 and 1914, the textile industry was not at the forefront of this development because it operated on a smaller scale and did not require extensive managerial hierarchies. In the Southern states, the masters or principal stockholders prided themselves on daily contact with their workers, exchanging banter and keeping an eye on progress (Hall *et al.* 1987: 91–2). F. C. Dumaine, who managed the Amoskeag textile works in New Hampshire during the early decades of the present century, was a former office boy, hired on a whim, who acquired his training on the job. Not surprisingly, Dumaine did not believe in management training. He held that the ability to run a company was a natural aptitude, largely consisting of having the right hunches (Harevan and Langenbach 1978: 79–81, 90). Amoskeag, it should be added, did not prosper after the First World War.

By contrast, the expanding Burlington empire in the South, in the 1930s, had a more Chandlerian attitude towards management. Business school graduates were hired, and the company even preferred this type of recruit to applicants with degrees in textile engineering (Hall *et al.* 1987: 269; A. C. Wright 1995). Burlington was the exception rather than the rule among American textile manufacturers in the interwar period. It was also the most successful American textile producer of this era, suggesting that high-quality management gave it a competitive advantage over its rivals. Japan's large textile firms introduced professional managers at an early stage in their history. In the early twentieth century, Kanegafuchi recruited twelve graduates each year. Within a decade these recruits could expect to manage a mill, and in their forties the most able of them would become company executives. Both science and social science graduates were hired in large numbers by Japanese textile firms (Yonekawa 1984). Japanese managers were of a commendable quality. It was partly due to these managers' initiative that Japanese mills in China overcame their Western and local competitors in the 1920s and 1930s (Kuwahara 1992). Japan had no tradition of the self-made manufacturer. Japanese firms were determined to catch up with their Western rivals, hence they had no alternative to the appointment of professional managers and engineers. The Japanese government's policy of increasing spending on higher education made this response feasible. The examples of Burlington and Kanegafuchi lend support to the hypothesis that professional managers were more likely to be appointed in newer firms than in those which had built a tradition of the self-made man. In the UK, in 1936, less than half of the board of Courtaulds possessed university degrees, and there was a strong bias in favour of the appointment of ex-public schoolboys (Coleman 1969b: 223). If Courtaulds had wanted to employ business graduates, which was not the case, it would have been hampered by a paucity of suitable degree programmes.

A rising sense of panic led some of the more traditionally minded Western textile producers to take an interest in modern management education and methods after the Second World War. Courtaulds and English Sewing Cotton helped to establish a Centre for Business Research at Manchester University in 1961. Its mission was to promote research into business problems and facilitate the cross-fertilization of ideas between academics and managers (Wilson 1992: 20). Frank Kearton, who became chairman of Courtaulds in 1964, placed more emphasis than his predecessor had done on the selection of professionally competent managers, and the Textile Institute provided appropriate advice to firms which planned to follow his example (Textile Institute 1969; A. Knight 1974: 71–2). Although business academics, and not least business historians, such as Chandler and Lazonick, have come to regard family management as antiquated, it has persisted in many areas of the textile industry. It would be a mistake to draw too rigid a distinction between efficient professional management and bumbling family management. Leading textile firms in Hong Kong did not accept that family management was incompatible with professionalism, and the Hong Kong spinners were nothing if not successful (Wong 1988). Italy's Benetton, a family-led company, was an outstandingly successful clothing company in the 1970s and 1980s, and it has been suggested that the problems encountered by Benetton during its diversification in the late 1980s stemmed from decisions taken by non-family executives (Glover 1993).

The quality of managers in Asia's growing textile industries has been far from uniform. One response to the shortage of managerial talent, in the nineteenth century, was to set up special managing agencies. But this device was largely confined to British India (Sengupta 1974). At the level of the small firm it would be unrealistic to expect MBA graduates to be employed. For example, Mr Choi, the proprietor of a successful knitting works in Korea in the 1970s, had very little formal education and learned how to manage by practical experience. He was assisted by fifteen supervisors and kept his own rather simplistic accounts, although he intended to hire an accountant when his firm was incorporated (Jones and Sakong 1980: 316–19). Larger businesses in Korea have been employing specialist managers since the 1950s. About 9 per cent of employees in the Korean textile industry were classified as administrators in 1983. Of these, 83 per cent were unrelated to the owners (Amsden 1989: 166). As a rough comparison, in 1983, 19 per cent of employees in the British textile industry were classed as administrative, technical or clerical workers (United Kingdom, Central Statistical Office 1990: 115). Many South Korean business leaders were highly qualified. Jong Hyn Choi (who was no relation of the previous Choi), the man who saved the Sunkyung textile company from disaster, was trained in chemistry, economics and management. His motto was that a firm should exist throughout eternity (S.-M. Lee 1989: 185). Taiwanese firms were also moving towards the professionalization of management in the 1970s, notwithstanding the suspicions of their proprietors, who liked to advertise their superiority over their underlings at every opportunity (Silin 1976). Thailand's largest textile producers, Thai Blanket Industry and Saha Union, provide an instructive contrast of management styles. Sukree, the head of TBI, was a one-man-band, unwilling to transfer any responsibility to outsiders. He needed technical advice, but made sure that those who provided it were kept in their place. Disgruntled managers often left to set up their own firms. Saha Union was organized in a more systematic fashion and managerial jobs were open to outside talent, but it still suffered from a shortage of capable middle managers, as did the rest of Thai industry (Doner and Ramsay 1993). Both groups continued to prosper in the 1980s, since the key to success in Thailand was the cultivation of ministers and high officials.

Cooperation between local firms and those from more advanced countries, especially Japan, has helped to raise the standard of management in Asia. But it must be admitted that in countries which rely on cheap labour for their competitive advantage, management is of secondary importance. Management becomes more central to the generation of competitive advantage once the earliest phase of textile development has passed. Even so, it is doubtful whether good management is a sufficient condition for the establishment of an enduring competitive advantage in textiles or clothing. Ease of entry, and the consequent high level of competition, makes the position of any business highly uncertain over the long run.

CAPITAL

Two types of capital are required by any manufacturing business: fixed capital, or buildings and machinery, and working capital, or the funds to purchase inputs, pay wages and hold stocks in the interval between the beginning of each round of production and the final receipt of payments from customers. In textiles and clothing, it is usually the case that working capital predominates. Scarcity of capital, and the inadequacy of financial institutions, are major constraints on the growth of industry in developing regions. Since the textile and apparel industries were at the forefront of the industrialization drive in many countries, the pioneers in this sector had to overcome primitive conditions in the capital markets. On the other hand, in comparison with such enterprises as railways, it was relatively inexpensive to begin production on the lowest rung of the textile industry, so that the difficulty of obtaining capital was in some measure alleviated.

During the establishment of factory textile industries in the UK and USA, a crucial role was played by networks of business leaders, often merchants, who were able to mobilize finance in the absence of modern banks or stock markets. The Boston Associates were the most famous of these early networks. These prosperous New England merchants established a number of textile mill companies after 1815, at a time when the banks were unwilling to lend to manufacturers. Interlocking shareholdings and directorates encouraged a common ethos among the companies established by this group. The group's first venture, the Waltham mills, required a capital of $400,000, three-quarters of which comprised working capital. This was a huge investment by the standards of other mills (Davis 1958; Dalzell 1987). However, it was trivial in comparison with the cost of the early trunk railroads, some of which were capitalized at between $17 million and $35 million (Chandler 1977: 90). Their early adoption of the joint stock form of organization suggests that the Boston Associates were financially more sophisticated than the first British cotton masters. For legal reasons it was virtually impossible for British manufacturers to employ the joint stock technique before the mid-nineteenth century. Most British textile pioneers had to rely on their own savings and the contributions of partners to raise their initial capital. Small firms could begin by hiring a room in a factory, and a connection to the steam engine, thereby eliminating large initial investments in fixed capital (Farnie 1979: 291–5; Lloyd-Jones and Le Roux 1980). Lancashire was particularly badly served by the banks before 1820. The main contribution of the banks to industrial development in Britain was in the provision of working rather than fixed capital, although a recent study of the Yorkshire textile industry indicates that their willingness to supply long-term finance may have been underestimated (Hudson 1986: 218–23). Arkwright had several business partners during his career, including Jedediah Strutt and Samuel Need, who had made their money as merchants in the hosiery industry of the east Midlands. The profits from the handicraft textile industry were channelled by Need and Strutt into the development of factory production. It is inconceivable that Arkwright, who was of relatively modest means, could have built his cotton empire without these financial alliances (Shapiro 1967; Chapman and Butt 1988). Later on, when joint stock textile mills became legally permissible, enthusiastic local share markets emerged, but many of the older firms remained closed partnerships. In Oldham, in the second half of the nineteenth century, joint stock companies were able to tap the savings of artisans for investment in mills (Farnie 1979: 209–76).

Merchants, especially the Parsis, invested large sums in the mechanized textile industry which was established in India from the mid-nineteenth century onwards. Wealthy Bombay merchants were able to raise additional funds on the local stock exchange (Yonekawa 1987). But, particularly in the Ahmedabad region, the local merchants operated on a smaller scale and the capital markets were more primitive. Unable to raise sufficient finance, the Ahmedabad merchants relied on managing agents to supply the balance of the capital, as well as managerial expertise (S. D. Mehta 1954). The Japanese banks, like those in Britain, the USA and India, did not play a leading role in the initial provision of capital to the textile industry. Osaka Boseki and Kanegafuchi Boseki in the 1880s, were established through the combination of capital belonging to private merchants and aristocrats. A stock market boom led to the successful flotation of a number of cotton spinning companies in the late 1880s (Yonekawa 1987: 574–9). The *zaibatsu* were reluctant to build textile mills on their own account because of the expense and risk such ventures entailed, but they did buy shares in mill companies floated on the market. Sumitomo had shares in Osaka Boseki, while Mitsui took a stake in Kanegafuchi (Morikawa 1992: 27). Mitsui did not gain control over Kanegafuchi until 1890, when the Mitsui Bank was forced to intervene in order to resolve a financial crisis in this textile firm. Equity finance, raised by joint stock companies, soon became the typical source of funds for new mills (Yamamura 1978: 238–44). The financial systems in Britain, the USA, India and Japan were adequate to the task of building modern textile industries. As such, they made a contribution to competitiveness. However, only the most acute capital shortage could have thwarted the relatively modest demands of this sector.

Growing textile and clothing businesses in Asian countries since 1945 have encountered a somewhat different financial environment. Frequently, the opportunity to raise substantial amounts of capital has depended upon the goodwill of the state. In both South Korea and Taiwan, capital was accumulated by former landlords who received compensation for acreage redistributed to peasants shortly after the Second World War. Some compensation took the form of shares in new manufacturing enterprises. Other landlords invested in small businesses. In addition, nationalized banks were important in South Korea in the 1950s and 1960s. These banks enabled the government to channel capital into businesses run by its supporters. Smaller firms had to survive on the savings of their founders and could expect few favours from the public sector (Ho 1980). The allocation of capital for large-scale manufacturing projects was largely a matter of politics. Privileged access to the banking system for loans at a favourable rate of interest could be bought by those who made generous donations to the coffers of the ruling party. Some firms also benefited from American foreign aid, although this was offset by the South Korean government's nationalistic reluctance to accept foreign investment (McNamara 1992). Mr Ham, who built up a small silk weaving factory in the 1960s, relied on capital supplied by his family, plus the American aid authorities, for whom he had once worked (Jones and

Sakong 1980: 324–7). Ham's story contrasts in stark fashion with those of the founders of the *chaebol*, who were given every assistance from the public sector in return for political obedience. Textile production was a favoured sector in the late 1950s and early 1960s (Amsden 1989: 72–4; Clifford 1994). Involvement by the state in the provision of capital was even more direct in the case of Indonesia, where a group of mills was founded by the state (H. Hill 1982). In the 1960s and 1970s, the Korean *chaebol* were required to invest in heavy industry rather than textiles, so that in this period government control over the capital market could have restricted the growth of the textile sector (Hong and Park 1986). The state deliberately distorted the allocation of capital in South Korea. It is unclear whether the textile and clothing sector was a net beneficiary of this policy, since in some periods the government advocated investment in textiles, whilst in others it regarded this sector as a low priority. The possibility cannot be ruled out that the textile industry would have gained if capital had been allocated according to market principles, especially since some of the heavy industrialization projects of the 1970s were failures. But there can be little doubt that the government's overall strategy of fostering high savings was of great value to industry in general. High savings ratios have been a common feature of successful Asian economies since the Second World War (World Bank 1993: 203–45).

Hong Kong's textile industry was given a head start in the 1950s by the transfer of capital from Shanghai. It is estimated that up to HK$200 million was invested in the colony by migrant textile capitalists by 1951, principally in the establishment of large spinning concerns (Wong 1988: 44–5). Among smaller Hong Kong textile and clothing firms in the 1980s, the source of initial capital requirements was quite different, and almost three-quarters of the founders of such enterprises claimed to have entered business equipped with only their own savings (Sit and Wong 1989: 149). Although Taiwan also received some capital from the Shanghai entrepreneurs, it was not such an attractive destination for migrants. Many Taiwanese business groups originated in the pooling of capital by relatives or acquaintances from the same district. These groups established small enterprises, often in textiles or clothing, and then used any profits to set up further businesses. Not all members of the network invested in every enterprise, but there was a high degree of overlap (Numazaki 1993). There were similarities between Taiwanese practices in the 1950s and 1960s and those of the Boston Associates and the English cotton pioneers, in the sense that networks of investors cooperated in sequential projects. But, whereas Western and Japanese textile capitalists tended to confine themselves to a narrow range of activities, firms in South Korea, Taiwan and other Asian countries quickly adopted a strategy of diversification. Textile profits formed a pool of capital for employment in the development of other sectors.

Countries blighted by deep racial divisions between indigenous populations and residents of Chinese descent, such as Indonesia and Malaysia, did their best to prevent the Chinese from tapping into state-controlled sources of capital, in the hope of fostering new businesses owned by national ethnic groups. These policies generally failed because the Chinese textile and clothing producers were able to turn to their own banks and financial networks. The Chinese remained a powerful force in the textile industries of such countries. No doubt the textile industries of Indonesia and Malaysia would have been more dynamic if Chinese firms had been given the same freedoms as those which they enjoyed in Hong Kong (Robison 1986; Yoshihara 1988; Jesudason 1990; Redding 1993).

Inward foreign direct investment (FDI) was another important source of capital for the textile industries of developing countries. Some countries were more open to FDI than others. Japanese capital has been of particular importance in fostering large-scale textile and clothing enterprises in Asia (Yoshihara 1978: 91–132). Almost 98 per cent of the paid-up capital of textile firms located in the Malaysian free trade zones in 1987 was of foreign origin and, in 1988, foreign investors accounted for 77 per cent of the proposed capital investment in the entire Malaysian textile industry. Japan was the main investor in Malaysia (O'Connor 1993: 238; Rasiah 1993: 128). Foreign investors were prone to establish factories which focused on export markets. In Mexico, in 1986, foreign-affiliated companies provided 6 per cent of the employment, but 36 per cent of the exports of the textile, leather and clothing sector (UNCTAD, Division on Transnational Corporations and Investment 1994: 34). The importance of inward FDI has not been uniform across the developing world. In the 1950s, foreign investment was relatively unimportant in Taiwan and South Korea, although US economic aid was to some extent a substitute. Japanese FDI in Asian textile and clothing production was not substantial before the mid- to late 1960s. The countries which welcomed inward foreign investment reaped considerable benefits. Countries which shunned foreign investors, such as Indonesia before the late 1960s, suffered a diminution in industrial growth (H. Hill 1988).

Capital was more readily available to textile firms in the advanced industrial countries, although the generally perilous condition of this sector made it a less than attractive proposition for many investors (Singleton 1991: 141–67). Some major Japanese textile firms benefited from their participation in networks of allied businesses, drawn from various industries, such as chemicals, engineering and steel. These *keiretsu* or *kigyo shudan* invariably included a bank and a trading corporation, and were often revived versions of the previous *zaibatsu* groups. Firms in these alliances traded with each other more intensively than they did with outsiders, and during crises the weaker members were assisted by purchases of equity and the offer of loans from their partners (Gerlach 1992; Okazaki 1995: 93, 95). Diversification into more profitable industries may have helped some textile firms to generate revenue, which could be ploughed back into their core businesses. Mergers with firms in other sectors could result in the injection of fresh capital into the textile industry. For example, the American hosiery manufacturer, Hanes, merged with Sara Lee, a leading food processor and distributor. Since the merger, the textile activities of Sara Lee have prospered and the group has increased its presence on the international stage, acquiring plants in Australia, Europe, Asia and Latin America (Finnie 1994a). Governments provided some financial help for textile firms in the form of grants for the scrapping of obsolete capacity, and subsidies for re-equipment. These concessions were designed to moderate the pace of industrial decline. Even import protection could be regarded as an indirect source of capital because it enabled firms to maintain their profit levels and thereby purchase new plant and machinery. Inward FDI constituted a further source of capital for the textile sectors of developed economies, although this was offset by outward FDI. Foreign-owned establishments were responsible for 7.5 per cent of the jobs in the US textile industry, and 2.3 per cent of those in the apparel industry, in 1990 (Howenstine and Zeile 1994: 37). Clearly, the textile and clothing industries of the developed economies gained from their access to sophisticated capital markets. Although small firms in the developed countries often complained of difficulties in obtaining finance, their problems were modest in comparison with those of businesses in poorer countries.

Lack of adequate access to capital is a more pressing constraint on new firms in developing countries than it is on established businesses in economically advanced countries. Nevertheless, many firms in developing countries, such as England in the 1780s and South Korea in the 1960s, succeeded in finding a reliable source of capital, and this helped them to generate a competitive advantage, if not to sustain it indefinitely. Attempts by governments to increase the supply of capital in the developing Asian economies, since 1945, have had impressive results at the level of the manufacturing sector as a whole. It is probable that textile industries in these countries found it easier to obtain finance than they would have done in the absence of policies encouraging high savings. Whether or not the distribution of the enlarged pie favoured textiles over other industries is less certain.

KNOWLEDGE

Porter (1990: 75) defines knowledge as a stock of scientific, technical and marketing information. Knowledge may be stored in research institutes or laboratories in either the public or private sectors, in technical journals or in networks of highly skilled individuals. In many instances, knowledge is imported from other countries, but it must originate in research activity somewhere. Porter's approach to knowledge downplays the practical know-how and rule-of-thumb methods which are especially prominent in the earlier stages of industrialization.

Knowledge is currently being manufactured at a relatively slow pace in the textile industry. R&D spending in the textile sectors of the advanced economies is a rough indicator of efforts to increase the stock of relevant knowledge. In developing countries, most R&D is devoted to the mastering of imported knowledge, so that R&D figures for these states need to be considered in a different light. In the USA, between 1958 and 1983, R&D accounted for 0.11 per cent of the sales revenue of the textile and apparel industries, making this the least research-intensive sector of American industry. The average share of R&D in sales revenue in the US industry was 4.22 per cent. Predictably, aircraft and missiles led the field, spending 21.66 per cent of their revenue on R&D, while office computing ranked second at 15.81 per cent. The annual rate of growth of R&D expenditure in textiles and apparel was only 1 per cent in real terms between 1958 and 1983, compared with an average of 3 per cent across American industry (Lach and Rob 1992: 6). These figures understate the amount of R&D which was of use to the textile sector, since they exclude research in related industries such as textile engineering and chemicals, and R&D conducted in the public sector. Innovations in machinery and dyestuffs were more common than those in finishes or processes (Chakrabarti 1990: 263). Similar difficulties, in attributing R&D to the most appropriate sector, occurred in a wide range of industries; for example, car manufacturers benefited from R&D in the glass, steel and electronics complexes. R&D and other knowledge-enhancing activities tended to be concentrated in substantial firms, if not always the largest ones.

Textile sectors in other leading industrial nations also spent little on R&D, although their efforts were relatively more substantial than those in the USA. In Germany in 1979, R&D as a share of sales was 0.6 per cent in textiles and 0.4 per cent in clothing and leather, but 3.3 per cent in all manufacturing (Schatz and Wolter 1987: 98). Private sector R&D as a proportion of sales was 1.23 per cent in Japanese textiles in 1986, compared with an average of 3.03 per cent in Japanese manufacturing as a whole. As a share of sales, R&D in Japanese textiles doubled between 1970 and 1986, but this was no better than the average growth rate of R&D in manufacturing (Tamura and Urata 1990: 131). This growth in R&D spending as a proportion of sales illustrates the attempts of Japanese textile firms to upgrade in the face of competition from other Asian producers. But increasing R&D expenditure was only one of several strategies open to firms experiencing new competition. Some transferred production to other Asian countries or Latin America. Perhaps the expected returns from R&D were judged to be rather limited in comparison with the returns from these other strategies. An examination of Italian industry in the 1980s (Table 2.3) suggests that R&D conducted inside textile and clothing firms did not play a key role in bringing about major innovations. R&D's contribution to innovation in textiles and clothing was well below the average figure for Italian industry. The purchase of new textile machinery was the most important aspect of the innovation process. This study confirms that textiles and clothing are relatively passive with

Table 2.3 Major sources of innovation in Italian textiles and clothing in the 1980s

	Textiles	*Clothing*	*All industries*
R&D	1.1	1.3	2.1
Design	1.8	2.1	3.1
Inside proposals	1.8	1.9	2.3
Purchase of technology	0.3	0.3	0.5
Raw materials	1.0	1.2	1.2
Intermediate goods	0.5	0.6	0.8
New machinery	4.5	4.1	4.0
Human skills	0.8	0.9	1.2
Professional training	1.8	2.2	2.2
Customer needs	2.1	1.7	2.3
Suppliers	1.5	1.4	1.6
Joint ventures	0.1	0.2	0.3
Industrial exhibition	1.2	1.5	1.5
Public institutions	0.1	0.0	0.3
Consultants	0.5	0.6	0.6
Imitation	1.6	1.6	2.0

Source: Malerba (1993: 238–9)
Note: Each factor is graded on a scale of one to six

respect to the generation of technical innovation. Although R&D statistics are notoriously unreliable, it is obvious that textiles and clothing are not knowledge-intensive industries. At the level of the individual firm, many of the decisions which are likely to make or break its fortune must be taken in the areas of design and marketing. These elements of strategy require the application of substantial amounts of skill and knowledge, but the knowledge in question is of an artistic or commercial, as opposed to a technological, nature.

Despite the qualifications made in previous paragraphs, some research institutions have made valuable contributions to the knowledge resources of the textile industry. The Shirley Institute in the UK, founded in 1919, has been funded from a mixture of public and private sources. Its original purpose was to conduct research on behalf of Britain's cotton industry. Most of the firms in this industry were too small to be able to justify the construction of in-house research facilities. In recent times the Shirley Institute has been involved in a variety of projects, including the development of non-woven (thermally bonded) fabrics, joint research with glass manufacturers into the production of woven fibreglass fabrics, and work on the use of nylon yarn in the manufacture of aircraft windscreens (Shirley Institute 1988). Although the efforts of the Shirley Institute could not prevent the slide of the UK textile industry, its activities did help some British firms to upgrade and enter lucrative niche markets. The modest but enduring success of the Shirley

Institute weighs in the balance against the argument that collaborative research facilities are inherently unsatisfactory (Mowery 1984). In 1993, the American government announced plans for collaborative research in the textile industry, involving a combination of private and public sector facilities (Finnie 1994b: 44–5). Amongst the more important recent innovations in textiles, as opposed to textile machinery, are the application of wrinkle-resistance to garments made from pure cotton and the development of non-woven technologies. Much of the research in these fields has been carried out by man-made fibre producers and their subsidiaries rather than by textile producers themselves. This illustrates the importance of clustering between the textile and related industries (Noonan 1994).

Non-technical forms of knowledge, such as the experience and judge-ment of decision-makers, and the established routines and know-how of the firm, are more difficult to quantify and value (Nelson and Winter 1982). Mass and Lazonick (1991: 42–3) stress that the superior skill of the Japanese in cotton blending was one of the reasons for the strength of Japanese textiles in the first half of the twentieth century, and this point is also made by Otsuka, Ranis and Saxonhouse (1988: 30), in their historical comparison of the Japanese and Indian textile industries. Knowledge is embedded in networks of producers, financiers and distributors, which may include firms in several countries. The knowledge flowing through these networks includes information about a partner firm's reliability. Trust is a form of knowledge, in so far as it is based on an informed assessment of the behaviour of a supplier or customer (M. Casson 1991). Non-technical knowledge may be relatively more important in textiles than in other industries, simply because the amount of formal scientific knowledge used in textiles is quite modest.

The textile and clothing industries of the Asian industrializers and other developing countries follow a strategy of economizing in the area of R&D. Comparatively little new research is conducted in most of these countries, and the focus of R&D is on the assimilation of techniques imported from Japan and the West. Data are scarce, but a reasonable amount of evidence is available for South Korea, as befits its status as a rising industrial nation. As a proportion of sales, R&D in South Korean textiles was 0.92 per cent in 1985, compared with an average of 1.51 per cent across the country's manufactur-ing sector (Wakasugi 1989: 339). One substantial Korean textile company, established in 1955, began to conduct its own R&D in 1976. This firm employed twelve R&D workers in 1984 (Amsden 1989: 249). By the 1980s, South Korea was entering the ranks of the developed world, and its attempts to generate knowledge were far in advance of those made by the following wave of countries, such as the Philippines and Vietnam. Significant R&D expenditure in South Korea is a sign that its textile sector is upgrading, in response to a lengthy period of protectionism in the West and growing competition from less developed countries.

Scientific knowledge is less important in the textile industry than it is in most other types of economic endeavour. As a result, it has been relatively easy for countries with a deficiency in knowledge pertaining to the textile industry to acquire or copy information from abroad. New knowledge has made a smaller contribution to the development of the textile industry in the twentieth century than it has to many other industries. It is hard to think of an equivalent in textiles of the introduction of the aeroplane, which transformed long distance transport, or of the television, with its widespread implications for mass communications.

RAW MATERIALS

Under most conditions, it is not important for modern textile-producing regions either to grow their own cotton or to keep their own sheep. In peacetime, these basic commodities are readily available on international markets. The ability of Hong Kong to sell textiles and garments at internationally competitive prices, despite its almost complete lack of natural resources, is adequate testimony to this principle. There appears to be no correlation between a region's competitive advantage in the production of natural fibres and the success of its textile and garment sector.

An abundance of sheep failed to stimulate the development of efficient wool textile industries in either Australia, New Zealand or South Africa. In the main, these major sheep-rearing nations exported their wool to factories in Europe, the USA and Japan. The history of New Zealand's wool textile industry, for example, has been marked by a protracted struggle for survival among a small number of modestly sized firms. New Zealand's wool textile industry was stunted by a combination of capital shortages, high labour costs and restricted domestic markets. Geographical isolation and a limited degree of protection gave firms a measure of relief from import competition, but they remained vulnerable. Export opportunities were severely circumscribed, except for the highest quality goods (Stewart 1975; McLean 1981). The British cotton textile industry stood at the opposite end of the spectrum, with respect to the local availability of raw materials. But Lancashire was not seriously disadvantaged by the absence of cotton plantations in the British Isles. Cotton could be imported from the West Indies, Egypt, India and the USA, as long as international sea routes were free of obstruction. In the nineteenth century, the cotton districts of the Southern USA were an economic colony of Lancashire (Willoughby 1993). Without British demand, the development of the cotton belt would have been considerably delayed. The American South was, in a sense, part of the economy of north-west England, just as parts of many Asian countries are now integrated into the textile economy of the Osaka region. Shipping shortages during the world wars reduced the British cotton industry's access to imported raw materials, but these were exceptional periods (Lacey 1947; Singleton 1994). Arguably of more interest was the 'cotton famine', during the American Civil War. It is still commonly believed that the Northern blockade of Confederate ports resulted in a severe crisis in the British cotton manufacturing districts. But the depression in Lancashire during the early 1860s was the consequence of a cyclical fall in demand for cotton goods on the Indian market. Supplies of cotton from the Confederacy were severely cut, but British mills substituted raw material from Egypt, India and even Japan (Farnie 1979: 135–70). Matters might have been different if the British demand for cotton had been high during the Civil War. What remains clear is that, except in time of war, the British cotton industry was not put at a competitive disadvantage by its lack of domestic cotton plantations. Japan's cotton industry found itself in a similar position. Although Japan was a producer of raw cotton in the nineteenth century, once its cotton industry began to mechanize, it became apparent that Japanese agriculture would not be able to satisfy the increase in demand for raw material. Japan began to import raw cotton from India, China, the USA and Japanese colonies such as Formosa and Manchuria. Wool had to be imported from the 1900s onwards. Australia became an important supplier of wool to Japanese mills in the 1920s and 1930s. Japan, however, remained an important producer of silk (Seki 1956: 104–6; Tsokhas 1990; Park and Anderson 1992).

Imports of natural fibres have been crucial to the growth of East Asian textile industries since 1945. Between 1965 and 1969, East Asia (i.e., Japan, Hong Kong, Taiwan, South Korea, China and the ASEAN states) accounted for 24 per cent of the world's imports of natural fibres, and their share rose to 37 per cent in 1985–7 (K. Anderson 1992: 12). These Asian countries were unable to sustain the expansion of their textile sectors on the basis of domestic supplies of raw material. South Korea and other interventionist Asian states subsidized the raw cotton imports of successful exporters. India, which lost its main cotton-growing districts, during partition in 1947, attempted to stimulate raw cotton production in new areas. Imports of raw cotton and man-made fibres were restricted and prices were kept high in order to assist domestic cultivators. This policy resulted in rising costs for Indian textile producers (Nayyar 1976: 68; Mazumdar 1991: 1201). By contrast, Pakistan, after its separation from India, possessed an abundance of cotton fields, but few textile factories. The Pakistani government aided indigenous entrepreneurs to establish a textile industry to use this raw material. Despite the advantage of easy access to raw materials, Pakistan's cotton industry failed to match the performance of its rivals in Hong Kong, South Korea and Taiwan (Adams and Iqbal 1983: 175–204). From time to time, even large producers of natural fibres may encounter troublesome shortages. In China during the 1980s there were severe shortfalls in wool deliveries. The liberalization of controls over the textile and clothing industries, and their subsequent expansion, put increasing pressure on the wool-growing sector, which did not undergo institutional reform until somewhat later (Findlay 1992).

It could be argued that the development of man-made fibre industries in the twentieth century represented a defensive response by countries, such as Britain, Germany and Japan, which had a deficit in trade in natural fibres. For instance, the Nazi government deliberately fostered man-made fibre production for strategic reasons. Germany was particularly vulnerable to blockade, and it was not a major producer of natural fibres (Chandler 1990: 580–1). But this line of reasoning cannot be pursued very far. The USA, a country with abundant domestic supplies of cotton, also became a leading producer of man-made fibres. Man-made fibre industries were in the main developed with the objective of adding variety to existing textile sectors. Their purpose was not to overcome a chronic shortage of natural fibres, which usually did not exist.

World trade in natural fibres has been relatively unrestricted, hence the textile manufacturers of most industrial countries have been able to import cotton and wool at world prices, adjusted for transport costs and the undervaluation or overvaluation of currencies. Agricultural protectionism has largely focused on the production of foodstuffs. Raw cotton could not have been produced at a reasonable cost in northern Europe, but it could have been grown in southern Europe or Japan. However, its price would have been exorbitant.

CONCLUSION

A plentiful supply of standardized labour is crucial in the early stages of textile development. Although the eighteenth-century textile inventions were emphatically labour-saving (Chapman 1987: 20), the stimulus which they gave to the industry led to a huge increase in demand for cheap labour. Regions lacking adequate supplies of factory labour, such as New England, found it difficult to compete with densely populated districts, such as Lancashire. Perhaps the need for further economies in the use of labour spurred the Americans on to the invention of the ring frame and the automatic loom. Capital shortages may have induced the Japanese to develop lighter and cheaper automatic looms, such as the Toyoda. The upgrading of textile and apparel production in the developed countries after 1945 was a reaction to the growing scarcity of cheap standardized labour, while the establishment of low-technology textile industries in South Korea, Taiwan and Indonesia was a rational response to comparative factor disadvantages in capital, knowledge and skills. Selective factor disadvantages clearly played some role in the development of modern textile industries.

But it is difficult to imagine an industry which does not have at least some relative factor disadvantages. The early American automobile industry lacked a domestic supply of rubber, while the Japanese car industry in the 1950s was severely deficient in technical knowledge and had to import it from Europe. Every successful industry has had to struggle to overcome selective factor disadvantages. During the 1950s and 1960s, textile and apparel produ-cers in Taiwan and South Korea took great strides forward towards master-ing their selective factor disadvantages. But their competitors in Indonesia and the Philippines were less successful. Perhaps this reflected differences in the commitment of governments to the fostering of industrial development. Selective factor disadvantages generate positive responses in some situations, but fail to do so in others. The process by which these disadvantages are overcome remains somewhat mysterious.

Factor conditions exert a major influence on the growth and survival of industries. It is understandable that they should occupy a prominent place in the diamond. Textile and clothing industries are relatively intensive users of some factors, including standardized labour and entrepreneurial skills, but relatively sparing users of others, such as fixed capital and formal technical knowledge. The evidence suggests that favourable input conditions are unlikely to confer a permanent competitive advantage on a textile industry. Cheap labour, if it is reasonably competent, may provide competitive advan-tage for a time, but sooner or later other countries with even cheaper labour will undermine this source of vitality. Textile industries must learn to adapt and upgrade, installing more advanced machinery, increasing their R&D and searching for niche markets. Investment in higher-quality inputs enables producers in mature economies to retain some of their competitive advan-tage, especially in more specialized markets. As textile industries move along their life cycles, they progress from a situation in which cheap disciplined labour is the foundation of competitive advantage to one in which technical knowledge and management skills are critical.

3

DEMAND CONDITIONS

Favourable domestic demand conditions are an important element in the home base of many industries. A secure home base is often the platform from which a successful export campaign is launched. Porter (1990: 86–100) identifies three key aspects of the domestic demand environment: the composition of demand; its absolute size and rate of growth; and the extent to which preferences in the home market can be imprinted on consumers abroad.

The composition of domestic demand has a number of significant features (ibid.: 86–92). Porter stresses that the quality of home demand may be more important than its absolute size. Firms are in a better position to monitor and interpret the needs of customers in their home region than they are of the requirements of purchasers in distant places. Information gathered about customer requirements may have a major impact on decisions about the introduction of new products and the styling of existing lines. For example, the British healthcare products company, Smith & Nephew, forged close links with hospitals in the vicinity of its factories, so that information could be gathered about the performance of its bandages and other medical textiles, and about the needs of doctors for new products. This information was used in the development of improved medical textiles. Since British hospitals were relatively sophisticated customers, Smith & Nephew was in a good position to expand into international markets on the basis of its domestic success (Foreman-Peck 1995: 126–7). Sophisticated customers in the home market force producers to upgrade. The same argument applies to the market for fashionable apparel. Home consumers who are in advance of world trends are an asset to domestic firms.

The implications of the volume and rate of growth of domestic demand are somewhat less straightforward, as Porter (1990: 92–7) concedes. In industries, such as chemicals and motor vehicles, which are marked by large technological economies of scale, an extensive home market is of enormous importance. But a large home demand is not essential if the minimum efficient scale of production is modest. With the exceptions of man-made fibre production and finishing, economies of scale are quite limited in the textile and clothing industries. But strong home markets may be desirable for other reasons. For instance, if domestic demand is thought to be less unstable than exports, an extensive home demand may be necessary to stimulate the investment that is required to establish a platform for exporting in future decades. On the other hand, firms could become complacent and unenthusiastic about exporting if they have access to large home markets. A limited domestic market acts as a powerful incentive for companies to seek export orders. High domestic demand will not facilitate the development of competitive advantage, unless it is for products which are popular in other countries. The implications of the growth rate of domestic demand are equally ambiguous. A high growth rate could act as a launching pad for exporters; but a buoyant domestic market could also lead to the neglect of exports. On balance, Porter (ibid.) believes that a large and dynamic home market is preferable. There should also be a large number of domestic purchasers, since undue concentration of buying power could result in the squeezing of manufacturing profits and a fall in investment. Demand for new products should increase rapidly and reach saturation point at a relatively early stage, so that producers are under constant pressure to look for new ideas.

Under some circumstances, domestic demand patterns can be internationalized. Multinationals operating abroad are likely to favour the purchase of inputs from their home country. Domestic tastes may be exported by the entertainment industry, and through tourism and emigration. Political ties, such as those between Britain and its empire, helped to replicate some aspects of British domestic demand overseas, especially in countries such as Australia, New Zealand and South Africa. American cultural hegemony since 1945 has had an even greater impact on consumer behaviour around the world (ibid.: 97–9).

Porter's analysis of domestic demand can be put into context by comparing it with the standard microeconomic theory on this subject. A major difference between Porter and the textbooks is that Porter regards the geographical origin of demand – whether domestic or foreign – as significant. Microeconomic theory contends that the quantity demanded of any good or service depends on its price, the level of income, the prices of other goods (especially substitutes and complements), tastes and population. It is important to note that Porter concentrates on the non-price factors that influence demand. The composition of demand is a matter of tastes and income, while the size and rate of growth of the domestic market are determined by income and population. It is not clear where prices enter into Porter's analysis of demand. Upgrading is the focus of Porter's work, but a competitive price is surely of importance when a firm makes the leap into export markets.

This chapter emphasizes the composition and quality of domestic demand, rather than the ability of the home market to generate economies of scale. It also recognizes that the composition of demand in any country is liable to change as it progresses along the road of economic development.

SIZE OF MARKET

The United States was the single largest final consumer of textile products, accounting for almost 18 per cent of the world total, in 1992 (see Table 3.1). US consumption would have been even higher in the absence of import controls which raised internal prices and constrained demand. Although the European Union as a whole possessed a home market to rival that of the USA, the individual EU states did not have large domestic markets by American standards. Consumption in the former Soviet bloc suffered in the late 1980s and early 1990s, as a result of political and economic upheavals. China was the dominant fibre consumer in the developing world, reflecting its enormous population and its comparatively high per capita fibre consumption. China ranked second in the world as a final consumer of fibre products. East and South-east Asia constituted a smaller market than did Japan for textile products. World consumption of textile products grew at 1.61 per

Table 3.1 Final fibre consumption by selected countries and regions, 1980–92

	Final consumption ('000 tons)			*Annual change (%)*	*Fibre consumption per head (kg)*	
	1980	*1986*	*1992*	*1986–92*	*1980*	*1992*
Developed countries						
USA	4,749	6,055	6,800	1.95	20.8	28.1
EC(12)	5,123	5,454	6,550	3.10	15.2	19.3
Other Western Europe	815	848	950	1.91	15.1	17.0
Japan	1,961	2,136	2,800	4.61	16.8	23.0
Eastern Europe	1,207	1,246	700	−9.16	12.7	7.1
Former USSR	3,894	4,127	3,300	−3.66	14.6	11.7
Other	1,012	1,186	1,300	1.54	12.8	14.6
Total	18,760	21,052	22,400	1.04	16.0	18.2
Developing countries						
China	3,944	5,569	6,200	1.80	4.0	5.7
Latin America	1,961	2,145	2,250	0.80	5.5	5.4
South Asia	1,773	2,138	2,700	3.97	2.0	2.6
East & South-East Asia	1,195	1,432	2,150	7.05	3.5	5.4
Other	2,252	2,292	2,400	0.77	3.5	3.0
Total	11,125	13,576	15,700	2.45	3.4	3.8
World total	29,885	34,628	38,100	1.61	6.8	7.1

Source: Coker (1993: 16, 18)
Notes: 1992 figures are estimates. China includes Taiwan. As a result of downward revisions of population estimates, the figures for consumption per head overstate growth since 1980

cent between 1986 and 1992. East and South-east Asia, Japan, South Asia and the EU enjoyed growth rates of consumption that were substantially above the world average. Fibre consumption per capita was highest in the USA, followed by Japan and then the EU, as one would expect in view of their comparative prosperity. Per capita consumption of textiles in the developing world remained very low in the early 1990s. Final fibre consumption per capita in the USA was four times the world average, and seven times the average for developing countries.

There seems to be little or no relationship between the absolute size of the home market for textiles and the possession of competitive advantage. Porter (1990: 292) shows that the biggest market in the world, the USA, lacked competitive advantage in any final textile product in 1985. Although Hong Kong, South Korea and Taiwan suffered from limited home markets, they became major textile and clothing exporters during the 1960s and 1970s. China has a huge domestic market and now has the potential to become the leading force in the world textile industry. The high rate of growth of domestic consumption in East and South-east Asia, between 1986 and 1992, benefited producers in this region. However, high consumption growth in this region was the consequence of earlier industrial success rather than an original stimulus to expansion.

The small scale of establishments in countries with thriving textile and clothing industries militates against the argument that a large home market is a precondition for competitive advantage. In Italy, in 1981, the average size of textile plants was eight workers, while that of clothing, footwear and leather plants was six workers (Navaretti and Perosino 1995: 183). Establishments with between 20 and 200 workers were responsible for three-quarters of the value added generated by the textile and clothing sector of Hong Kong in 1989 (UNIDO 1993: 540). This does not mean that a home market is unimportant, especially during the early stages of industrialization. Even though the scale of production may be low, and the home market small, preferential access to domestic outlets gives firms an opportunity to master new technologies and improve their organizational and marketing skills. Import substitution normally precedes expansion into foreign markets. Domestic demand was vital in the early days of the British cotton industry, during the eighteenth century (Lemire 1991). Small domestic markets supplied an adequate stimulus to the South Korean and Taiwanese textile and clothing industries during their import substitution phases in the 1950s (Ho 1978: 186–223; Amsden 1989). Hong Kong did not follow this route, since it had several unique advantages in the 1950s: an inflow of experienced entrepreneurs from the Chinese mainland, bringing with them plentiful supplies of capital, and free entry into the British market until 1959 (Wong 1988). Small countries, such as South Korea and Taiwan, turned to exports at a relatively early stage in their industrial development, in the 1960s, because their home markets could not sustain rapid growth for more than a few years.

Larger countries, such as India and Indonesia, may have suffered as a result of the greater scope which their economies offered for a protracted period of import substitution. The histories of the textile industries of Britain, Japan, South Korea and Taiwan all indicate that it is advantageous to reduce dependence on the home market sooner rather than later. Much later, as competitive advantage begins to wane, the home market may enjoy a new phase of importance as a refuge from more difficult conditions in inter-national markets.

INCOMES, DEVELOPMENT AND DOMESTIC DEMAND

Countries vary in the configuration of their textile and apparel markets. Wealthy countries differ from poor, largely agricultural states. We would also expect to find considerable diversity among nations occupying similar income levels, due to varying tastes.

A recent study, employing 1990 data, illustrates the cross-sectional rela-tionship between per capita income and final fibre consumption (as opposed to mill consumption) in a large group of countries (Coker 1993: 20). Per capita final fibre consumption increased quite rapidly as per capita incomes rose to about US$5,000. Nations in this very low income group included China, India, Pakistan and Bangladesh. Economic growth in these countries resulted in a large increase in fibre demand. At per capita incomes above US$5,000 and, even more so, at those above US$15,000, the relationship between income and fibre consumption became more problematical. Per capita fibre consumption rose more slowly in the income bands occupied by the wealthier countries. In some cases, the connection between income and fibre consumption appeared to break down. Switzerland, Australia and the Netherlands all recorded per capita incomes above US$15,000 in 1990. Although income per capita in Switzerland was approximately double that in Australia and the Netherlands, all three countries consumed roughly the same quantity of fibre per head of population. France and Germany had very similar levels of per capita income, but German consumers used considerably more fibre per capita than their French neighbours.

These differences suggest that, especially among nations which have attained high income levels, there were significant variations in preferences for textile products relative to other goods and services. As a further illustra-tion of the relationship between income and apparel consumption, we could examine the share of clothing in consumer budgets in EU countries, in 1991. The poorer states, including Spain (9.2 per cent), Portugal (9.0 per cent) and Greece (8.9 per cent), tended to devote a larger share of total consumer spending to clothing and footwear than did the more prosperous ones, such as Denmark (5.4 per cent) and France (6.4 per cent). Consumers in the wealthier EU states allocated larger shares of their expenditure to other goods and services because their need for clothing was largely satisfied. However, Italy, which is no longer one of the poorer nations of Europe, devoted 10 per cent of its consumer expenditure to clothing and footwear. National preferences, in the Italian case, determined that clothing occupied a more prominent place in consumer budgets than one would have expected in an advanced economy (Leyland 1994: 98). Tastes in apparently closely related areas may be difficult to reconcile. It is curious that the Italians are less adventurous than northern Europeans in home furnishings, preferring plain sheets, towels and carpets (Stogdon 1993: 149).

Income elasticity of demand is a measure of the responsiveness of consumer expenditure on a product to changes in income. Income elasticity can be measured over various intervals, with different results. A high short-run income elasticity of demand would indicate that the industry under investigation was rather vulnerable to cyclical variations in unemployment and real incomes. A low long-run income elasticity would suggest that the prospects for rapid long-term growth in home demand were limited, making the industry less attractive to potential investors. Houthakker and Taylor (1970: 69–70, 84, 166-7), using US data from the 1930s to the 1960s, calculated that the short-run income elasticity of demand for clothing was 1.14; this figure was in the middle of a range which included most other consumer products and services of the mid-twentieth century. Spending on clothing and household textiles varied pro-cyclically. Most items of clothing were quite durable, so that purchases could be delayed when times were hard and accelerated when conditions improved. Consumers behaved in a similar manner in their expenditure on cars and washing machines. Apparel had one of the lowest long-run income elasticities (0.51) in Houthakker and Taylor's survey. This industry did not offer much prospect for rapid secular increases in demand. The long-run income elasticity for home furnishings (0.65) was not much higher. For comparison, 3.0 was the long-run income elasticity for radio and TV receivers, records and musical instruments. Estimates of the long-run income elasticity of demand for apparel, in the USA, between the mid-1960s and mid-1980s have produced disconcertingly varied results: either 0.85 or 2.1, depending on the source of data employed. Moreover, it is not easy to distinguish between the effects on clothing expenditure of fluctuations in income, changes in relative prices and demographic phenomena, so that there must be some doubt about the accuracy of calculations in this area (Cline 1990: 46–7). Despite these difficulties, the broad picture is clear. Demand for clothing rises slowly over the long run in developed economies. Once a certain level of income has been reached, consumers prefer to spend a rising share of any additional income on optional items rather than necessities. The twentieth century has witnessed the invention of new consumption goods, such as TVs, VCRs and personal computers. Air travel has also come within the reach of ordinary consumers since the 1950s. As a result of this expansion in the range of alternative goods and services, the opportunity cost of using extra income to buy clothes or household furnishings has increased (Jacobs and Shipp 1990). Lebergott (1993: 91) shows that the proportion of personal expenditure allocated to clothing and jewellery, in the USA, rose from 13.7 per cent in 1900 to 17.1 per cent in 1920, but thereafter it fell to 9.9 per cent in 1960 and 6.4 per cent in 1990. Between 1900 and 1990 per capita spending on clothing in the USA rose by 238 per cent in real terms, compared with increases of 2,060 per cent for household appliances, 1,136 per cent for recreation and 2,166 per cent for automobiles (ibid.: 76). It is interesting to note that, in 1990, urban households in China spent 13.4 per cent of their budget on clothing, a very similar proportion to that in the USA in 1900 (Chai 1992: 730; Anon 1996). Although we should not press the comparison between China and the USA too far, perhaps we should expect the demand for apparel in China to grow less quickly than Chinese incomes during the twenty-first century. Textile and apparel producers in wealthy countries should be aware that they are operating in a slowly growing home market, compared with firms in other industries. This should be an incentive to them to seek out export markets and to upgrade, in order to obtain a share of the market for higher value-added textile and apparel products.

Income elasticities differ from country to country. One study of seventeen countries, occupying varying rungs of the development ladder during the years 1955 to 1968, found that the expenditure elasticity of demand for clothing was highest in middle-income countries, but that it fell in both lower- and higher-income countries (Lluch, Powell and Williams 1977: 54). While such findings should be treated with caution, a reasonable explanation would be that, in middle-income countries, the purchase of more stylish clothing was a symbol of new-found prosperity, since more expensive items, such as cars, were not yet within the grasp of most consumers. Expenditure elasticities of demand for apparel may have been lower in the poorest countries because clothes were almost a basic necessity. The expenditure elasticity may have been lower in the richest countries because more valuable goods, such as cars, were the most sought-after status symbols.

Consumer units in the top quintile (or top 20 per cent) of the US income distribution in 1988 spent more than five times as much on apparel and footwear as those in the bottom quintile. Male consumers in the top quintile bought more than seven times as much clothing as males in the lowest quintile. Females in the lower quintiles of the income distribution consumed almost twice as much apparel as their male counterparts, but females in the highest quintile bought only 30 per cent more apparel than men in the same group. Poor men, it would seem, had very little interest in their appearance, in comparison with poor women. Expenditure on clothing increases with educational level, although this phenomenon could be a by-product of the more important relationship between education and income. Lower-income groups in the USA bought about one-seventh of their clothing second-hand in the 1960s (Magrabi, Chung, Chu and Yang 1991: 129, 131). In the 1970s and 1980s, higher income groups in the USA actually spent a bigger percentage of their budget on clothing than poorer people (Magrabi, Chung, Chu and Yang 1991: 130; United States, Office of Technology Assessment 1987: 18). Prosperous countries contain many consumers who are willing and able to pay for apparel of a high quality. Other things being equal, this segment of the market should provide a secure base for domestic manufacturers.

Men and women clearly do not have identical spending patterns with respect to apparel. Over short periods, the Houthakker and Taylor (1970: 69–70) study indicates that men had a higher income elasticity of demand for clothing than women, suggesting that men were more willing than women to adjust their apparel purchases to fluctuations in income. Over longer periods, women had a higher income elasticity of demand for clothing than men, possibly reflecting the greater interest of women in clothing, at least in the mid-twentieth century. A recent study of demand conditions in France found that per capita consumption on apparel in 1993 was as follows: boys, aged two to fourteen, 1,870 fr.; men 1,910 fr.; girls, aged two to fourteen, 2,225 fr.; women 3,165 fr.; and babies 4,560 fr. (Lewis 1995: 64). Although high expenditure on babywear could be due to the rapid physical growth of infants, there is also an element of competition among mothers to spend money on their babies. One could speculate that the babywear and childrenswear market may have grown in relative importance during the twentieth century, because children are no longer regarded as income-earning assets, but rather as sources of emotional satisfaction.

Demographic and social changes affect the pattern of demand for textiles. Rapid increases in population in Asia, Africa and Latin America have created growing markets for local manufacturers of basic textiles. But supplying low-quality textiles to the burgeoning masses of poor domestic consumers may not be the best preparation for an assault on world markets. If increasing population does have a favourable impact on the textile sectors of developing countries, it is more likely to operate through downward pressure on the wages of textile and clothing workers. The changing age distribution of the world's population also has implications for textile and apparel manufacturers. Older consumers currently spend significantly less on clothing than the young. Retired people have lower incomes, larger stocks of old clothing and a declining interest in fashion. Approximately 16 per cent of the population of the developed countries were at least sixty years old in the mid-1980s. By 2025, it is expected that about 25 per cent of the population of the developed world will be at least sixty years old. In the less-developed regions, the proportion of people aged sixty or more is also predicted to increase, from between 6 and 7 per cent in the mid-1980s to about 12 per cent in 2025. There is some evidence to suggest that, in the economically developed democracies, the growing electoral influence of the elderly will be used to increase their incomes relative to younger people (Kono 1989). A policy of raising taxes to fund better state pensions and medical care for the aged would limit the spending of the more fashion-conscious younger age groups, without leading to a compensating increase in spending on apparel by the elderly. The ageing population of the rich countries presents the apparel and textile industries with some problems.

Domestic textile markets are segmented by fibre. Cotton remains the dominant fibre at the global level, constituting 48.8 per cent of final consumption in 1990, compared with 38.9 per cent for synthetics, 7.2 per cent for cellulosic fibres (rayon) and 5.1 per cent for wool. Climate and income largely explain the relative usage of the two main natural fibres in different parts of the world. Wool products, which are both expensive and more suitable for cooler climates, are most popular in the high-income countries of the temperate zones. By contrast, cotton's popularity is greatest in the developing world, where its share of final fibre consumption is 66 per cent, compared with a mere 40 per cent in the developed countries. Cotton has fared better in the USA than in most other developed countries, partly because of government subsidies and partly because of consumer loyalty to a home-grown fibre. Synthetics, and synthetic–natural mixtures, rose to popularity in most countries in the 1960s and 1970s. Since 1980, however, natural fibres have fought back in the richer countries, where consumers have started to attach greater value to products made from natural materials (Morris 1994; Roche 1994). A similar return to traditional preferences occurred in the second half of the nineteenth century, among the middle and upper classes of Britain, and this created opportunities for specialist fabric and carpet designers such as William Morris (Harvey and Press 1991). Meanwhile, in the developing countries, the durability of synthetic fabrics, and the ease with which they can be given bright colours and designs, are highly marketable features. Between 1977 and 1986, the share of man-made fibres in the textile and apparel purchases of the bottom quintile of the Indian income distribution rose from 14 per cent to 39 per cent. This reflected a fall in the relative price of man-made fibres (Roy 1993: 212). It is a moot point whether variations in local demand for different fibres are a key determinant of regional differences in competitive advantage. Despite a large home demand for cotton fabrics, in the nineteenth and twentieth centuries the USA never succeeded in gaining a strong competitive advantage in world markets for cotton textiles. Britain and Japan, however, did succeed in building internationally competitive cotton industries on the foundations of strong home demand. Was England's competitive advantage in supplying woollen cloth in medieval times due to the high domestic demand for woollen garments in a cool climate, the suitability of the land for maintaining sheep or other factors? It is difficult to provide brief answers to such questions, since it is necessary to consider the interaction between all of the relevant variables. Perhaps too much weight should not be placed on a single factor, such as domestic demand.

In developed economies, the market for home furnishings and technical textiles is relatively large. About 36 per cent of all fibres used by the textile industry in the EU in 1992 were converted into household furnishings, including carpets, and 18 per cent of all fibres were channelled into technical applications, including tyre cord (Anon 1994b: 95). Industrial uses of fibres have become steadily more important during the twentieth century. Motor vehicles and aircraft are significant consumers of fabric, in the form of material for strengthening tyres, and upholstery. Until the 1940s, fabric was also widely employed in the manufacture of aircraft fuselages. As well as providing a further domestic outlet for fabric, the growth of the motor vehicle and aircraft industries had a positive effect on textile exports, because fabrics were embodied in shipments of transportation equipment. Collins & Aikman, now one of the largest textile companies in the USA, was a medium-sized Philadelphia firm, of no particular importance, until the 1920s. Collins & Aikman then took advantage of the shift from open-topped to closed-compartment cars, which was accompanied by the replacement of leather upholstery with seating fabric. The company entered into long-term contracts to supply GM and Ford, and prospered in the wake of the rise of the motor vehicle industry (Scranton 1989: 165, 325, 396). Firestone's investment in textile production in New England in the 1920s, which was made with a view to supplying cotton cord for its tyre plants, contributed to the survival of the textile industry in this ailing region (Lief 1951: 1927). Existing textile producers, such as the Lancashire firm of Bottomleys, converted mills to the production of tyre cord, in the interwar period, in response to the better prospects offered by working for the motor vehicle industry (Hess 1957: 35–7). The benefits received by textile industries from the increase in tyre manufacturing were limited by the tendency of tyre producers to establish factories in foreign markets, as opposed to supplying these markets by exports. This trend was already highly developed by 1939 (G. Jones 1984; French 1987). Cotton was the most extensively used fibre during the early development of the tyre industry. By the late 1930s, rayon was taking over from cotton in many countries, because of its strength. Polyester, on account of its cheapness, was adopted for light vehicles in North America and Japan, from the 1960s onwards, although rayon remained popular in Europe. Nylon and steel are used in the manufacture of tyres for vehicles which need to be of rugged construction. During the 1980s, Japan replaced France as the world's leading exporter of tyres. The five largest tyre exporters in 1990 were, in descending order: Japan, France, West Germany, the USA and the UK. South Korea was the only developing country with large tyre exports, as befitted its status as a successful car producer. These new markets have assisted South Korea's now mature textile industry to defend its position. South Korea also had the highest ratio of tyre exports to imports of any country, in 1990 (Barlow, Jayasuriya and Tan 1994: 210, 226–31). Advanced non-woven textiles also find uses in the motor vehicle industry. Freudenberg Group, the world's largest non-woven textile producer, manufactures filters from staple fibre for use in the interior of cars at its factory at Weinheim, Germany. As well as supplying German car manufacturers, Freudenberg exports filters to other European countries and their car factories. The group's plant at Colmar, France, has recently added capacity for the production of a new roofing substrate (Noonan 1994: 32). Overall, textile manufacturers in the economically advanced countries have gained a great deal from the emergence of new industrial uses for fibres.

As countries develop their economies, home demand for textile and apparel products is likely to grow at a diminishing rate. The share of textile products in final consumer expenditure falls, although it remains of significance. Domestic consumers become increasingly sophisticated as their incomes rise, and textile and apparel producers must learn how to respond, if they are either to retain their home markets and develop higher value-added products for export. We have seen that one successful answer to these challenges is for firms to move into industrial textiles. Another approach is to emphasize fashion.

THE INFLUENCE OF FASHION AND DISTRIBUTION

Tastes and fashions are far from identical across international boundaries, and may even vary within an individual country. In fashion there are leaders and followers. Apparel producers located in regions which are centres for the diffusion of new fashions have a competitive advantage measured in time.

Fashion goods occupy a large slice of the market in wealthy countries, although it must be remembered that fashion may not be synonymous with quality. Three broad sub-categories of the apparel market were identified in the USA in the mid-1980s: a fashion segment, with a product life of ten weeks (35 per cent of the total); a seasonal segment, with a twenty-week product life (45 per cent); and a basic segment, consisting of products sold at a steady rate throughout the year (United States, Office of Technology Assessment 1987: 16). Basic textiles predominate in poor countries, but luxury items, including silks, are not entirely absent, and may be worn for special occasions such as weddings and religious festivals. In India, silks are also draped around the statues of gods. Silk constituted 2 per cent of the textile and apparel purchases of India's lowest quintile of consumers in 1986, compared with 12 per cent for the wealthiest quintile. Since India is the second most populous nation in the world, it constitutes a large market for high quality textiles (Roy 1993: 126). Similar extravagance could be found in early twentieth-century Lancashire, where girls wore dresses made from luxurious material when they marched in the religious and ethnic processions on Whit Monday (Roberts 1984: 161).

Variety and conformity in clothing arise from a mixture of practical and cultural considerations. Garments have two main purposes in every culture:

first, to protect people from the elements and, second, to decorate the wearer in a manner which has some kind of social meaning. Some items of apparel convey an explicit meaning. Young English ladies who supported the rising of Bonnie Prince Charlie, in 1745, wore garters into which were stitched seditious mottoes, such as 'Our Prince is brave, our cause is just' (Monod 1989: 289). Potential suppliers have considerable scope to add value in both areas. A wet towel gives some protection against heat and flames, but specialized protective clothing is required for efficient firefighting. There is nothing to stop people in Europe from wearing identical Chairman Mao suits, but in practice the vast majority purchase garments which incorporate some degree of elaboration. Those who either cannot afford new clothes, or base their decisions solely on price, buy second-hand garments.

Clothing is a form of communication, although it is not a precise one. Apparel influences how people are assessed by others, especially strangers. In previous centuries, sumptuary laws tried to ensure that people of lower status did not wear clothing judged to be suitable only for their betters, since this could lead to social confusion. Today it is a crime to impersonate a police officer. A business suit or a white medical coat gives the wearer a certain authority. Of course, the message transmitted by clothing could be either accidentally, or deliberately, misleading. A burglar could dress as an estate agent or a lunatic could masquerade as a surgeon. The interpretation of clothing depends on the context. An England football shirt has one meaning when it is worn on the field of play, but another one when worn by a hooligan fighting with the riot police. People use dress to associate themselves with a particular group, draw attention to themselves, or make themselves invisible (McCracken 1988: 57–70). Certain rules of clothing are almost immutable, for no apparent reason, other than tradition. The most obvious example is the rule that men do not wear skirts, except in Scotland and Greece. Despite the efforts of eminent designers, including Lorenzo Riva and Jean-Paul Gaultier, this taboo remains powerful (Franklin 1995). Such a convention reduces the options of apparel producers throughout the Western world, except in Scotland and Greece.

Differentiation in clothing is related to the level of a country's economic and cultural development. According to a contemporary report, 80 per cent of the British population bought at least some ready-made clothing by 1860 (Chapman 1993: 5). However, for men in particular there was little variety. Jackets and trousers, and a sombre suit on Sundays, were the norm during the early twentieth century. Working-class couples with young children had little money to spare for clothing, although young unmarried women with jobs, who lived at home with their parents, could afford to dress smartly (Meacham 1977: 82–4). A respectable young man, recalled the Labour politician, Roy Hattersley, was expected to look like an undertaker's assistant. This state of affairs was undermined, in the mid-1950s, by growing prosperity and changes in popular culture (Mort and Thompson 1994). In 1960, the British press was shocked to find that both young men and women were beginning to spend lavishly on clothing (Benson 1994: 67). But the development of fashion-consciousness, especially among men, did not proceed at a constant pace across national boundaries. The British remained comparatively reluctant to spend their earnings on apparel. In 1991, British consumers devoted 5.8 per cent of their budgets to clothing and footwear, whereas the Italians spent 10 per cent on these items. Only the Danes and the East Germans, in the EU, spent a lower proportion of their budgets on clothing than the British (Leyland 1994: 98).

Conspicuous consumption, in clothing, and other goods and services, could have several motivations. People who are ascending the social ladder may choose expensive clothes either to distance themselves from less successful groups or else to identify themselves with their new peers. Those who are sliding down the ladder may be prepared to spend freely in order to keep up appearances. As well as being an expression of vertical social relationships, conspicuous consumption reflects competition within social groups (Veblen 1922; R. Mason 1981). For example, the aspiring youth of Eastern Europe compete with each other to acquire jeans displaying the most popular foreign labels. The higher the price, the more exclusive the garment, and therefore the greater the demand among those engaged in the competition. Interest in fashion now begins at an early age – fourteen or fifteen in New Zealand, according to one leading Wellington department store. The label was a critical attribute of any garment, according to press interviews conducted in New Zealand in 1994. One young man, Robbie, aged seventeen, said that higher prices made clothing more appealing and did not deter purchasers. Rikki (also male), sixteen, added that it was important for boys to wear 'label' clothing because girls would have nothing do with boys who were badly dressed. Colours fluctuated in popularity from year to year. Poo, a yellowish-brown, was the preferred colour in New Zealand's lower North Island, in early 1994 (Daniel 1994).

Increasingly demanding domestic tastes do not guarantee a bright future for the New Zealand apparel industry. Local manufacturers should gain some comfort from the knowledge that not all consumers worry about price. But appealing designs, efficient distribution channels and effective marketing are necessary before a promising local market can be converted into a lucrative regional base. Even if New Zealand manufacturers can satisfy domestic consumers, they may find it difficult to succeed in export markets, where tastes may be subtly different. A visitor to New Zealand, in 1996, compared student fashions in Wellington with those in Manchester in 1985.

Young Japanese consumers are even more fashion-conscious than young New Zealanders. Time, place and occasion (TPO) are said to be vital considerations in Japan and, in consequence, young consumers require an extensive array of garments. According to a survey conducted in the early 1980s, Japanese shoppers paid less attention to labels than to quality and design.

Although imported fashion goods, especially European brands, had considerable appeal, foreign apparel was not always suited to local tastes and fits. Markets were highly segmented. A 1981 study identified seven distinct looks among young women, ranging from 'Yokohama Trad' to 'Rock and Roll'. Japanese women aged fifteen to twenty-four regarded fashionable dressing as an important form of self-expression (Brummett 1987). Opportunities clearly existed for Japanese clothing producers to modify popular Western styles to cater for local tastes and conditions. The case of worsted suits demontrates that some parts of the Japanese clothing industry have responded positively to the increasing sophistication of domestic demand. Japan is the world's largest market for worsted men's suits, since wool is held in particularly high esteem by Japanese consumers. Ichinomiya is the centre of the Japanese worsted wool textile industry. The surrounding region has accumulated a wealth of technical knowledge and experience, and reaps economies of scale in dyeing. Apparel manufacturers currently dominate the distribution chain for worsted suits, and respond quickly to electronic sales information flowing from retailers. Foreigners, such as the South Koreans, who have a smaller home market, less experience in suit manufacturing and an insecure foothold in the Japanese distribution system, have found it difficult to compete. Given Japanese firms' high costs and the strength of the yen, however, it is possible that they will choose to relocate their plants overseas (Miwa 1994). In the mid-1980s, apparel as a whole was one of the industries in which Japan's competitive advantage was weakest (Porter 1990: 391, 393–4). The existence of a sophisticated domestic market has so far failed to give Japanese textile and apparel producers the momentum which they need, if they are to overcome the grave obstacles to their competitiveness.

Sophisticated tastes in the home market have contributed to the international success of the Italian textile and clothing sector. Italy's competitive advantage in clothing has been most pronounced in the medium- and higher-quality segments of the market (Buxton 1988; Bigarelli and Crestanello 1994). Kay (1993: 297–8) suggests that branding, reputation and efficient mechanisms for gathering, processing and responding to information underpinned the Italian knitwear industry's excellent performance during the 1980s. Demanding home consumers forced Italian firms to hone their production and marketing techniques. Firms which could satisfy the Italian market were in a good position to expand their sales abroad. The industrial district of Carpi exported substantial quantities of cheap knitwear to Germany and other West European countries in the 1960s. Facing increasing competition in the late 1970s and 1980s, producers in Carpi altered their strategy and began to export more fashionable garments (Bigarelli and Crestanello 1994: 134–5). Their ability to change course with such success reflected their experience in satisfying home consumers. During the 1990s, however, the tag 'Made in Italy' has lost some of its market value, as foreign consumers have increasingly demanded that the quality of garments live up to the expectations generated by their labels (Navaretti and Perosino 1995: 178). Perhaps it is in the nature of things for reputations to become debased, especially in atomistic industries such as clothing.

In the mid-1990s, French textile and apparel producers were planning to follow the Italian strategy. The French hoped to exploit their reputation for high quality and design, and increase their sales of middle-of-the-range and top-of-the-range garments in Asian markets. French consumers are not particularly extravagant in their spending on textile products, although they do constitute a sophisticated domestic market by global standards. Moreover, the name of France as a centre of high fashion is a reputational asset which can be utilized by the apparel industry. Exclusive distribution agreements have been signed by French producers in countries such as South Korea, Thailand and Hong Kong, which possess increasingly prosperous middle classes. French producers state that they were encouraged to start exporting to Asia by cuts in tariffs in Asian countries in the Uruguay round of GATT. Success for French clothing manufacturers has been limited to the areas of medium-and high-quality apparel. It remains to be seen how French medium-fashion goods will fare against competition from other West European countries and the USA, where large numbers of firms are thinking along similar lines (Lewis 1995).

High fashion (as opposed to high street fashion) constitutes a relatively small, but influential, segment of the clothing market. Its significance derives from its delayed effect on the styling of clothing for the general consumer. The market value of fashion goods bears no relation to the cost of the material inputs and wages of production workers, although it may bear a close relation to the cost of hiring the designers and models. Barthes (1983) argues that written clothing and actual clothing are different phenomena. Fashion experts pronounce certain fabrics, colours and styles as either desirable or undesirable, and appropriate or inappropriate for particular occasions. These rulings may change from year to year. The market value of a new dress from Paris or Milan is determined by what is said about it. Public confidence in the special powers of the expert is an essential element of this process. However, the designer and the fashion critic cannot afford to depart too radically from the norms of the surrounding culture. It is unlikely that people could be induced to buy dresses made from pieces of bacon, whatever may be said about the merits of bacon. The most important fashion shows are held in the most sophisticated markets. They enhance the reputations of the apparel industries of the cities and regions concerned. Since firms in these regions face high costs, their participation in the fashion industry is vital for the defence of their competitive advantage. Star models lend further weight to the drive for competitive advantage by demonstrating products manufactured in the high fashion industry or adding glamour to more ordinary brands of apparel. Naomi Campbell promoted garments supplied by Swish, in the mid-1990s (Levine 1995a: 77). Since Ms Campbell was British, and Swish was Italian, this was an international joint venture: the consumer bought a combination of Italian apparel and Naomi Campbell's glamour. Bendon, a New Zealand lingerie manufacturer, signed the Australian model Elle Macpherson in the late 1980s to promote a line of economical underwear called Elle Macpherson Intimates. Ms Macpherson earned US$1.5 million per annum from Bendon sales, on which she received a 6 per cent commission (ibid.: 76). Kmart hired the TV star, Jaclyn Smith, to promote its apparel in 1984 (Wolf 1992).

A sophisticated domestic distribution network may provide an additional stimulus to competitive advantage. Such a system puts manufacturers under intense pressure to improve the quality of their products. Britain's efficient merchanting system helped its textile industry to achieve a competitive advantage in the eighteenth and nineteenth centuries, although the atomistic structure of its distribution network, particularly in relation to exporting, has been severely criticized on the grounds of its unsuitability to twentieth-century conditions (Lazonick 1983: 225–7; Chapman 1992).

Porter (1990: 90) stresses the advantageous features of the Italian clothing distribution network. In 1989 in Italy, 70 per cent of all clothing was sold by independent retailers. Specialist multiples supplied another 12 per cent of the market and local street markets were also quite prominent. But general department stores and mail-order firms made only a small contribution to total sales. By contrast, in the UK in 1989, independents sold just 20 per cent of the clothing bought by consumers. Specialist multiples (28 per cent) and department stores (31 per cent) dominated apparel retailing in Britain, and mail-order suppliers (10 per cent) also played a significant role. France and Germany occupied an intermediate position: consumers in these countries purchased 38 per cent and 44 per cent respectively of their garments from independent retailers (Stogdon 1993: 146). Marks & Spencer alone was responsible for 15 per cent of UK clothing sales in the 1980s, and was even stronger in areas such as underwear (Tse 1985: 2). Mass garment retailing began in the mid-nineteenth century with firms such as E. Moses & Son of London (Chapman 1993). Apparel retailing in the USA is also dominated by mass retailers, such as Wal-Mart, Kmart, and Sears, Roebuck and Co. Discounters, such as Wal-Mart and Kmart, have grown at the expense of traditional mass merchandisers (like Sears) and department stores, but they continue to aim at a fairly undifferentiated market. TV home shopping has prospered, since its introduction in the mid-1980s, and mail order has regained some of its popularity, leaving comparatively little room for specialist and independent stores (Tedlow 1990; Finnie 1994b: 40–1). In the 1960s, specialist outlets sold 69 per cent of the suits purchased by American men, but their share fell to 44 per cent by 1981, indicating that the mass retailers were taking over. Most American men were not prepared to pay for well-made suits (Harrigan 1983: 166). British and American consumers accepted a relatively high degree of regimentation in style.

The fact that Italian shoppers patronize boutiques, whilst Americans buy clothes from TV shows and Britons get their underwear at Marks & Spencer, does not necessarily imply that the Italian distribution complex is more sophisticated than those of the USA and the UK, although it clearly demonstrates that Italian consumers are more sophisticated than Anglo-Saxons. Clothing manufacturers are faced with demanding customers under both regimes. While the predominance, in Italy, of independent and specialist clothing outlets, encourages the production of a wider range of styles, under the British and American systems, apparel manufacturers are under continuous pressure to minimize costs (Taplin 1994; Taplin and Winterton 1995). Long-term alliances do exist between retailers and clothing producers in Britain and America, but these relationships involve a high level of dependency (Steedman and Wagner 1989; Bull, Pitt and Szarka 1991). British and American manufacturers must respond with a minimum of delay to the directives of their major customers, and the discount stores often express a preference for lower costs rather than better designs. Intensification of effort may be substituted for the upgrading of products. The upgrading of processes may be confined to the installation of labour-saving as opposed to skill-enhancing machinery. Information flows between retailers and suppliers can be computerized under either the American or the Italian systems. Sophistication in distribution takes several forms, but it is legitimate to conclude that the Italian approach results in a more differentiated product, which is less vulnerable to competition from the developing world and has greater prospects of exports to other advanced countries. India, in the late nineteenth century, provides a radical contrast to modern distribution systems. Itinerant carriers hawked locally manufactured textiles from village to village, following a seasonal schedule. Goods were distributed some months before payment was due. Some of these traders were members of a special caste. They transported their cloth by cart, pack animal or sometimes carried it in a bundle on their heads (Roy 1993: 153–4). Such procedures were hardly conducive to the formation of an international competitive advantage.

The peculiarities of domestic tastes may act as a form of protection against imports. European textile manufacturers never fully understood Indian preferences in design and colour, and this factor contributed to the survival of a large textile and clothing sector on the subcontinent, using handicraft techniques, during British rule in the nineteenth century (ibid.: 116–17). Traditional Japanese textile producers were sheltered from foreign competition, during the late nineteenth and early twentieth centuries, by the resilient domestic demand for types of cloth suitable for converting into kimonos (Kawabe 1989: 33–4). The domestic merchants who resisted foreign imports were not the same as those who were so successful in opening the Chinese market in the 1890s. Japanese yarn exports were pushed by the Japan Cotton Spinners Association and Mitsui Bussan, two of the spearheads of the modernization drive (Sugiyama 1988b). Protection is less likely to be derived from traditional preferences today, since fundamental differences in tastes and lifestyles have been eroded. In the nineteenth century, people in European cities and those in Japan wore completely different garments, but nowadays the variations in style between Europe and Japan are quite subtle. Nevertheless, a substantial part of the Japanese distribution chain is descended from the pre-industrial cloth merchants. For example, the leading retail group, Matsuzakaya, has its roots in the kimono distribution network of the Edo period. The intricacy and inefficiency of the distribution system made it relatively difficult for imports to penetrate the Japanese home market after the Second World War, but this obstacle is no longer as difficult to surmount, due to the growing influence of supermarkets and discount stores (Tatsuki 1995).

Discerning home consumers provide textile and clothing manufacturers with an incentive to upgrade, and a convenient source of market information to assist them in this process. Producers in developed countries are to some extent protected from low-cost competition by home demand for fashionable goods of a reasonable quality. A strong home base can be the launching pad for missions to sell apparel in other developed countries and in the growing middle-class markets of the newly industrializing world.

THE INTERNATIONALIZATION OF DEMAND

The transplantation of domestic patterns of demand to other countries is not a new phenomenon. When ancient Rome ruled Europe and much of the Middle East, its cultural influence stimulated demand for apparel made in the Italian peninsula. Cloaks from Brindisi, for instance, were imported by the Palestinian provinces of the Roman empire (Safrai 1994: 389).

As Western Europe extended its power over the globe, in the seventeenth century, European tastes were exported. Settlers from Europe demanded clothing from home. In 1688, blue, purple and scarlet hose, manufactured in England, were in high demand among the English residents of Jamaica. Zahedieh (1994) maintains that the strong demand of colonists, in America and the West Indies, for standardized hats and garments encouraged London apparel manufacturers to specialize, introduce technical innovations and lengthen their production runs. Colonial orders contributed to the development of London's competitive advantage in the late seventeenth century. British dominions, such as Australia, New Zealand and South Africa, remained loyal to the products of the British textile industry, even after it had lost markets in other parts of the world, although this preference was fading by the late 1950s (Singleton 1991: 118). European clothing styles have influenced the dress habits of non-European races. The suit, for example, has become the global business uniform. During the twentieth century, the inhabitants of southern India, a region with a traditional preference for draped (i.e., unstitched) garments, began to wear increasing numbers of stitched garments, under the cultural influence of Europe (Roy 1993: 118–19).

The exportation of Western notions about appropriate clothing did not create a sustainable competitive advantage for the bulk of the Western textile and apparel sector. Long-distance international trade in garments was uncommon before the Second World War. Consequently, most Western-style apparel was actually produced in non-Western countries, and its manufacturers had no particular incentive to use imported fabrics, unless they represented good value for money. Indians who needed cheap trousers did not import them from New York or London. Only in a minority of cases did prestige confer a sustainable competitive advantage on Western firms in trade with non-Western countries. An example would be the persistent high demand in Japan for Italian designer-suits (Miwa 1994: 35). It is open to domestic firms to attempt to capture a share of this prestige market. In 1964, the Japanese retailer Matsuzakaya hired tailors trained in Britain to work in its shops, with the promise that they would cut suits for their customers in the style worn by English gentlemen (Tanner 1992: 130). Some Western sportswear manufacturers have competitive advantage bestowed upon them by the global popularity of Western sports, and the endorsement of their products by Western sports stars. In 1982, foreign branded sportswear, which was either imported or made under licence in Japan, held 60 per cent of the Japanese market (Brummett 1987: 211).

The history of denim shows that it is possible for the traditional fabric of one nation to be captured by another nation, and marketed around the world as a universally recognized expression of the latter's popular culture. Denim was a fabric worn by peasants in the south of France. In the 1860s, an American firm, Levi Strauss & Co., decided that denim pants would make excellent work clothing for miners, industrial workers and farmers. By the 1930s, due to the free advertising provided by cowboy films, jeans were becoming fashionable. After 1945, American popular culture, and jeans with American labels, swept the world (Rourke 1992). There is some debate about whether young consumers in the affluent countries are becoming more homogeneous or more differentiated in their tastes, in the last decade of the twentieth century. One view asserts that teenagers are the first global consumers, and that their preferred brands are American, such as Levis, KFC and Coca-Cola. This interpretation suggests that American cultural hegemony, established in the mid-twentieth century, remains unchallenged. The alternative view states that the influence of American tastes on the spending patterns of young European and Japanese consumers is starting to wane. Europe is re-emerging as a rival purveyor of popular culture and fashion (Miller 1995). The success of products that are based on an attempt to internationalize either genuine or imagined domestic tastes may well be transitory. Laura Ashley apparel and furnishings achieved popularity in other developed countries in the 1980s because of their perceived Englishness. But

71

fashions moved on, and, in 1995, the company announced that it would have to close up to one-fifth of its 190 North American stores (Levine 1995b). It appears that the exportation of American tastes has given US firms a more robust competitive advantage in labels and logos than it has in the products attached to them. If American firms own the most attractive labels, they could reap the accompanying rents, while subcontracting the manufacturing process to businesses in less developed countries.

Internationalization of domestic demand patterns has encouraged significant exports of apparel only under rather limited circumstances. Textiles, in comparison with apparel and home furnishings, are a basic commodity, hence it makes little sense to think in terms of the internationalization of domestic demand for textiles. An examination of the rapid strides made in export markets by Asian apparel manufacturers in recent decades must conclude that these countries replicated Western styles. Asian styles of clothing have not had a great deal of impact on Western preferences, although there are markets for traditional clothing in immigrant communities.

CONCLUSION

Since the minimum efficient scale of production in most branches of the textile and clothing sector is comparatively small, an extensive home market is not essential. This does not mean that home markets are unimportant to textile and apparel industries. New businesses in industrializing countries can gain useful experience by supplying domestic customers before they expand into international markets. Textile and apparel producers in more advanced economies derive information and ideas from their contacts with sophisticated home consumers and distribution networks. This information may help them to prepare products for equally sophisticated foreign markets. Domestic demand for industrial textiles preserves the international position of some textile mills, such as those working for the tyre and car industries. If a country acquires a reputation as a centre of fashion, its exports will benefit from inflated foreign perceptions of their value. The USA and Western Europe have managed to internationalize their tastes as a result of five centuries of political and cultural imperialism. Western countries still reap some rewards from this domination in the fashion segments of the market, but it is not difficult for countries in the developing world to copy the more standardardized forms of Western garments.

4

RELATED AND
SUPPORTING INDUSTRIES

No industry is a completely self-contained entity. It requires inputs manufactured by other industries. In the case of textiles and clothing, the most
important related and supporting industries are the production of textile
machinery (including certain types of electronics) and chemicals (especially
man-made fibres). Porter (1990) argues that clusters of mutually supporting
and related industries are stronger than isolated industries. This is not a
matter of the ready availability of textile machinery or chemicals since, if
necessary, they can be imported. Rather, the benefits of clustering arise from
opportunities for cooperation between firms engaging in related activities.
Flows of information, and informal contacts between personnel, are likely to
be more intensive where businesses in related sectors are located near to each
other. Shared national pride and a common business culture may also
improve the effectiveness of collaboration in this setting.

Neighbouring textile producers and machinery manufacturers are likely to
discuss the types of equipment which are most suitable for local mills.
Knowledge gained in such consultations is used in the design of new generations of machinery. Similarly, close proximity facilitates the rectification of
defects in new machinery. It also makes it easier for machinery producers to
advise users on how to operate their spinning frames and looms. Chemicals
are required in a variety of textile processes. Hence, the potential fruits of
cooperation between chemical suppliers, textile mill companies and the
makers of textile machinery are of considerable value. Since the introduction
of man-made fibres, the scope for profitable cooperation between textile
and chemical firms has increased. Porter gives several examples of strong
industrial clusters that are related to textiles, including embroidered goods
and embroidery-making machinery in Switzerland, and silk, synthetic fibres
and textile machinery in Japan (ibid.: 100, 105). An extensive group of
related industries, including clothing, weaving, leather, synthetic fibres, textile
and leather-working machinery and design services, is to be found in Italy
(ibid.: 424, 443–4). The USA, however, lacks a successful cluster of textile-
related industries (ibid.: 288, 292).

The concepts of vertical integration and the industrial district are closely related to that of clustering. Chemicals production and textile machinery manufacture are links in a chain of processes supplying households and industrial consumers with textile commodities. Consequently, when speaking of a cluster of textile, chemical and textile machinery firms, we are describing an industrial structure in which vertical integration is incomplete. If integrated corporations produced all of the machinery, man-made fibres, and chemicals used in textile production, as well as yarn, cloth and apparel, the concept of a textile cluster would be redundant. But complete vertical integration is costly. Textile machinery, dyestuff and man-made fibre producers have more to gain from being part of wider engineering and chemical industry networks. These linkages keep firms in touch with important developments in applied engineering and chemistry. Different industrial clusters overlap to varying degrees. For instance, the textile cluster and the automobile cluster could be linked through the engineering industry. Toyota provides an example of this phenomenon. The Toyoda Automatic Loom Works began producing motor vehicles in 1935. Although vehicle production was spun off to form a separate business called Toyota Motor Corporation, cooperation continued between the Toyoda textile machinery and Toyota motor businesses (Rouland 1991). Such activities as the manufacture of tyre cord and upholstery could be treated as parts of both the motor vehicle and textile clusters.

Porter's emphasis on regional clustering serves to connect his work with that of Marshall (1921: 599–603) on the industrial district. It is argued that external economies develop in an industrial region. In an area exerting a large demand for dyestuffs, chemical fibres and textile machinery, the local chemical and engineering firms have an incentive to focus on these specialities. Local educational establishments will specialize in textile science rather than in more general forms of vocational training. As a result of this concentration of effort, suppliers of inputs to the textile industry should be able to attain high levels of expertise and productivity. Cooperation between textile and clothing firms and their suppliers, in the development of new processes, has already been introduced as one of the advantages of clustering.

The relationship between the textile and clothing sector and its supporting and related industries evolves over time. Developing countries tend to import their textile machinery, either new or second-hand, because they possess few trained engineers. Chemical products required in textile factories are also imported. Before a recognizable cluster can emerge, the textile sector must become sufficiently large to provide an adequate market for local machinery and chemical producers, and the country must assimilate the relevant technologies and train cadres of skilled workers, technicians and managers. Clusters are likely to emerge only in reasonably highly developed economies. But, as we shall discover, in some advanced economies the textile cluster may prove illusory or brittle. Proximity between textile firms and their suppliers does not guarantee effective cooperation. Elements of the cluster may progress along divergent paths and they may be overrun separately by their competitors.

TEXTILE MACHINERY

During the formative years of mechanized textile production, the manufacture of spinning machinery was an integral part of the textile industry, rather than a separate endeavour. This reflected the novelty of mechanized textile production. The capacity to design and construct his own machines gave the most successful of the early British cotton textile magnates, Richard Arkwright, his competitive advantage. Arkwright invented the water frame in 1769, one of several machines developed at this time to enable a number of threads to be spun simultaneously. Secrecy, patents and litigation were used by Arkwright, with varying degrees of success, to protect his inventions from piracy. Arkwright sold patented machinery to other firms. Although some unscrupulous mills attempted to copy patented machines, few craftsmen fully understood how to replicate them. Spinning machines were high-technology devices in the late eighteenth century (Fitton 1989). Mechanized spinning technology was gradually diffused and became part of the common domain. The mule, a hybrid machine, combining elements of the water frame and the earlier spinning jenny, established itself as the dominant technology in the early nineteenth century. Capable machine builders were in a strong position in the cotton textile complex. One of Manchester's leading spinning enterprises of the early nineteenth century, M'Connel and Kennedy, originally built its own machinery. Only later did the firm decide to concentrate on spinning (C. H. Lee 1972). Early textile machinery was made of wood and could be constructed in a small shed. Firms which combined spinning with the manufacture of spinning frames were able to exert greater control over the quality of their equipment, and this was an important consideration at a time when machine-building skills were scarce. Textile factories were powered by waterwheels or steam engines. Britain's leadership in these power technologies was an asset to its textile industry. Builders of waterwheels and producers of steam engines occupied important places in the textile cluster (von Tunzelmann 1978).

Early American mills commonly supplied their own textile machinery. Matters were complicated by the fact that the British government tried to prevent the transfer of technology to the American republic. Textile machines constructed in the USA were more or less accurate copies of British models. Samuel Slater, who had worked in an Arkwright-type mill in England, brought the Arkwright spinning technology to the USA (Jeremy 1981: 76–91). Components and plans were smuggled out of Britain, but they were useless without skilled personnel to interpret them. A Scottish immigrant, William Gilmour, tried to replicate the British power-loom at Lyman Mills, Providence, in 1816–17 on the basis of memorized knowledge.

Although Gilmour was an excellent mechanic, the help of an Englishman trained in weaving was required before the power-looms could be coaxed into action (ibid.: 97–8). A mill boasting someone who understood how to make textile machinery enjoyed a competitive advantage over its rivals, particularly if this expert could be persuaded to remain loyal to the firm. In-house design and manufacture of textile machinery continued in some specialized trades which were not served by the major machine makers. When the US corset industry moved from a handicraft to a factory basis in the late nineteenth century, corset producers designed their own machines for this type of work (B. Smith 1991).

As the market expanded for textile machinery, specialist textile engineering firms emerged in Britain and the USA. Several of the most successful American firms, such as the Lowell Machine Shop, began their careers as in-house machinery producers for major mills, and were later spun off as separate businesses. In a sense, this process could be regarded as a form of vertical disintegration. A different route was taken by the Draper organization. This leading New England manufacturer of textile machinery did not originate as a mill machine shop, but it drew its personnel from the reservoir of engineering talent created by the region's cotton mills and agricultural machinery workshops. One of Draper's strategies was to establish joint ventures with the holders of important patents, such as Jacob H. Sawyer, a mill agent of Appleton Mills, Lowell, who devised the fuel-saving 'Sawyer' spindle in 1871. The Sawyer spindle, however, proved most popular in Europe (Mass 1989: 886–91). Many of New England's best textile technicians and inventors were hired by Draper. It was a highly research-intensive business by the standards of the time. James H. Northrop, a Draper employee, made a series of inventions in 1889–91, which led to the production of the first successful automatic bobbin-changing loom. Experiments with the new loom were carried out at several New England mills, and Draper bought shares in the first mill to be fully equipped with Northrop looms, at Burlington, Vermont, believing that this would help to advertise the product (ibid.: 893–921). Weavers could tend higher complements of Northrop automatic looms than of standard power-looms. Labour costs were lower on the Northrop looms, and this was a very important consideration in a high-wage economy such as the USA. The Northrop loom was a major technical advance, and its development owed much to the exchange of information and personnel between Draper and the New England mills.

Whether or not the appearance of the Northrop loom enhanced New England's competitive advantage in weaving is more doubtful. New England's main domestic competitors were in the Southern states, and these were the most enthusiastic purchasers of the Northrop loom. First, the rate of new mill construction was highest in the South. Second, automatics were more suitable for the weaving of the coarser fabrics made in the Southern states. Third, Northrop looms economized on the use of skilled labour, and this was particularly scarce in the Southern textile region (Feller 1966; 1974). The Draper company inadvertently employed skills developed in New England to further the competitive advantage of a rival region. Thus, New England's textile cluster generated very large externalities.

Platts of Oldham was the largest British textile machinery producer in the second half of the nineteenth century. It too had a rather curious relationship with the surrounding textile industry. Platts was the world's premier exporter of textile machinery and was especially well-known for its spinning equipment. Ring frames became a leading export of Platts in the 1880s. Demand for ring frames was growing in most countries and ring spinning was gradually replacing mule spinning. British firms, however, lagged behind the rest of the world in the adoption of ring spindles. They continued to order mule spinning equipment until the First World War, because mules were well-suited to the fine yarns made in many British mills. Between 1905 and 1909, Platts exported 78 per cent of its production of ring spindles, but only 16 per cent of its output of mule spindles (Farnie 1991: 168). Platts had risen to prominence on the basis of domestic orders, but in the ring era it assisted overseas countries to mechanize, and hence to displace exports of yarn and cloth from Britain. The UK supplied 56 per cent of world textile machinery exports in 1913 (Farnie 1993b: 148). Of course, if Platts had not exported textile machinery, overseas mills would have obtained equipment from continental or American engineers, and the effects on Britain's cotton industry would have been identical. What is interesting about Platts and the Draper company is that they became increasingly detached from their regional textile clusters. The same could be said of Singer. Singer plants in New Jersey and Scotland manufactured 75 per cent of the world's sewing machines in the late 1880s. The Scottish factory exported to markets in Europe and Asia. Singer was concerned with global markets, and it had no particular interest in the competitive advantage of the American apparel industry (Hounshell 1984: 67–122; Thomson 1987; Chandler 1990: 66).

Since India did not have an indigenous textile machinery industry in the late nineteenth and early twentieth centuries, it had to rely on imports. British firms had a virtual monopoly of exports of modern textile machinery to India, until the 1930s (Kirk and Simmons 1981: 784–5). The Indian cotton mills were owned by financiers and traders, whose ignorance of engineering left them dependent on British technicians for advice on the purchase of equipment. Some of these mill technicians worked on commission for British engineering firms, so that their recommendations were not impartial. Others simply chose the equipment which they had been used to in England, without enquiring into its suitability under local conditions. As a result, many Indian firms continued to install mule spindles. Rings would have been a more appropriate choice, since Indian mills concentrated on spinning low counts of yarn, and the country laboured under a shortage of skilled mule operatives (Kiyokawa 1983). Other factors, such as the absence of cotton mixing, and social obstacles to the employment of cheap female labour, militated against the speedier adoption of ring spinning in India (Otsuka, Ranis and Saxonhouse 1988: 55–60, 82–3). But the lack of a textile engineering base undoubtedly influenced the choice of technology for the worse.

Spinning mills imported British machinery, especially from Platts, during the early years of mechanization in Japan. Unlike the Indians, however, the Japanese soon learned to make their own machinery. Power-looms were easier and cheaper to copy than either mules or ring frames. By the mid-1870s, Japanese handloom makers were beginning to replicate the Western power-loom. Toyoda and Kubota were prominent machine builders in the 1890s. Their power-looms were significantly lighter and cheaper than Western models. By making their own looms, the Japanese were able to save foreign exchange and gain experience in engineering. Their machines were ideally suited to weaving the fabrics popular in local markets. Toyoda cooperated with Mitsui Bussan, which was in turn the sponsor of the Kanegafuchi spinning company.

Toyoda's connection with Mitsui helped it to develop improved machines and to market existing ones. It took Japan much longer to acquire the capacity to produce spinning machinery, but a factory making spinning equipment was eventually opened by Toyoda in 1921 (Nakaoka 1982). Toyoda also operated cotton spinning and weaving factories in Japan and China, from which it derived useful information about technical requirements. In 1925, Toyoda perfected a light automatic loom, which multiplied labour productivity in weaving by up to nineteen times. The Toyoda automatic loom was so successful that Platt Brothers paid £83,500 for manufacturing rights, and the proceeds of this transaction were invested in the automobile industry (Mass and Lazonick 1991: 41; Rouland 1991: 636). The Japanese, unlike the Indians, were determined not to be the passive recipients of Western technology. Japan trained its own cadre of engineers and succeeded in developing and adapting a textile machinery industry to meet local needs. Although Japan's rise to prominence as a modern textile producer and exporter was due to the interaction of a number of factors, the rapid establishment of an independent capacity to design and produce textile machinery stood it in good stead. Japan developed a cluster of supporting industries around its textile core. The fact that India lacked such a cluster put it at a disadvantage (Otsuka, Ranis and Saxonhouse 1988: 91–6). Even China was in advance of India in the manufacture of modern textile machinery. A Shanghai factory was making stocking-frames at the time of the First World War, and shortly after the war Shanghai's Dahrlong Engineering Works started to produce copies of foreign looms and other equipment (Elvin 1991: 12, 18–19).

Our analysis of Britain, the USA, India and Japan indicates that it was desirable for textile regions to possess strong textile machinery industries. The history of textiles in industrializing Britain cannot be separated from the history of the revolution in textile machinery. Due to the British embargo on machinery exports until 1843, the US textile industry depended on the ability of American workshops to replicate foreign equipment. Japanese textile machinery makers successfully adapted Western technology to Asian conditions. By the second half of the nineteenth century, textile machinery producers in Lancashire and New England were equipping rival textile regions. This partially offset the external benefits which they conferred on their home regions. Some regions which continued to rely on imported machinery, such as Bombay and Ahmedabad, did not make the best selection of equipment. But Southerners in the USA were in a more favourable position, since they were well-informed about the equipment being manufactured in other parts of their own country.

Table 4.1 illustrates some recent developments in the competitiveness of the producers of textile and leather machinery. In 1970, all of the leading exporters were established industrial nations, with long records of success in textile engineering. Less developed countries, such as South Korea and Hong Kong, had negligible exports of textile machinery, due to such factors as their technological backwardness and their comparative advantage in light consumer products. Between 1970 and 1993 there were some major changes in world market shares. Britain and the USA lost a considerable amount of ground. Switzerland also experienced a decline in market share, although its performance remained impressive for a country of its size. Italy gained market share. Japan's share of world exports almost doubled. It is significant that Hong Kong and South Korea joined the top ten exporters during this period. Hong Kong's exports of textile machinery exceeded those of either Britain or the USA in 1993. If the statistics of export market shares in 1993 are broken down into sub-categories, there emerges an interesting pattern of

Table 4.1 World export market shares of textile and leather machinery, 1970, 1993

1970	%	1993	%
West Germany	30.4	Germany	26.6
United Kingdom	12.3	Japan	22.5
Japan	11.4	Italy	12.4
Switzerland	11.3	Switzerland	7.8
United States	9.7	Hong Kong	5.6
Italy	9.4	United States	5.0
France	5.6	France	3.4
Belgium–Luxembourg	2.4	United Kingdom	2.9
The Netherlands	1.4	Belgium–Luxembourg	2.3
Sweden	1.1	South Korea	2.1

Sources: Calculated from United Nations, Department of Economic and Social Affairs (1975: 160); United Nations, Department for Economic and Social Information and Policy Analysis (1995: 170)

specialization. Japan (37.5 per cent) dominated the export trade in sewing machinery (Standard International Trade Classification (SITC) 7243). Germany (16.5 per cent) was a distant second, followed by Hong Kong (13 per cent). China, Brazil, South Korea and Singapore were also among the top ten exporters of sewing equipment. Germany (38 per cent) led in spinning machinery (SITC 7244), followed by Japan (23 per cent). The Japanese (30 per cent) were the leading exporters of weaving equipment (SITC 7245), with Germany in second position (22 per cent). Switzerland still had a strong presence in the export of looms, although it was losing ground quite rapidly to Japan. In the light of the previous exploits of Draper, it is worth noting that, in the 1990s, the USA was no longer one of the top ten loom exporters. The strengths of Italy, and the weaknesses of the USA and Britain, were spread across a range of categories (United Nations, Department for Economic and Social Information and Policy Analysis 1995: 604–12).

A record of excellence in textile engineering is consistent with the relative success of Germany as a producer of higher-quality textiles and clothing. German engineers found it impossible to compete with the British in standardized textile machinery in the nineteenth century. Like Germany's textile industry, its textile engineering firms adopted a strategy of specializing in niche markets. Machines were customized and built to high technical standards. This approach bore fruit in the twentieth century, because it helped the Germans to attain a superiority in engineering over their British and American rivals (Sabel, Herrigel, Deeg and Kazis 1989: 385–91). Switzerland's case is more unusual. The achievements of the Swiss in textile engineering have decisively overshadowed their performance as textile producers. Although Switzerland contributed 45 per cent of the world's exports of weaving machines in 1985, woven fabrics did not register among the country's principal exports in that year (Porter 1990: 309). The Swiss textile machinery industry was originally a supplier to local firms making embroidered goods and silks. But Switzerland's strategic position at the centre of Western Europe gave its engineering industries access to adjacent export markets. Swiss machinery producers were effectively incorporated into the German textile cluster (Schröter 1993: 49–53). Their expertise in textile machinery making is exemplified by the firm of Sulzer Brothers. Sulzer was famous in the early twentieth century for its diesel engines, although it had a diverse range of products. During the depression of the 1930s, Sulzer bravely diversified into the manufacture of industrial weaving equipment. The Sulzer shuttleless loom was a technical breakthrough because it dispensed with the slow mechanical shuttle. This innovative product became a global market leader after the Second World War. In the 1970s, Sulzer entered the industrial electronics and robotics sector. The company also established a joint venture with the Toyoda Automatic Loom Works in Japan (Classe and Classe 1991; Rouland 1991: 638). When Sulzer entered the textile machinery sector in the 1930s, it was not starting from scratch. It already had an impressive record of achievement in precision engineering. The fact that Sulzer was able to bring a new perspective to the design of textile machinery, combined with its strict technical standards, may have given it a competitive advantage over the traditional giants of textile engineering, such as Platts and Draper. These British and American firms had narrower horizons than those of Sulzer. Platts had a history stretching back to the days when textile engineering was more of a craft than a science.

The last few years, however, have been difficult for the Swiss textile machinery industry. Switzerland's share of world loom exports (SITC 72451) fell from 45 per cent in 1985 to 18 per cent in 1993, illustrating how quickly competitive advantage can be undermined (United Nations, Department for Economic and Social Information and Policy Analysis 1995: 611). Italy's share of world textile machinery exports doubled between the early 1960s and early 1990s, but it remained a long way behind the two leading exporters, Germany and Japan. Italy overtook Switzerland as an exporter of textile machinery in the mid-1980s. The resilience of the rest of the Italian textile cluster, and its demands for high quality equipment, stimulated innovation in the textile machinery industry, which in turn reinforced the competitive advantage of the textile industry. When a region's textile industry declines, its textile machinery producers are also likely to suffer. The great achievement of the Swiss may have been their ability to extend the interval between the loss of competitive advantage in textiles and textile machinery.

Japan's textile machinery industry recovered from the war by focusing on the production of relatively unsophisticated equipment. In 1945, Japan possessed a large stock of machine tools and a surplus of mechanics. Many of these skilled workers turned their attention to the manufacture of sewing machines on a small scale. Large new factories were established somewhat later, in the 1950s, and Japan became the world's leading exporter of sewing machines during this decade (Tsuru 1993: 78–81). Despite this success, the Japanese sewing machine industry did not produce the increasingly complex machinery which was needed in the more advanced sections of the nation's textile cluster. Thus the sewing machine industry was not fully integrated with the Japanese textile sector. While continental European textile machinery producers cultivated markets in other developed economies, the Japanese (and to some extent the British) exported the bulk of their machinery to industrializing countries, especially those in Asia. Japanese textile machinery makers, such as Toyoda, Ishikawa and Howa, were in effect assisting overseas mills to displace Japanese yarn and cloth. In this respect, the Japanese machinery exporters were following a pattern set by Platts in the nineteenth century. But there were significant differences between the British and Japanese cases. Many of the East Asian mills constructed during the 1960s and 1970s were either wholly or partially owned by Japanese textile interests. These overseas plants formed an important element in the Japanese textile and clothing complex (Yoshihara 1978: 91–132). Japan's textile machinery industry, notwithstanding the setbacks of the 1940s, gradually improved its technical standards. Its progress may be illustrated by examining the number of patents held in connection with open-end rotor spinning. Japan possessed just one patent relating to this process in 1966, compared with Czechoslovakia's nineteen and West Germany's eight. By 1984, Japan had accumulated 219 patents in this field, and was not far behind Czechoslovakia's 230, although West Germany still led with 512 patents. Americans held only 66 patents (Antonelli 1989: 277). Japan has taken great strides forward in the production of machines suitable for both developing and advanced countries.

The British textile and textile machinery industries encountered serious difficulties after 1950. Britain's share of world exports of textile machinery collapsed from 30 per cent in 1954 to 11 per cent in 1975 (Rothwell 1980: 128). There are no grounds for believing that the decline of British textile engineering caused the collapse of the UK's traditional textile industries. Domestic firms which were not satisfied with British machinery were free to import equipment, at least once the post-war foreign exchange crisis had eased. Foreigners supplied two-thirds of the textile machines that were newly installed in Britain in 1975–6 (Saunders 1978: 91). Causation ran in the opposite direction: a weak textile industry resulted in an increasingly backward capital goods sector (Rothwell 1980). Many British textile mills did not demand sophisticated machinery. As a result, the product ranges of British textile engineers became outdated in comparison with those of competitor firms in Switzerland, Germany and Japan. Once a gap in performance had opened up, it was difficult for the British to close it. Consequently, they were unable to take full advantage of the growth in overseas demand for more complicated spinning and weaving machines. Of course, unsophisticated and demoralized domestic customers were not the only problems confronting the UK textile machinery industry. Poor management, the loss of imperial business and a lack of qualified research workers also played their part in the process of decline. Platts finally bowed out in 1982, after the firm had failed to keep up with the competition in such specialities as open-end rotor spinning (Farnie 1991: 163).

American textile machinery builders also struggled to adapt to new technological opportunities, and entered a long and fatal period of decline in the 1940s. The record of Draper is instructive. At the end of the Second World War, Sulzer Brothers offered to supply Draper with a licence to manufacture shuttleless looms in the USA. Draper declined this offer, believing that it could produce a competitive shuttleless loom on the basis of its own research. Draper and Sulzer became deadly rivals. But Sulzer always kept one step ahead in terms of the quality and reliability of its looms. It took a decisive lead over Draper in world market share in the 1970s. Rockwell International, an American electronics company, acquired Draper in 1967. Although Rockwell attempted to regenerate Draper through the development of a promising new loom, the DML, the firm's hopes of recovery were nipped in the bud. A financial crisis enveloped Rockwell in 1974, and it decided that it could not afford to pay for the introduction of the new loom. This withdrawal of support effectively terminated Draper's career as a leading textile machinery manufacturer (Mass 1990).

The failure of the American textile machinery industry was partly the result of defective managerial strategies. New England machine builders attempted to control costs by achieving long production runs. They were unwilling to customize their machines and reluctant to make incremental improvements to them, on the grounds that small changes were inconvenient and expensive. Such an attitude was short-sighted because an accumulation of small improvements sometimes led to the appearance of greatly superior products. Furthermore, the evidence suggests that American textile machinery was often uncompetitive in price with European and Japanese equipment (Kravis and Lipsey 1971: 331–9). European firms captured many export markets from the Americans. The Europeans' policy of meeting the customer's precise technical requirements paid dividends in the long run (Sabel, Herrigel, Deeg and Kazis 1989: 381–5). The American textile cluster lacked cohesion. US textile mills exerted little influence over the machinery made in the engineering works. It is unlikely, therefore, that the decline of such firms as Draper and Saco–Lowell did much harm to the American textile industry. Textile producers could obtain better service from foreign suppliers. The USA was the largest non-communist importer of textile machinery throughout the 1980s and early 1990s. In recent years, labour productivity and total factor productivity in US textiles have exceeded the levels obtained in the German and Japanese textile industries (Golub 1994: 294, 296). Imported machinery helped American textile firms to maintain high levels of productivity, although these did not translate into internationally competitive costs.

Both Hong Kong and South Korea were insignificant textile machinery exporters until the 1980s. Rapid growth in exports of textiles and clothing from these Asian countries began twenty years before the emergence of strong textile engineering sectors. The development of the South Korean textile industry necessitated large imports of machinery from the advanced economies. Amsden (1989: 254) recorded the machinery purchases of an anonymous South Korean textile firm, 'L', between 1963 and 1984. L's principal suppliers of ring frames were Platts and Howa. It was not until 1983 that the company bought domestically produced ring frames from an Anglo-Korean joint venture called Samwhan Platt. L's imports of automatic looms came from Howa, Enshu (Japan) and Picarol (Belgium). In 1980, some shuttleless looms were acquired from Ishikawa (Japan). Open-end spinning equipment was bought from Ingolstadt (West Germany) in 1979, and Schlafhorst (West Germany) in 1984. Korean textile firms with less sophisticated requirements were more likely to buy locally manufactured capital goods. A study of a sample of Korean textile firms found that, in the mid-1970s, about 40 per cent of their stock of machinery was made in Korea. Textile machinery plants connected to the *chaebol* were among the earliest exporters of this type of equipment (Westphal, Rhee, Kim and Amsden 1984). Hong Kong's textile and apparel industries also relied on imported capital goods for many years. Japanese equipment came to dominate the market in Hong Kong, with American and European firms trailing a long way behind. Mainland China was becoming an important source of textile equipment for Hong Kong in the 1980s (Sit and Wong 1989: 169). Attention has already been drawn to the growth of an internationally competitive sewing machine industry in Hong Kong. It made sense for machinery makers in Hong Kong to specialize in sewing machines, rather than in more complex spinning, weaving and finishing technologies, since European and Japanese competition was more intense in the latter fields.

Textile machinery production in India commenced in 1937 (Otsuka, Ranis and Saxonhouse 1988: 131). The Birla group, which managed six cotton mills, a rayon mill and two jute mills, established a branch to make textile machinery and parts in 1939 (Bhagwati and Desai 1970: 48–9). But India did not develop a substantial textile machinery industry until the 1960s. Priority was given to the production of capital goods for use in other sectors. Indian textile machinery producers tended to manufacture simple equipment, a choice which was fully justified in an economy with an immense supply of cheap labour. Attempts were made by Indian firms to enhance their engineering knowledge through collaboration with companies from Japan and the West. But some foreign partners proved reluctant to transfer their skills to Indian personnel, and they sometimes forced the Indians to buy raw materials, such as steel, at inflated prices. Collaboration could result in the exploitation of the technically backward partner (Balasubramanyam 1973: 75, 83). Factories controlled by foreign firms accounted for only 7 per cent of the sales of the Indian textile machinery industry in 1980–1, and it follows that this sector was mainly home-grown (N. Kumar 1988). Indian firms slowly improved their capacity to make acceptable engineering products. Machinery produced in India was ordered for the Birla group's joint venture textile and rayon mills, in Indonesia and Thailand, during the 1970s. Although the choice of equipment for these mills reflected nationalistic and corporate as well as purely economic considerations, it demonstrated that Indian machinery was now worthy of consideration (Lall 1982: 136–7). The most rapidly growing segment of the Indian weaving industry, after independence, utilized second-hand power-looms instead of new machinery. Second-hand machinery was quite appropriate in a country with low wages (Pack 1977). Overall, it would be impossible to argue that the domestic textile machinery industry has made a great contribution to the Indian textile and clothing cluster.

China's textile machinery industry is substantial. It comprised 800 factories in 1993, although only about forty of these produced modern equipment with a realistic chance of finding export markets (Glasse 1995: 106). The Chinese currently export textile machinery to South-east Asia, but China's exports are greatly outweighed by imports. In fact, in 1993, China was the world's largest importer of textile and leather machinery, taking 19 per cent of global exports (United Nations, Department for Economic and Social Information and Policy Analysis 1995: 170). Under the Eighth Five Year Plan, of 1991–5, the Chinese government placed increasing emphasis on the creation of a modern textile machinery industry. Joint ventures were planned between Chinese establishments and engineering and textile machinery companies from Japan, Taiwan and Hong Kong. Shuttleless looms were to be constructed in the Shanghai area (Bow 1993; Glasse 1994: 106–11). European textile machinery producers, facing the continuing relative decline of their domestic users, are eager to become involved in joint ventures in China and India (Spinanger 1995: 7). Given China's relative factor prices, however, it is by no means clear that the optimum strategy for its textile sector is to install the most modern equipment. Simpler technology may be quite satisfactory. According to a detailed study of technology choice in the textile sectors of developing countries, there is a tendency for the larger mills in such countries to opt for machinery which is too capital-intensive, on the basis of misleading or biased foreign advice (Amsalem 1983: 45–7, 156–63).

Electronics have become an important branch of the textile machinery sector since the 1960s. A link has thus been forged between the computer industry and the textile cluster. The design and preparatory processes in the clothing industry are amenable to the use of computer technology. Even the more straightforward elements of garment assembly can be automated with the assistance of computers. Electronics companies, such as Gerber Scientific Inc. of the USA and Laser Lectra of France, began supplying equipment to textile and apparel mills. IBM and other companies developed software for use in conjunction with computerized textile and apparel machinery (Hoffman and Rush 1988). Established manufacturers of sewing machines, including Brother and Pfaff, acquired capabilities in electronics, so that they could introduce equipment of greater sophistication. Singer took this strategy to unexpected extremes. The Singer company diversified into electrical goods, electronics and defence equipment in the 1960s and 1970s. Singer eventually decided that the prospects were poor for its sewing machine business, and this part of the group was spun off as SSMC in 1986. This left Singer, renamed Bicoastal, to concentrate on defence production (Anon 1990). Information technology has found many applications on the commercial side of the textile cluster. Levi Strauss operates an extensive information network, which incorporates the bar-coding and scanning of products, electronic ordering and invoicing, and the collection and manipulation of sales data (Hammond 1993: 196–9). Benetton's information-gathering and processing network used IBM and Siemens mainframes in the late 1980s, while agents were linked to the company by IBM PCs (Rullani and Zanfei 1988a: 67, 70–1).

Now that electronics are vital to the textile and clothing complex, countries with powerful electronics industries, such as Japan and the USA, could gain an advantage over the Europeans, who are comparatively weak in this sphere. However, some smaller European companies are making progress. Bonas, from Tyneside, a region without a strong textile tradition, invented the world's first electronic jacquard in the 1980s. The jacquard, invented in 1805, is a punched card device, attached to a loom, which controls the pattern of the weave. One in eight Bonas employees was involved in R&D in 1993, and its most famous product was exported all over the world. The company's electronic jacquard was also manufactured under licence by Yamada, the leading Japanese firm in the field (Purkiss 1993: 36–7). Bonas is small compared with Toyoda and Sulzer, but its success illustrates that technical breakthroughs can occur in unexpected places.

The evidence suggests that a resilient textile industry and a strong textile machinery industry are often found in the same region. Lancashire in the nineteenth century and Japan in the twentieth century are prime examples of this mutually supporting relationship. But the textile histories of Lancashire and the USA also illustrate the tendency for decline in one part of the textile cluster to spread through the entire group of related industries. Even the Swiss textile machinery industry may be suffering from its isolation within the regional economy.

CHEMICALS

Modern textiles could not be produced without the assistance of the chemical industry. Bleach and dyestuffs are required in order to render the final product more appealing to customers. Even the uniforms worn by the inhabitants of Mao's China were dyed green instead of being left in their natural greyish state. More sophisticated forms of chemical treatment are needed in, for example, the waterproofing of clothing or the adding of lustre to fabrics. Chemical procedures are also employed to great effect in the manufacture of rayon and synthetic fibres, thereby widening, and in many cases cheapening, the range of products on offer to the consumer.

Until the late nineteenth century, British firms led the world in the production of chemicals for use in the textile industry. But this commanding position was not maintained in the face of Germany's growing expertise in chemicals. British manufacturers of bleaching materials fell behind their European competitors in the replacement of the Leblanc process by the Solvay process, although the significance of this particular episode should not be exaggerated (Sandberg 1981: 113). Britain also failed to capitalize on W. H. Perkin's discovery of a means of producing dyestuffs from coaltar. This major British breakthrough was seized upon by the Germans.

Germany's excellent system of technological education enabled its chemical firms to enter fields which required a high degree of scientific knowledge. Germany produced over 85 per cent of the world's output of industrial dyestuffs in 1913, and Switzerland was ranked in second place. The largest firms in this sector were BASF, Bayer and Hoechst. Germany's success, argues Chandler, stemmed from the willingness of its firms to invest in worldwide marketing networks, the construction of large-scale plants and the systematic pursuit of R&D (Haber 1958; 1971; Chandler 1990: 474–81). Edgerton and Horrocks (1994: 219–20) point out that British chemical producers did have laboratories and some R&D staff before 1914, but it would appear that their labours were comparatively unsuccessful.

Germany's leadership in artificial dyestuffs was not a serious handicap to textile producers in other countries until 1914. British firms could import German dyestuffs free of duty, and the Germans thoughtfully established subsidiary plants in major foreign markets, including the USA and UK. During the First World War, however, the cessation of trade with Germany created difficulties for textile firms in Britain, France and their allies. The British government intervened to relieve the situation by establishing a new enterprise, British Dyes, and by extensively subsidizing R&D in this field. After the war, the state encouraged the reorganization of the British chemical industry, through the formation of larger groupings, and set in train a process which led to the creation of the Imperial Chemical Industries (ICI) combine in 1926 (Reader 1970; 1975; Edgerton and Horrocks 1994). Together with Du Pont of the USA, and I.G. Farben, which had been established through the merger of prominent German chemical suppliers in 1925, ICI was one of a triumvirate of firms which dominated the global chemical industry in the 1930s. The First World War also prevented Japanese textile mills from obtaining supplies of German dyestuffs. Mitsui Mining and the Japanese government were in the vanguard of attempts to develop an indigenous dyestuffs industry between 1914 and 1918. When the first Japanese factories ran into technical problems, they had to solve them without foreign help. This was very expensive in the short term, but at least it ensured that Japanese technicians gained plenty of experience. During the 1920s, German firms tried to restrict the flow of technical information to potential rivals, and refused to supply Japan with manufacturing licences. The determination of Mitsui Mining and Nihon Senryo to perfect their capacity to manufacture dyestuffs eventually thwarted the Germans, and in the 1930s market-sharing agreements were signed between the top Japanese and foreign firms (Kudo 1994). Both Britain and Japan, by dint of great effort, succeeded in fostering the development of competent dyestuffs sectors. But it is difficult to calculate the benefits to the British and Japanese textile industries of this activity. Britain's textile sector was beginning to decline in the 1920s, while that of Japan was at its most dynamic between the wars. The possession of a modern dyestuffs sector was a marginal factor in the determination of their overall success or failure.

Man-made fibres started to make an impact on world textile markets in the 1900s, when rayon, or artificial silk, made its commercial debut. The most successful rayon-producing technology did not originate in an advanced chemical laboratory. In fact, the crucial experiments were conducted in a small workshop near the Kew Gardens underground station in London. Rayon was taken up by the southern English textile firm of Courtaulds, which was looking for a product to replace its traditional, but faltering, line of mourning crape. Before the First World War, Courtaulds built large rayon manufacturing plants at Coventry in England in 1905 and, through its subsidiary, the American Viscose Corporation, at Marcus Hook in Pennsylvania in 1911 (Coleman 1969b: 1–119). Several alternative types of rayon-producing technology were developed among the leading industrial countries of Europe and the USA (Markham 1952; Robson 1958). Du Pont, which would later become a dominant force in the nylon industry, started to manufacture rayon in 1921 (Hounshell and Smith 1988: 161–82). The rise of man-made fibres resulted in a gradual blurring of the edges between the textile and chemical industries. Chemical and textile firms had much to learn from each other, in areas such as the details of chemical processes and the organization of textile mills. Sometimes textile companies, for example Courtaulds, were in the forefront of the development of new fibres. At other times, the chemical producers, including Du Pont, were the driving force.

Rayon production began in Japan in 1915, with the construction of the Yonezawa plant by an offshoot of the general trading company, Suzuki Shoten. This factory went on to become the nucleus of the giant Teijin group. In the 1920s and 1930s, many of Japan's leading cotton and chemical manufacturers established rayon factories, using technology imported from Britain, Europe and the USA. For example, Kanegafuchi, one of Japan's largest cotton textile producers, opened its first rayon plants in 1935 and 1936, on the basis of Italian technology (Yamazaki 1992a; 1992b; Abe 1993: 8). By the late 1930s, the Japanese rayon industry possessed large export markets and was worthy of comparison with its rivals in Europe and North America. Rayon factories competed with the producers of natural fibres such as cotton plantations. In its continuous filament form, rayon was also a threat to the spinning industry. But rayon goods were woven on ordinary cotton looms, providing additional work for mills in ailing textile regions. And staple rayon, which was produced in short strands resembling cotton fibres, could be spun on existing machinery in cotton mills. Mixed fabrics of rayon and natural fibres were produced by many firms. Some textile firms, notably Burlington, chose to specialize in the processing of rayon, and grew despite the depression of the 1930s (A. C. Wright 1995). Rayon's emergence, and its incorporation into the textile clusters of Western Europe and the USA, acted as a break on the relative decline of these areas as textile producers, but it could not reverse this process. The rapid adoption of rayon by the Japanese textile cluster served to limit the boost which this fibre gave to the competitive advantage of Western textile producers.

Synthetics constituted the next generation of man-made fibres. To a much greater extent than was the case with rayon, advanced research by large firms was required to create and develop the synthetic fibres. Du Pont scientists produced the first synthetic fibre, nylon, in 1930 (Hounshell and Smith 1988: 223–48, 257–73). This event was a major breakthrough, although its full exploitation did not occur until after the Second World War. Firms in other countries were eager to proceed along the same path. Toyo Rayon (Toray) of Japan succeeded in making a pirate version of Du Pont's nylon yarn in 1939, but further progress in Japan was cut short by the war (Ozawa 1980: 134–5). Terylene, the first polyester fibre, was developed in 1940 by researchers employed by the Calico Printers' Assocation, a large but somewhat old-fashioned cotton textile finishing business in England. But the Calico Printers' Assocation was not in a position to make the heavy investment required to produce Terylene on a commercial basis. ICI, working in conjunction with Courtaulds and Du Pont, acquired the production rights. In the USA Terylene was called Dacron (Reader 1975: 381–2). Research into the third main type of synthetic fibre, acrylic, was conducted by I.G. Farben and Du Pont in the late 1930s and 1940s. Du Pont's acrylic fibre, Orlon, entered production in 1950 (Read 1986).

A series of agreements between the European and American man-made fibre producers, and especially between ICI and Du Pont, resulted in widespread exchanges of technical information and production licences. The commercial development of synthetic fibres involved a collaborative effort among leading chemical and textile firms in the USA and Europe. Alliances between large firms in different countries were formed in order to reduce the incidence of costly struggles for global domination. Any country with a capacity for advanced research in chemicals was able to join the club. Synthetic fibres could not be monopolized by any single region, and leadership in this area was difficult to sustain.

In Britain, after 1960, the man-made fibre industry was worried about the poor performance of the textile cluster and decided to intervene with some vigour in its affairs. Profits generated in the fibre industry were used to reorganize the textile industry. The 1960s witnessed a series of acquisitions of textile and clothing firms by Courtaulds and companies acting on behalf of ICI. These acquisitions were followed by the closure of surplus capacity and the construction of new plants on greenfield sites. But Courtaulds' strategy was a symptom of its own weakness, and the lifeline thrown to the textile industry proved illusory. Courtaulds had earlier failed to make the transition from rayon to synthetic fibres. This made it increasingly desperate to prevent the collapse of its rayon outlets in northern textile mills, which were facing severe competition from Asia. Courtaulds had its roots in textiles instead of chemicals, and was more likely than other fibre producers to contemplate an initiative in textiles. Once Courtaulds had taken the plunge, ICI had to follow suit, in order to stop Courtaulds from gaining a stranglehold on the domestic fibre-using industry. Both Courtaulds and ICI later regretted their decisions to become embroiled in the textile sector, since they were unable to restore its competitiveness and lost large sums in the attempt (Singleton 1991: 209–30; Blackburn 1993). In principle, Courtaulds' strategy of intervening in the textile industry was not misguided. But it had little hope of success, since both the fibre and the textile companies were already in considerable difficulties. By the mid-1980s, Britain's textile cluster was looking increasingly thin (Porter 1990: 490, 494). Contact between the textile industry and related activities served to emphasize the cluster's weaknesses rather than its strengths.

The man-made fibre industries of Western Europe, the USA and Japan found it increasingly difficult to fill their order books in the 1970s and 1980s. Excessively optimistic forecasts of demand led to the construction of many new plants in both developed and developing countries. Overcapacity emerged at prevailing prices. The plight of the chemical fibre industry was deepened by the rising cost of inputs, especially oil, during the 1970s (Shaw and Shaw 1983). European man-made fibre producers formed a crisis cartel in 1977. Firms agreed to reduce competition by concentrating on the production of just one or two fibres. Redundant capacity was eliminated, although there was a tendency for this condition to recur (Dolan 1983: 593–6; Shaw and Simpson 1988; S. Davies 1995). Even Toray descended into crisis in the late 1980s, as a result of the appreciation of the yen and growing competition from other Asian countries. Katsunosuke Maeda, who was appointed president of the company in 1987, concluded that Toray's long-term survival was under threat unless it reduced its dependency on fibres and textiles. Maeda's Action Plan 2000 called for more bulk fibres to be produced abroad, and for the Japanese core of the business to concentrate on speciality fibres. He also thought that the group would need to diversify into areas such as pharmaceuticals and plastics (Anon 1993a). His assessment of the situation was the opposite of that made by Courtaulds in the early 1960s.

Neither Du Pont, the largest man-made fibre producer in the USA, nor the leading German chemical fibre firms, judged it advisable to copy the Courtaulds strategy of annexing substantial portions of their countries' textile mill industries. A sharper distinction between the textile and man-made fibre sectors was preserved in the USA and Germany. Whilst introducing some new fibres, such as Kevlar, Du Pont's main response to difficulties in the textile industry was to acquire firms in other industries, including Conoco in oil, Seagrams in liquor and Remington Arms, and to diversify into biomedical products (Anon 1988). The Germans substituted long-term co-operation agreements between fibre and textile producers for formal vertical integration (Kenis 1992: 60–4). Such arrangements limited the liability of fibre producers to suffer the effects of instability in textile and clothing markets. Porter (1990: 364, 367) argues that the German textile cluster is not very deep, and that it would not carry much weight in the absence of a powerful textile engineering industry. But the position of the German textile cluster has been reinforced by outward processing, especially in Eastern Europe. This extension of the influence of German textile firms provides an answer to some of the problems posed by high labour costs in the domestic economy (Spinanger and Piatti 1994). It also provides a better market environment for the German man-made fibre producers. The German experience suggests that it is possible to manage without an evenly balanced cluster of textile and related industries. Parts of the textile cluster can be transferred abroad, while control remains in the hands of producers in the core countries. Firms in less-developed countries acquire technology from the West, and companies in Germany acquire cheap labour power in Eastern Europe, the Mediterranean and Asia.

Italy's man-made fibre producers were more willing than their German counterparts to take direct control of capacity in the textile industry. Chemical fibre firms, such as Snia Viscosa, are regarded as textile firms in Italy (Kenis 1992: 63, 155). As was the case in the UK, the forward integration of fibre producers in Italy was not a great success. Indeed, the most dynamic part of the Italian textile and clothing sector has escaped domination by the large man-made fibre producers. Italy's competitive advantage in textiles derives from agglomerations of small, design-intensive firms in industrial districts (Piore and Sabel 1984: 213–16; Camagni and Rabellotti 1992; Bigarelli and Crestanello 1994). Companies such as Benetton, which focus on marketing and retailing, are the main coordinators of the textile and clothing sector. Italian man-made fibre producers were to some extent sidetracked and relegated to the poverty-stricken southern periphery, where they were invited to participate in joint ventures with the state, to develop a modern industrial base. The role of synthetic fibre producers in the revitalization of the Italian textile and clothing cluster has been a comparatively minor one. Italian apparel manufacturers would not have found it difficult to substitute imported for domestically produced fibres.

There is a high degree of multinational activity in the man-made fibre industry (Clairmonte and Cavanagh 1981; Read 1986). This has implications for the relationship between the man-made fibre industry and the textile sector. Product or process innovations developed by textile firms in one country, in conjunction with a fibre multinational, are likely to be disseminated across international boundaries with rapidity. The man-made fibre industry of Germany has widespread international connections. In 1980, five foreign man-made fibre manufacturers possessed affiliated production units in West Germany: AKU (Netherlands), Du Pont (USA), ICI (UK), Rhone Poulenc (France) and Monsanto (USA). The largest German firms, Hoechst and

91

Bayer, had majority shareholdings of their own in eight fibre companies in other countries (Kenis 1992: 61). Hoechst acquired one of the USA's leading man-made fibre producers, Celanese, for $2.84 billion in 1986, and BASF acquired American Enka (Finnie 1990: 69). Italy presents an interesting contrast because in 1980 there were no foreign multinationals operating fibre subsidiaries in this country. Whether or not this relative isolation materially assisted Italy to retain the fruits of technical cooperation between its fibre and textile firms is uncertain. Italian fibre producers, such as Montefibre and Snia Viscosa, did have overseas affiliates, through which information could be disseminated. The globalization of the man-made fibre sector has reduced the probability that cooperation between fibre and textile producers in one location will foster a lasting competitive advantage.

Since 1945 the capacity to produce synthetic fibres has spread from the USA and Western Europe into Eastern Europe, Japan, the newly industrializing countries of Asia, Latin America, and elsewhere (Hufbauer 1966: 132–4). Many governments of developing countries regard the construction of a man-made fibre complex as an essential part of the drive for modernization, equivalent to the establishment of a steel industry or a state airline. Such plants evidently increase the prestige of the countries concerned, may save foreign exchange and help to train cadres of domestic technicians. This is not the place to comment on the logic of development plans involving large investments in capital-intensive technologies. Developing countries offered generous terms of assistance to the projectors of synthetic fibre plants. In Taiwan, for instance, the effective rate of protection applying to synthetic and artificial fibres was 88 per cent in 1965 (Sun 1969: 114). Between 1975 and 1985, Taiwan and South Korea increased their combined share of world productive capacity in rayon and synthetic fibres from 6.7 per cent to 14 per cent (Kenis 1992: 45). Productive capacity underwent a rapid expansion in Latin America, where the Dutch firm AKZO was a major investor. By 1976, AKZO was involved in chemical fibre joint ventures with local firms in Argentina, Brazil, Colombia, Ecuador and Mexico, as well as in India and Nigeria. These joint ventures provided advice to local textile producers on the use of synthetic fibres in fabric production (Montavon 1979: 63–111; Tattum 1990). By the early 1990s, Taiwan had become the world's leading producer of polyester fibre, and the USA was relegated to second place. China ranked third, illustrating the speed with which the relevant technology has been disseminated since the 1950s (E. Anderson 1993; Glasse 1995: 77–86). Synthetic fibre plants are becoming commonplace in developing economies. PT Indorama Synthetics of Indonesia, already a major synthetic fibre producer, opened a $115 million computerized polyester plant in 1992, using Japanese and German technology (Selwyn 1993). Indian policy towards synthetics was quite different. High duties were imposed on imports of synthetic fibres, and only four relatively small polyester factories were built before the 1980s. The thinking behind this strategy was that growers of natural fibres should be protected from competition (Mazumdar 1991: 1200–1). Thus, although India avoided adding to world overcapacity in synthetic fibres, its textile mills were unable to import synthetic fibres at world prices for processing into exportable fabrics.

The Japanese state viewed the promotion of a synthetic fibre industry as a key factor in its plans to strengthen the textile industry. In 1949, the government decided that only Toyo Rayon (Toray) and Kurashiki Rayon had sufficient technical ability to proceed with synthetics. Other interested firms, including Kanegafuchi and Toyo Boseki, were told to keep out of the production of synthetics for the time being. Toray obtained the rights to produce Du Pont nylon, and also developed its own nylon, based on the version originally introduced by I.G. Farben. Other firms were allowed to enter production once they had upgraded their technical skills. This stimulated greater competition and encouraged the development of new fibres, usually with the cooperation of more technically advanced Western firms. By 1956, Japan's output of synthetic fibres was second only to that of the USA. Japan's policy reduced the chances of confusion and mistakes in the early stages of the development of synthetics. But the high profits earned by the pioneers attracted too many entrants in the long run, leading to overinvestment and excess capacity by the 1970s (Ozawa 1980).

Did the growth of the Japanese synthetic fibre industry increase the competitive advantage of the Japanese textile industry? In the early 1950s, importing synthetic fibres would have been cheaper than producing them in Japan. Strict import controls were enforced by the Japanese authorities, especially in the 1950s, in order to economize on foreign exchange and to enable the government to protect those firms which it regarded as national champions in high-technology industries (Komiya, Okuno and Suzumura 1988). Japanese textile firms did not have a free choice between imported and home-produced fibres, and in consequence they had to pay more for lower-quality fibres. However, in the long term, the Japanese textile industry was not to be disappointed with the price or quality of domestic fibres. But these benefits were partially offset by new side-effects. Once the Japanese synthetic fibre industry had reached maturity, it began to export, thereby supplying the foreign mills which were undermining Osaka's supremacy. Japanese man-made fibre firms entered into close association with foreign textile interests. Toray took a 50 per cent stake in Textile Alliance Ltd in 1971. This Hong Kong firm was in the process of opening textile mills in South-east Asia (Read 1986: 212). By joining forces with Textile Alliance, Toray secured large new overseas outlets for its fibres, at the expense of the textile sector in Japan. The introduction of synthetic fibres was not a panacea for textile industries that were losing their competitive advantage. Japan occupied an intermediate position with respect to the degree to which the textile and man-made fibre sectors fell under unified ownership. Japanese fibre producers were encouraged by the government to collaborate with textile companies. Nippon Rayon, for example, merged with the Nichibo cotton spinning company in 1969, to form Unitika, a combination of interests which was to prove reasonably successful in the 1970s (O'Leary 1992: 387). But mergers and acquisitions were not the only strategies of the fibre producers. There was also a tradition of cooperation between large fibre and spinning firms, and small weavers and clothing workshops, which fell well short of formal vertical integration (Dore 1986: 153–81).

South Korea began to produce nylon in 1960, acrylic in 1964 and polyester fibre in 1966. Korea's move into synthetic fibres received state approval and encouragement. The Korean government was concerned to upgrade the products of the national economy. Early Japanese synthetic fibre makers sought Western technical assistance, but shunned Western FDI and management. The Koreans, given their greater technical backwardness, could not avoid sanctioning inward FDI. Joint ventures were arranged with Toray and Teijin. One of the Korean businesses engaging in polyester fibre production was Cheil Synthetic, which was established as a joint venture with Toray in 1972. Cheil Synthetic was part of the Samsung *chaebol* group, and therefore it was related to Cheil Wool Textiles (Jones and Sakong 1980: 351). As soon as it was practically possible, Korean synthetic fibre makers invested in their own R&D facilities, and by the early 1980s they had acquired the capability to design their own plants, devise new variations of basic fibres and export technology to less-developed countries (Tran 1988). South Korea had assimilated man-made fibre technology at a rapid pace. Japanese involvement in Korean fibre enterprises was systematically reduced in the late 1970s and early 1980s. In the mid-1980s, Japanese multinationals such as Toray were finding it hard to compete with synthetic fibre plants in Korea and Taiwan, which they had earlier helped to spawn (Anon 1993a).

Porter (1990: 461), using export figures for 1985, found a very strong cluster of industries in textiles, synthetic fibres, apparel, footwear, luggage and accessories in Korea. Of course, Korea's synthetic fibre plants were heavily protected, especially in their formative years. Textile and apparel firms in South Korea could have obtained cheaper synthetic fibres from abroad, but the government ordered them to use locally manufactured supplies. The state compensated fibre users for this inconvenience, by subsidizing their inputs and exports, and enabling them to charge exorbitant prices in local markets. It must be asked whether the Korean textile and apparel sector gained from the forced growth of a domestic synthetic fibre industry. If the state had been unwilling to fix the outcome of the market process, then local textile producers would have borne a heavy burden, at least for a number of years. The most powerful supporting industry related to the Korean textile sector was not synthetics, but the government bureaucracy, especially during the export boom of the 1960s. In Japan, South Korea and other Asian countries, the links between textiles and their related and supporting industries were often strengthened through their mutual participation in alliance systems, such as the Japanese *keiretsu*, and conglomerate groups, such as the Korean *chaebol*.

The message of this section is that the benefits of clustering among textile and man-made fibre industries, whilst important, should not be exaggerated. Close ties with man-made fibre producers have not enabled declining textile regions, such as northern England, to regain their competitive advantage. In countries blessed with a relatively successful textile sector, such as Italy, it is doubtful whether the synthetic fibre industry makes a great deal of difference to the cluster's overall competitiveness. If textile producers are free to import man-made fibres, and tariffs are set at moderate levels, it now makes little difference whether fibre is procured domestically or abroad. In partially closed economies, such as post-war Japan and Korea, the textile and man-made fibre cluster was carefully fostered by the government, and eventually became an asset. But it would be difficult to prove that the strength of the textile and fibre clusters in any of these cases was greatly in excess of the sum of the individual parts.

CONCLUSION

Strong domestic textile machinery or chemical fibre industries may in some circumstances make a large contribution to the success of a textile cluster, but the presence of these factors is not absolutely essential, since highly developed international markets now exist for these inputs. Perhaps the regional cluster was of greater moment in previous generations, when enduring international links between textile producers, chemical firms and engineers were more tenuous. The interests of textile, textile machinery and man-made fibre businesses located in the same region are unlikely to be identical. In reality, apparently strong regional clusters may be no more than collections of industries with common origins which have since grown apart. Machinery and man-made fibre producers are keen to export their products, thereby facilitating the rise of rival textile industries. In the very long run, a successful textile cluster may contribute to its own destruction. Platt Brothers of Oldham helped to dig the graves of the Oldham spinners, and more recently Toyoda has assisted the Indonesians and Koreans to dig the graves of the Osaka spinners. Some powerful clusters of related industries may extend across several countries and contain firms of various nationalities. The German textile cluster includes multinational fibre producers, German engineering firms and textile and clothing businesses in a number of low-wage countries as well as those in Germany itself. Alongside traditional regional clusters of industries, there are international clusters. It may be possible to detach some parts of the cluster and attach new ones, in line with the requirements of the coordinating interest.

5

FIRM STRATEGY

Strategy concerns the choices made by firms in relation to the creation or defence of a favourable competitive position (Rumelt, Schendel and Teece 1994). Use of the term 'strategy' implies that firms have the ability to influence their fate by deliberate action. Obviously, in any given period, some firms have more freedom of manoeuvre than others, depending on the characteristics of their environment and their initial attributes and condition. The quality of strategic decision-making by a company's leaders may have an enormous impact on its position relative to its rivals. But strategic insight is not the sole determinant of a firm's success. Most crucial decisions are taken under conditions of uncertainty, so that chance plays a part in distinguishing between good and bad strategies. Furthermore, firms may be carried along by the tide and achieve profitability despite a poor choice of strategy in a rapidly expanding industry, whilst even the best managers may be unable to save their businesses in a contracting industry (Porter 1994).

Three generic strategies are identified by Porter: overall cost leadership, differentiation and focus. Overall cost leadership and differentiation have as their objective the establishment of an industry-wide competitive advantage. Focus involves concentrating on a segment of the market, and may be pursued by means of either cost minimization or product differentiation. Firms which fail to make a clear choice of strategy are less likely to succeed (Porter 1985: 34–41). Strategy also entails choosing how to compete, if at all, on the international stage. Having made a decision to compete internationally, it is necessary to choose among strategies of exporting from the home base, establishing production facilities in each foreign market and operating them in isolation, or creating an integrated global production and distribution network. International businesses also need to make a selection between policies of overall cost leadership, differentiation and focus (Porter 1986; 1987).

The most common strategy may change over an industry's life cycle. During periods of rapid expansion, cost leadership in standard products may be adequate to ensure profitability. In a saturated market, differentiation and focus become more important. Even in a declining industry, firms may choose from several plausible strategies, and Porter (1980: 267) identifies these as the drive for leadership, the defence of a profitable niche, the harvesting of short-term profits with a view to eventual exit, and immediate divestment.

Porter (1990: 108; 1994: 451–5) adds that the selection of a strategy may be strongly influenced by the regional or national environment. Countries with highly competent and well-motivated business personnel are more likely to produce firms with strategic insight. The diamond of forces within the industrial region affects the flow of information to business leaders and modifies the structure of incentives. A textile diamond which includes strong engineering firms, sophisticated consumers, high-quality human capital and healthy rivalry offers constituent firms better information and a wider range of opportunities than a diamond blighted by failure. It should be possible to discern different national strategies, and these may be expected to evolve over time, reflecting changes in the diamond. Toyne *et al.* (1984: 130–71) distinguish between the strategies of textile producers in different countries in the 1960s and 1970s. They argue that choice of strategy reflected leaders' perceptions of the homogeneity or heterogeneity of their home markets. Large British and American firms viewed their domestic markets as homogeneous, and invested heavily in capital-intensive machinery, with the objective of achieving economies of scale. This strategy failed because capital-intensive plants could not compete with cheap imports of standard textiles from developing countries. Firms in some other countries, including Italy, Germany and, to an extent, Japan, viewed their markets as heterogeneous, followed strategies based on differentiation and focus, and achieved greater success. Businesses in developed countries could sustain a strategy of producing standardized textiles and clothing only by outsourcing the more labour-intensive processes to countries with low labour costs. Toyne *et al.*'s approach illustrates the importance of strategic decision-making, and shows how it relates to other elements of the diamond, such as perceptions about demand conditions, and the choice of technology.

Due to limitations of space, a decision must be made about whether to organize this chapter on a country-by-country or strategy-by-strategy basis. Either approach would be illuminating, but to attempt both would entail repetition. My strategy will be to proceed thematically.

GENERIC STRATEGIES

Three generic strategies – overall cost leadership, differentiation and focus – are open to firms. Choice among these strategies depends on the firm's environment and the ability of its decision-makers. Firms with incompetent decision-makers may find it difficult to identify alternative strategies, let alone choose between them, and could adopt a policy of drift by default.

Although strategies relating to international competition cannot be ignored here, they will be examined in more detail in the next section.

Generic strategies before 1939

In an industrial sector such as textiles and clothing, in which there are a number of distinct fibres and many types of garment, each requiring particular yarns, fabrics and finishes, it would be very difficult for any firm either to establish a cost leadership across the board, or to supply a superior version of every textile and clothing product. Firms must focus their activities to some degree. This tendency to concentrate on a restricted segment or niche of the market is not a recent phenomenon, although it is sometimes thought to be a response to increasing price competition from developing countries. In nineteenth-century Britain, for instance, firms specialized in either cotton or wool or silk textiles. Those firms which concentrated on cotton usually focused even more narrowly on one process, and within this process they focused on certain types of yarn or cloth. For instance, it was costly to make frequent changes in the count (or fineness) of the yarn spun because this necessitated time-consuming adjustments to the machinery. Once a firm had chosen to compete within a certain range of counts, it could seek to differentiate its yarn from that of its rivals by using better cotton or branding but, in general, competition between mills spinning similar counts took place on the basis of costs. The same principle applied in weaving (Robson 1957: 63–102). Cotton spinning and weaving firms clustered in separate towns, and there was even a powerful trend for individual towns to specialize in particular types of yarn or cloth. Bolton and its environs concentrated on fine yarn, and Oldham on coarse yarn (Farnie 1979: 301–13). Firms in the wool textile industry also specialized, and an important distinction was drawn between the producers of woollen and worsted fabrics, which required different sorts of wool and finishing processes (Jenkins and Ponting 1982).

Similarly, focus was central to the strategy of American textile firms in the nineteenth century. The 700 textile businesses of Philadelphia, in 1890, were divided into the following product sub-categories: carpets, cotton goods, dyeing and finishing, hose and knits, silk goods, upholstery, woollen goods and worsteds. A closer examination of each of these sub-categories would reveal even finer gradations of focus (Scranton 1989: 103). Scranton (1994) discusses the competitive strategies of apparel manufacturers in Philadelphia, in the early twentieth century. Some Philadelphia firms opted to pare costs to the bone by employing outworkers and minimizing overheads. Others tried to make apparel of a consistently higher quality, and chose to operate larger facilities so that they could monitor workers. Many businesses compromised between these two approaches. The relative popularity of these strategies ebbed and flowed, as styles, labour regulations and distribution patterns evolved. In New England, there was far less variety and the tendency was for large firms to produce standardized cotton yarn and cloth. Even here, however, some pockets of firms focused on narrower segments of the market, and New Haven and Bridgeport had become centres of the corset industry by the 1880s (B. Smith 1991).

As the economies of the USA and Western Europe became increasingly mature and prosperous, opportunities arose for more subtle forms of specialization. The social philosopher, expert in medieval arts and crafts, and businessman, William Morris, produced tapestries, carpets and printed textiles, to the highest standards for discerning clients, at his idyllic mill near London, during the Victorian era (Harvey and Press 1991). Courtaulds, another English firm, had great success as a manufacturer of mourning crape to satisfy Victorian tastes for elaborate funerals and extended mourning periods (Coleman 1969a). Burlington Mills, a weaving firm established in North Carolina in 1923, was not particularly profitable until its founder recognized that rayon was the rising fabric and decided to focus on the production of rayon material for bedspreads and women's dresses. Burlington became the largest textile producer in the USA within a few years (A. C. Wright 1995). Smith & Nephew, a retail pharmacist and manufacturer of cod liver oil, based in Yorkshire, established itself as a leading producer of textile products for medical purposes, and also of sanitary towels, in the early twentieth century. Demand for these products was growing because rising incomes fed through into expenditure on healthcare (Foreman-Peck 1995). In the First World War special fabrics were designed for use in the manufacture of Zeppelin envelopes and coverings for the wings and fuselages of aircraft. Fabric continued to be used in aircraft manufacturing between the wars, until it was superseded by metal (Singleton 1994: 606–9). Another industrial outlet for textiles was the burgeoning automobile industry. Collins & Aikman rose from obscurity in the 1920s as a result of its decision to produce seating fabrics and its subsequent collaboration with General Motors and Chrysler (Scranton 1989: 325, 396).

These innovative product strategies were adopted for a number of reasons. Burlington and Collins & Aikman were actively searching for alternatives to their existing and less than successful ranges of textile products. William Morris was anxious to promote a revolution in taste and to demonstrate the merits of traditional manufacturing methods. Courtaulds was experiencing increased import competition for most types of silk and found that crape was its most reliable source of revenue. Smith & Nephew came under the influence of Horatio Nelson Smith (the nephew), who had previously been employed by a textile company, and was in an ideal position to bridge the gap between healthcare and textiles. Smith & Nephew was diversifying backwards into textiles from the distribution industry. The producers of fabrics for airships and aeroplanes were responding to the lure of high wartime demand. The sustainability of the competitive advantage generated by these strategies was not uniform. Morris's business gradually lost its dynamism after his death, since it was grounded in his individual genius for design. Towards the end of the Victorian era, the obsession with mourning became less intense, and so did the market for black crape, but Courtaulds found an even more fruitful area of specialization in rayon (Coleman 1969b). Burlington and Collins & Aikman have survived as entities, despite many vicissitudes, although their product mixes have undergone several transformations in response to changing market conditions. Smith & Nephew continued to prosper, and after the Second World War it successfully added pharmaceuticals to its range of products (Foreman-Peck 1995: 161–82, 228–52).

Textile and clothing producers in Japan implemented a policy of focus at an early stage of their exposure to Western competition. A fundamental strategy of mechanized textile producers in late-nineteenth-century China and Japan was to avoid direct competition with Western firms in the higher counts of yarn and more sophisticated Western styles of cloth, since Asian workers and technicians could not match Westerners in the operation of modern techniques (B. L. Reynolds 1986). Firms specialized by fibre. Apart from cotton, there was a particularly strong silk industry in Japan. Producers in Japan were distributed between weavers of narrow cloth for traditional uses in the domestic market and weavers of broad cloth for the city and export markets. Choice of product and choice of technology were intertwined, and firms which continued to supply traditional Japanese textiles persevered with handlooms and outworking for much longer than businesses which aimed at exporting. Specialization in Japan, as in Britain, was pursued to the extent that individual towns and districts concentrated on certain types of cloth (Minami 1987: 173–256; Abe and Saito 1988; Abe 1992; Howe 1996: 176–200).

Strategy selection had implications for the choice of technology in the West. Firms which supplied a relatively standardized product, such as cotton yarn or grey (untreated) cloth, had no difficulty finding suitable machinery in the catalogues of textile engineers. Those producing less commonplace articles, such as the Connecticut corset producers, either designed and manufactured some of their own equipment or collaborated with machinery makers such as Singer to modify existing types of machinery (B. Smith 1991: 116–23). Much controversy has been generated by the choice of technology in the cotton industry in the late nineteenth and early twentieth centuries (Mass and Lazonick 1991). British cotton textile producers lagged behind their American rivals in the installation of ring spindles and automatic looms, and opted to remain with the older mule spinning method and the Lancashire (power-)loom. In 1913, 87 per cent of cotton spindles in the USA were rings, compared with 19 per cent in Britain. Automatic looms made up 40 per cent of cotton weaving capacity in the USA, but under 2 per cent in the UK (Lazonick 1983: 198). More yarn and cloth could be manufactured in the same time using ring spindles and automatic looms, raising questions about the rationality of British employers. Although the 'rings versus mules' debate is a complex one, it has been established that early ring spindles and automatic looms were unsuitable for the manufacture of the finer yarns and cloths, in which many British, but few American, mills specialized (Sandberg 1974: 15–92; Saxonhouse and Wright 1984a; 1984b). In view of their prior selection of strategy, British mills made a reasonable choice of equipment. The continued global domination of British cotton textiles before 1914, despite their use of an older generation of machinery, provides a further objective reason for vindicating Lancashire's choice of technology: in 1910–13, the UK supplied 70 per cent of world exports of cotton piece goods, while the USA supplied just 4.2 per cent (Rose 1991: 3). For a modern parallel, Amsden (1989: 256–7) suggests that South Korean textile firms may be guilty of entrepreneurial failure, since open-end rotors contributed a mere 0.72 per cent of their industry's spinning capacity in 1983.

Competitiveness was difficult to sustain, especially among producers of the most easily imitated and least knowledge-intensive products. Focus was an ingredient of success, as British textile producers learned in the nineteenth century. But existing specializations could be rendered obsolete by changing conditions. Between the world wars, Japan overtook Britain as the leading exporter of cotton textiles, for a number of reasons, including a favourable combination of low wages and efficient workers, supplemented by high quality management (Sandberg 1974: 175–206; Allen 1980: 63–82; Mass and Lazonick 1991: 37–50; Howe 1996: 201–31). Mass and Lazonick stress that Japan's competitive advantage between the wars resulted from superior strategy, citing the industry's vertically integrated structure, its superior choice of technology, its effective blending of cotton and its coordination of marketing and production. Unlike British firms, which regarded graduates with suspicion, the leading Japanese textile producers were eager to recruit students from local universities (Yonekawa 1984). Whilst it can be accepted that major Japanese firms were staffed by capable leaders who pursued sensible business strategies, it does not follow that their contribution to Japan's competitive advantage outweighed that of a cheap, efficient and well-disciplined labour force. British producers of coarse yarn and cloth were especially vulnerable to Japanese competition, because these were the least skill-intensive branches of the industry. It is doubtful whether any business strategy could have enabled these firms to compete successfully with Japan in the long run. British firms supplying other categories of textiles, such as fine yarn and sewing thread, were not directly threatened by Japanese competition and fared much better (Committee on Industry and Trade 1928: 38–9; Robertson 1991). Smith & Nephew, for example, was untouched by Japanese competition between the wars. Having discovered a congenial niche, Smith & Nephew continued to upgrade and differentiate its product range (Foreman-Peck 1995: 73). The producers of the least differentiated commodities faced the greatest risks before 1939, and we would expect to see the same pattern after 1945.

Generic strategies since 1945

The spread of mechanized textile production into new areas, particularly in Asia, since 1945 has not fundamentally changed the range of strategies open to firms, although it has caused many producers in developed countries to select different strategies from the shelf. Newly industrializing countries tend to focus on the least sophisticated product categories. This strategy reflects the poverty of domestic consumers, as well as skill shortages in design, production and marketing. Since apparel assembly is the most labour-intensive process in the textile and clothing sector, many newly developing countries have had their initial success in this field (Jones and Sakong 1980: 316–24; O'Connor 1993: 239, 241–2). In Thailand, in the 1950s and 1960s, the most successful strategy for mills with official connections was to focus on large military orders for basic commodities such as blankets and uniforms (Doner and Ramsay 1993: 694). Especially among smaller firms, this emphasis on cheap, standardized goods has continued into more recent times, even in increasingly advanced Asian economies. According to a survey conducted in 1987, small- and medium-sized Hong Kong textile and apparel producers regarded low prices rather than high quality as the key to competitiveness (Sit and Wong 1989: 176).

Econometric research into the quality of textiles and clothing manufactured in different parts of the world during the 1980s provides support for the hypothesis that the newly industrializing and developing countries supply commodities in the lower-quality ranges. Japanese and Italian firms produced the highest-quality textiles, while Italian and British firms made the best-quality apparel. There were signs, however, that some newly industrializing states, including South Korea and Hong Kong, were beginning to upgrade their wares (Barry and Dickerson 1987; Faini and Heimler 1991). For instance, some South Korean firms were turning to the manufacture of high-quality woollen fabrics in response to rising wage levels and loss of competitiveness in standard textiles (Park 1994: 149).

Increased price competition from developing countries has, since the 1950s, stimulated a variety of responses from textile manufacturers in developed nations. In the 1960s and 1970s, European and American firms sought to meet the Asian challenge head on. Major Western firms tried to compete in standard lines, building large mills equipped with the latest machinery, in the belief that unit costs could be reduced to levels comparable with imports. Courtaulds pioneered this strategy in the UK, and it was followed in France, the USA and, for a time, in West Germany. Courtaulds alone spent £57 million on textile machinery and the construction of new factories between 1962 and 1969. This strategy also involved seeking overall cost leadership. Prior to embarking on its massive investment programme, Courtaulds was principally known as a rayon producer. By 1970, however, the Courtaulds empire included large facilities in most branches of the textile sector (A. Knight 1974; Shepherd 1981: 32–9; Singleton 1991: 160–6, 209–30). By 1980, this strategy had proved a costly mistake, and relatively new factories were either closed or running at levels well below capacity. Toyne *et al.* (1984: 163) suggest that the failure of the Europeans was a consequence of the smallness of their home markets in comparison with the USA. But this argument is unconvincing, since economies of scale are relatively limited in textile production, and therefore a huge domestic market is not essential (Pratten 1971: 226–38). Moreover, Burlington also followed a strategy of producing long runs of standardized textiles in technologically advanced mills, during the 1970s, and met with equally unsatisfactory results (Schusteff 1992a). Generally speaking, textile firms in the developed countries underestimated the ability of their Asian competitors to make further rounds of cost reductions, and subsequently found that their initial predictions of relative costings were too optimistic.

A closely related strategy for responding to rising competition entailed the introduction of more sophisticated machinery. Open-end rotor spinning and shuttleless loom weaving became increasingly popular from the 1960s onwards. An open-end rotor head of 1984 vintage could produce four times as much yarn per minute as a modern ring spindle, although the higher initial capital cost of the open-end rotor system should be set against the lower spinning costs (Antonelli 1989). Shuttleless looms use jets of air or water to propel the weft, thereby reducing friction and saving time (Ray 1984: 38–51). Warp-knitting technology also underwent a dramatic transformation, supplying fabric producers with an alternative to the weaving system (F. A. Wells 1972: 179–82; Parsonage 1973). Table 5.1 shows the extent to which open-end rotors and shuttleless looms have been introduced in selected nations. It would appear that high-technology strategies were not confined to the developed capitalist countries. Both Czechoslovakia, where the open-end rotor was invented, and the USSR, recorded high levels of installation. Moreover, Hong Kong has outpaced Japan, Switzerland, the UK and the USA in the re-equipment of its mills with open-end rotors and shuttleless looms. Japan has been particularly slow to introduce the open-end rotor. The fact that Hong Kong's large mills are moving in a capital-intensive direction is a reflection of the colony's rising labour costs relative to nations at a lower stage of development. It is conceivable that the uneven rate of installation of open-end rotors among developed countries may reflect the tension between the incentive to buy the most modern machinery as quickly as possible, and the temptation to wait until an even better model is forthcoming. Another pertinent factor could be the rational decision of some firms to retain fully written down equipment of an older generation until it wears out, because it no longer bears depreciation charges. Moreover, if

Table 5.1 Open-end rotors and shuttleless looms as percentages
of total spinning and weaving capacity in selected countries,
1975, 1990

	Open-end rotors		Shuttleless looms	
	1975	*1990*	*1975*	*1990*
Czechoslovakia	19.6[a]	37.5	—	33.3
France	2.4	29.2	—	83.2
Hong Kong	13.8	46.7	1.0[a]	72.0
India	—	0.7	0.4[a]	4.8[c]
Italy	2.8	11.3	5.9[a]	83.9
Japan	5.2	6.4	8.0[a]	36.5[b]
Pakistan	0.1[a]	3.8	0.2[a]	33.3
Sweden	7.6	55.6	—	—
Switzerland	1.7	4.3	5.5	55.3
Taiwan	1.2	11.0	3.5[d]	36.5[c]
Thailand	0.3	4.3	0.4	6.3
United Kingdom	3.4	17.0[b]	18.3[a]	51.0
United States	2.6	17.4	6.9	61.8
USSR	10.1[a]	57.1	—	71.2
West Germany	3.9	18.0	—	86.6

Source: Lücke (1993: 1232–5)
Notes: — not available
     a 1976
     b 1988
     c 1989
     d 1977

firms eventually intend to withdraw from volume production of yarn and cloth, they have no incentive to buy new equipment. As is admitted by those who have studied the spread of open-end rotor spinning and shuttleless loom weaving, a complete explanation of the diffusion of these innovations remains elusive (Antonelli, Petit and Tahar 1992: 146–8).

Since the 1970s, some parts of the clothing sector have been revolutionized by microelectronics. The design and preparation stages of clothing manufacturing may be controlled by computers, enabling firms to reduce their employment of expensive skilled labour. Although programmable sewing machines and equipment for assembling collars and sleeves are also available, the automation of these tasks has been fraught with technical difficulties. Predictably, the USA, Western Europe and Japan have led the world in the introduction of computerized clothing technology (Hoffman and Rush 1988). It has been argued that the application of microelectronics to textiles and clothing, which has led to the introduction of more intelligent and versatile machines, could make it possible for high labour cost countries to regain some of their lost competitiveness in volume textiles (Kell and Richtering 1991). This remains to be seen, and it should be pointed out that computerization is not confined to developed countries. Keerthana Garments, of Tiruppur, India, successfully installed a computerized embroidery machine in 1988 and, by 1993, there were 300 such machines in this district, facilitating the supply of cheap garments of a consistent quality to Western retailers (McDonald 1994). Electronic techniques have also played an increasing role in the marketing of apparel and in the establishment of better communications between manufacturing and distribution units. Sales registers may be linked by computer to clothing firms and their subcontractors, reducing the time needed to respond to shifts in consumer taste from a matter of months to one of days (Rullani and Zanfei 1988a; 1988b).

One positive strategic response to enhanced competition is to seek a niche in one of the more sophisticated areas of textile and clothing production. Italian firms, such as Benetton, successfully positioned themselves during the 1980s as suppliers of fashionable, but not exclusive, clothing to young people. The strengths of Benetton's strategy have been in branding, image, electronic communications and subcontracting networks. Other firms in the Italian clothing sector have followed comparable strategies, with considerable success. It is significant that the thriving Italian clothing sector of the late twentieth century is populated by new firms, and that earlier generations of businesses have been destroyed. Even though established firms may fail to modify their strategies in the light of new competitive conditions, a region as a whole may succeed in adapting by recombining human capital into new businesses (Shepherd 1981: 34–6; Buxton 1988; Kay 1993: 287–318; Bigarelli and Crestanello 1994). Of course, the reconstitution of a moribund textile and clothing industry is far from automatic: the process of renewal has not been as marked in northern England as it has in Italy.

A greater emphasis on R&D, with a view to developing and mastering new products and processes, is another strategic option. Burlington opened an R&D department in the 1950s so that it could study the implications of the availability of synthetic fibres. However, it should be recalled that textiles and clothing is a sector which generally exhibits a low intensity of R&D. Burlington spent a mere 1 per cent of sales on R&D in 1961, compared with Du Pont's 7 per cent (A. C. Wright 1995: 54). Most R&D that is of relevance to textiles and clothing occurs in the textile engineering and chemical fibre industries. The appearance of non-woven fibres in recent decades, and their increasing penetration of the market for industrial textiles, has provided new opportunities for some long-established textile producers, including Toyobo and Canada's Dominion Textiles, as well as chemical producers and specialist non-woven firms (Noonan 1994). Increasingly sophisticated fibres and fabrics are required for specialized activities, such as sports and fire-fighting. Modern textiles have a wide range of novel uses. Textiles are needed by surgeons to replace worn-out blood vessels, and they are made into inflatable dams for flood control (United States, Office of Technology Assessment 1987: 16). Small firms, staffed by personnel with high levels of technical expertise, have been able to position themselves in some of these niches. For example, during the 1980s and early 1990s, the high-technology garment industry expanded in Scotland. Firms in this industry use special synthetic fabrics in the manufacture of leisurewear, protective uniforms for the armed forces and fire service, and clothing for the oil and fishing industries (H. Hall 1994: 282). Reduced levels of protection in New Zealand have forced surviving textile and apparel firms to concentrate on more sophisticated products. In 1994, Deane Apparel won a contract to supply fire-resistant trousers to the New South Wales fire brigade (*Export News* 21 Feb. 1994: 12). Levana, another New Zealand company, devoted itself to making speciality stretch fabrics, and won international awards for quality (*Export News* 7 Feb. 1994: 11). The sportswear market offers numerous openings, and some of the largest American textile and clothing firms, such as Guilford Mills, were focusing on this area in the mid-1990s (Rudie 1993: 18–20).

Strategies of diversification are common. Diversification may be directed towards lines of business with close connections to textiles, with the objective of strengthening the firm's existing base. Or else it may be a strategy for reducing a firm's dependence on textiles, by gaining a presence in more profitable industries. Porter (1990: 604–6) argues that diversification is unlikely to improve a firm's performance unless it builds upon the company's established position. Random diversification usually does more harm than good. The Bleachers' Association, a British textile finisher, acquired a diverse collection of businesses in engineering, laundering, timber merchanting and tanning, as well as carpet-making and knitting, between the 1930s and the early 1960s. Directors of the Bleachers' Association conducted takeover negotiations over drinks with golfing chums. They had no clear strategy about which industries to enter and which to leave alone. One of their selection criteria was that businesses should be located near the group's base in north-west England. The result was chaos (Jeremy 1993: 195–8). Not all British firms behaved as ineptly as the Bleachers' Association. Shiloh cotton spinners followed a diversification programme, in the 1970s and 1980s, which was sharply focused on such areas as knitwear, healthcare and protective clothing. Shiloh continued to prosper (Millington 1995). Far more glamorous companies than the Bleachers' Association have made serious errors of judgement. Benetton made an unsuccessful foray into the financial services sector in the late 1980s. Since 1989, however, Benetton has adopted a more focused policy, concentrating on products which are closely related to the group's existing business, such as ski equipment, skates, sports shoes, tennis rackets and bicycles (Glover 1993; Kay 1993: 310).

A major study of diversification among large American corporations between 1929 and 1954 examined four textile companies: United Merchants & Manufacturers, Cannon Mills, Armstrong Cork and Pacific Mills. By 1954, these companies possessed capacity in many industries, including apparel, paper, chemicals, rubber, stone, clay and glass, fabricated metal products, machinery, miscellaneous manufacturing, farming, mineral extraction, construction, wholesaling, retailing and finance. In four instances these textile firms had established themselves among the eight leading producers in the industries entered. Apparel and chemicals were the most popular sectors for these firms. But it is unclear what skills these textile companies brought to bear on mineral extraction and construction (Gort 1962: 28, 94, 131). Leading US textile producers exhibit a range of stances towards diversification. At the modest end of the spectrum, Milliken has slowly increased its involvement in the chemical industry (Jacobson 1992). Springs Industries bought a frozen food company in 1974, a manufacturer of window blinds in 1979 and later a producer of ceramic bath accessories. Window products and bathroom accessories were not unrelated to Springs's core business, since they could be sold in conjunction with the company's line of home furnishings (Ring 1992; Ozanian 1993). At the other extreme, we find Royal Little's Textron, a true conglomerate, with facilities in a number of industries from electronics to paint, in the 1980s. Textron originated in the north-eastern textile industry in the 1940s. It had completely abandoned textiles by 1963, in favour of what it considered to be more lucrative ventures in other fields (Bluestone and Harrison 1982: 278–82).

Non-textile sales of the big nine Japanese spinners rose from 12 per cent of total sales in 1973 to 16 per cent in 1979, while non-textile sales of the big seven fibre makers rose from 21 per cent of total sales to 37 per cent over the same period (Dore 1986: 216). Large Japanese textile firms occupied a middle of the table position, in terms of their degree of diversification, in the mid-1970s in comparison with large firms in the rest of Japanese industry (Goto 1981). In the aftermath of the Second World War, Kanebo (originally Kanegafuchi) divested itself of interests in chemicals, papermaking, pharmaceuticals, toiletries and wire manufacturing, but the increasing saturation of markets for Kanebo's cotton, wool and rayon textiles, during the late 1950s convinced the company's top managers to introduce a radical new strategy, involving forward integration into apparel, the production of nylon fibre and diversification into non-textile products. In 1962, Kanebo repurchased its former toiletry manufacturing business and developed a network of stores to market its goods. Kanebo also moved into food processing. These diversification measures, especially in the realm of cosmetics, were successful (Suzuki 1991: 111–13; Abe 1993: 15–16). The evidence from the USA and Japan suggests that, with some exceptions, textile firms have not been at the forefront of the diversification movement. This strategy could be portrayed as suitably cautious or unenterprising, depending on one's point of view.

The above strategies were accompanied by efforts to lobby governments for protection against cheap or 'disruptive' imports. Mass-market strategies were launched by such companies as Courtaulds, in the mistaken expectation that they would be granted increased protection until their new plants reached their full potential for cost savings. Some firms facing deteriorating sales have concluded that exit is the best strategy. Many traditional British cotton textile producers, encountering stiff Asian competition in the 1950s, pursued a strategy of making what profits they could in the short term, and making no provision for the replacement of machinery, while planning to quit in the long run (Singleton 1991: 153). The textile business network of the Bromley clan of Philadelphia also gradually declined. Bromleys withdrew from some activities in the 1950s, but continued to invest in those lines which, from time to time, showed prospects of recovery, until the pressure of competition from foreign and other American firms proved too great in the early 1990s (Scranton 1993: 113–14). Some firms abandoned manufacturing and became importers. Quitting textiles was not necessarily the end for entrepreneurs. Recognizing that its buildings and land were more valuable than its textile business, the Yorkshire firm of Mountleigh ceased production and, in the late 1970s and 1980s, became a successful property developer. Ernest Hall, one of Mountleigh's supremos, resigned in 1982, and devoted his fortune to converting the Crossley carpet mills into units occupied by an art gallery, a radio station, educational facilities and small businesses, thereby contributing to the much-needed gentrification of Halifax (Blackhurst 1992).

Obviously, there is no universally correct strategy for textile and clothing producers. Much depends on the ability of decision-makers to identify the best strategy for their particular firm under the prevailing conditions. Even the largest textile companies, such as Courtaulds and Burlington, may make very costly mistakes, while small family businesses in Italy and Indonesia may rapidly identify the strategies which promise success. The largest firms, with the greatest sunk investments, may be the most reluctant to read the writing on the wall.

INTERNATIONAL STRATEGIES

Firms are confronted with a range of possible international strategies. A strong domestic platform often helps firms to launch themselves into foreign markets. International strategies fall into four main groups, upon which are superimposed the additional options of cost leadership, differentiation and focus. The first broad category is an export-based strategy with decentralized marketing. Second, a firm could choose a 'simple' global strategy, where exports from the home base are sold in a coordinated manner around the world. Third, factories could be established in foreign countries to serve those individual markets alone. Fourth, elements of the production process could be dispersed across several countries, with marketing occurring at an international level in accordance with a global plan (Porter 1986; 1987).

Exporting strategies

Exporting from a secure home base, with or without the coordination of marketing in different countries, has been the usual strategy of firms making their debut on the international stage, from the cotton mills of early nineteenth-century England to the Asian tigers of recent times. The British cotton industry exported a growing proportion of the value of its final output: 52.8 per cent in 1819–21, rising to 78.8 per cent in 1899–1901 (Deane and Cole 1967: 187). At the height of its powers, in 1935, the Japanese cotton industry exported 27 per cent of its output of yarn, and 66 per cent of its production of cloth (Seki 1956: 313). The prior development of a competitive advantage in the production of certain types of cotton yarn and cloth underpinned the export drives of both Britain and Japan, and increased the probability that individual textile producers would market their yarn and cloth overseas.

It was necessary to weigh up the relative profitability of selling in domestic and foreign markets, and the outcome depended on a number of factors. In Britain and Japan, the decision to export was, at least in part, made by the merchant houses, when they placed orders for yarn and cloth. Especially in Britain, exporters did not follow a simple global strategy, because different merchants supplied different markets, and individual towns and manufacturers produced cloth which was specifically targeted at certain markets; Blackburn, for example, specialized in coarse cloth for India, while Preston made higher-quality textiles (Shimizu 1986; Chapman 1992). But not all firms adopted a passive attitude to the destination of their output. J. & P. Coats, the leading Scottish producer of sewing thread, began to export its thread direct to America in 1840 (Kim 1994: 188–9). In the 1920s, slack domestic demand encouraged the Sen'nan firm of Obitani Shoten to switch from producing narrow cotton cloth for the home market to weaving wider cloth for China. This change in direction proved to be highly advantageous and Obitani Shoten became Japan's largest independent weaving concern in the 1930s (Abe 1994: 16). After the early 1960s, when domestic markets became saturated, businesses in Taiwan and South Korea followed aggressive export strategies, bidding for and winning orders in excess of their productive capacity and subcontacting work to neighbouring firms in order to meet delivery times (Lam and Lee 1992: 109–12). Some firms, of course, were satisfied with the home market. For instance, late nineteenth-century American cotton textile manufacturers, who were enjoying the fruits of a large home market protected by high tariffs, put comparatively little effort into exporting, and seemed to regard foreign markets simply as outlets for any cloth that was surplus to domestic requirements. Consequently, the USA's performance in some export markets, especially Latin America, was patchy (Marrison 1975: 332–3).

Table 5.2 shows the propensity to export of various textile and clothing

Table 5.2 Exports as a percentage of output in branches of the textile and clothing industries in selected countries, 1989

	Spinning, weaving and finishing (SITC 3211)	Made-up textile goods excluding wearing apparel (SITC 3212)	Knitting mills (SITC 3213)	Carpets and rugs (SITC 3214)	Other textiles (SITC 3219)	Wearing apparel (SITC 3220)
Colombia[a]	6.6	25.1	1.0	0.3	31.4	39.7
Hong Kong[a]	44.3	64.7	15.6	82.3	50.3	—
Indonesia[b]	21.7	—	4.4	30.8	18.6	—
Japan[b]	13.4	1.4	1.9	2.8	9.5	2.4
Mexico[a]	22.4	—	4.3	40.0	15.8	28.9
Philippines[a]	6.6	26.6	2.3	80.3	4.9	61.0
South Korea[b]	31.5	51.0	20.0	49.6	36.7	—
Spain[b]	19.3	14.8	7.2	29.7	14.2	11.7
Sweden[b]	57.4	46.9	14.5	—	48.6	82.2
United Kingdom[a]	38.0	13.4	6.3	16.6	72.7	28.7
United States[b]	7.0	1.7	1.1	4.1	10.0	4.3
West Germany[b]	68.7	33.0	19.0	—	22.5	48.4

Source: UNIDO (1993: 375, 391, 397, 403, 405, 417, 428, 432, 436, 438, 442, 444)
Notes: — not available
    a 1988
    b 1989

producers, in the late 1980s. There was no obvious relationship between the level of a country's economic development and the export propensity of its textile and clothing sector. West Germany and Sweden had relatively high propensities to export, while the USA and Japan appeared to put more emphasis on supplying home consumers. Some of the comparisons are particularly intriguing. West Germany and Sweden exported larger shares of their production of spun, woven and finished textiles than did such countries as Colombia, Hong Kong, Indonesia, Mexico, the Philippines and South Korea. Sweden exported a higher proportion of its output of wearing apparel than the Philippines. Across all six categories of textiles and clothing, the UK had a higher propensity to export than Japan.

Although each country's experience has unique features, the figures in Table 5.2 are amenable to a broader interpretation. First, export-to-output ratios were distorted by political decisions. Trade in textiles and clothing was constrained by protectionism, which prevented the countries of Asia and Latin America from maximizing their ratios of exports to output. In Western Europe, trade discrimination against non-EU members enabled countries such as Germany and Britain to win orders in other member states which may otherwise have gone to outsiders. Second, the low export-to-output ratios of Japan and the USA were typical of the industrial sectors of these economies and reflected the pull of their large home markets. In 1987, Japan exported 10.7 per cent of its GDP and the USA exported 5.6 per cent. By comparison, the UK exported 19.6 per cent of its GDP, West Germany 26.2 per cent and South Korea 39.0 per cent (Porter 1990: 22–3). Third, textiles and clothing markets were highly segmented. Since the failure of the mass-market approach of the 1960s and 1970s, manufacturers in the developed countries tended to specialize in the production and export of higher-quality textiles and clothing. Developed countries could achieve high export-to-output ratios by avoiding direct competition with, for instance, Indonesia and China, which devoted their efforts to exporting less sophisticated goods (H. Hill 1991: 110–12; Crowley, Findlay and Gibbs 1992). Fourth, intra-industry and intra-firm trade plays an important role in the textile and clothing sector. Figures showing export-to-output ratios do not distinguish between firms following a straightforward exporting strategy and those engaged in a strategy involving the coordination of production in several countries.

The degree to which exporters choose to coordinate their marketing efforts in customer countries depends upon the circumstances. When most textiles were relatively undifferentiated, in the nineteenth century, coordination was less necessary than it is today in some of the more fashion-conscious branches of the industry. Benetton is an excellent example of a firm implementing a simple global strategy. Eighty-five per cent of Benetton's merchandise is manufactured in Europe, particularly in its home country of Italy. Yet clothing with the Benetton label is marketed around the world, in over 7,000 franchise stores in 110 countries (as of 1994). Each shop must conform to the Benetton image and must engage in constant communication with headquarters. The practice of using the same advertising in different countries is a further indication that Benetton thinks globally rather than in terms of dealing with separate foreign markets. Whether this approach has been entirely satisfactory is another matter, since research suggests that Benetton's advertising evokes a range of responses among potential consumers, even in reasonably similar north European countries (Evans and Riyait 1993; Glover 1993; Anon 1994a).

One of the problems of an exporting strategy, as opposed to a multi-national strategy, is that exporters are vulnerable to shifts in the global distribution of competitive advantage. Classical British cotton spinners and weavers relied almost exclusively on exports. During the twentieth century, these firms discovered that their yarn and cloth was increasingly uncompetitive on world markets. An unreflective exporting strategy may reduce a firm's chance of long-term survival.

Strategies involving production in several countries

Textile manufacturers have been establishing production facilities abroad since the nineteenth century. Foreign direct investment (FDI) has had several motivations, including tariff avoidance, the lure of cheap labour, the desire to exploit and protect the firm's superior technology, and the advantage of proximity to the market. Until quite recently, overseas facilities were designed to serve local markets, rather than to participate in a global production and marketing strategy.

Several examples can be given of early multinational activity in textiles. The Yorkshire textile manufacturers Isaac Holden and Samuel Cunliffe Lister formed a partnership with the intention of expanding their business activities abroad and opened the first of their three mills in France in 1849. As well as being businessmen, Holden and Lister were pioneers in the development of mechanical wool-combing, and their goal was to dominate wool-combing in France by acquiring all of the relevant patents and forestalling potential competitors. Although mechanical wool-combing methods could not be monopolized indefinitely, Isaac Holden et Fils (Lister withdrew in 1858) was a profitable venture and it continued to trade until 1938 (Honeyman and Goodman 1986). William Barbour & Sons of Lisburn, Northern Ireland, established an American subsidiary in 1865. This firm built mills in New Jersey and Pennsylvania, and became the leading flax thread manufacturer in the USA. New tariffs induced J. & P. Coats to set up a sewing thread factory in Rhode Island, in 1869, and British firms went on to dominate this branch of textiles in the USA. Most early FDI in American textiles originated in Britain. However, in 1903, the German woollen producer, Forstmann and Huffmann, erected a mill at Passaic, New Jersey, in response to the imposition of the Dingley tariff (Buckley and Roberts 1982: 47–50). The most ambitious and successful case of FDI in American textiles before 1914 was that of Courtaulds, which went into rayon production on a large scale in Pennsylvania in 1911 (Coleman 1969b).

Japan, by contrast, was not a major destination for foreign investment in textiles in the nineteenth century. While the Japanese acquired Western machinery and know-how, they did not seek direct financial involvement by Westerners in their mills. Language difficulties further militated against FDI in Japan, as did the comparatively low tariff regime. Japanese cotton spinners became multinationals at an early stage in their development, unlike their British counterparts. In the early twentieth century, Japanese spinners established factories in China. The Chinese market was an important one for Osaka. Chinese firms, assisted by new tariffs, were beginning to make inroads into Japan's market. The erection of Japanese-owned mills served to defend Osaka's position. British firms also invested in new Chinese mills, although there was an important difference between British and Japanese strategy. The British firms tended to be merchants, such as Jardene

112

Matheson, rather than experienced cotton spinners, and they formed joint ventures with local Chinese capitalists, instead of taking direct control. In the increasingly depressed conditions of the 1920s, competition intensified. This competition was won by the Japanese, and most Western mills failed. Japanese mills were more successful because their parent companies insisted on employing Japanese managers and imposing Japanese factory discipline. The Chinese managers who ran the western mills frequently did so in a haphazard fashion (Allen and Donnithorne 1954: 174–8; Kuwahara 1982; 1989; 1992). Japanese firms also invested in plants in their Taiwanese and Korean colonies. These facilities were confiscated at the end of the Second World War, and provided Taiwan and South Korea with a foundation upon which to build modern textile industries (Ho 1978: 74; Yoshihara 1978: 92). American textile firms, by contrast, were comparatively inexperienced as overseas investors before the Second World War. Julius Kayser & Co. manufactured branded garments in Canada, Australia and Germany before 1914, and the trading, mining and shipping giant W. R. Grace & Co. bought the largest cotton mill in Peru in 1917. In the 1920s, Americans invested in the production of yarn, carpets and tapestries in China, embroidering in the Philippines and carpet making in Turkey, but most of this activity was in the hands of small expatriate firms (Wilkins 1974: 28, 64–5).

FDI has become increasingly prevalent in the global textile and clothing sector since the Second World War. This trend is explained by the continuation, and in some cases reinforcement, of protectionist measures, combined with the rising labour costs and declining competitiveness of plants in developed economies. Japanese textile, synthetic fibre and clothing businesses were prominent in the race to establish factories overseas. Japan opened just one textile plant in South-east Asia (in Thailand) in the 1950s. A trickle of authorizations followed in the 1960s and then, between 1968 and 1974, Japanese firms were given permission by host governments to engage in 275 fibre, textile and apparel projects in South-east Asia. South Korea, which had discouraged investment by Japanese textile interests until the late 1960s, had the largest number of Japanese FDI projects in the region by 1974; Taiwan ranked second; Thailand third. Trading companies, including C. Itoh, Mitsui & Co. and Marubeni, were among the largest investors in overseas production facilities. These trading companies preferred to build joint plants with Japanese textile firms, in order to secure an alliance of commercial and industrial expertise. Host governments often required Japanese investors to form joint ventures with indigenous entrepreneurs. For local firms, a joint venture with a Western or Japanese company was a means of obtaining capital, technology and management skills. Most Asian countries sought to develop their textile industries behind protective barriers, and Japanese firms wishing to retain a strong presence in these markets had to set up plants behind the tariff walls (Yoshihara 1978: 91–132).

The search for cheap labour was a complementary reason for engaging in FDI, and in some cases it resulted in the use of overseas plants as bases for exporting. While many Japanese textile businesses engaged in FDI were small, the big firms also built up impressive lists of projects. Teijin's overseas assets were worth $116 million in 1973, and comprised twenty-five plants in South Korea, Taiwan, Hong Kong, the Philippines, Thailand, Singapore, Indonesia, the USA and Brazil. Kanebo's sixteen overseas factories in South Korea, Taiwan, Hong Kong, Thailand and Indonesia were worth $36 million in 1973 (Steven 1990: 73). Japanese FDI was a dominating factor in parts of East Asia (Arpan, Barry and Tran 1984: 136–54). In the Indonesian textile and garment sector, 80 per cent of the inflow of foreign direct investment between 1967 and 1989 came from the Japanese. By contrast, Europe and North America provided a mere 1 per cent of FDI in Indonesian textiles (H. Hill 1991: 101). In 1974, 65 per cent of accumulated Japanese FDI in textiles was located in Asian countries, while Latin America, with 25 per cent, was the second most important location. By 1988, accumulated Japanese FDI in textiles totalled $2,353 million, of which 52 per cent was in Asia, 18 per cent in Latin America, 17 per cent in North America and 10 per cent in Europe (Steven 1990: 68, 89). Western firms may have failed to match the Japanese in South-east Asia, but they did not entirely neglect this region. For instance, in 1990, Coats Viyella had a wholly owned subsidiary in Hong Kong and was the majority owner of joint ventures in Indonesia and Malaysia. The company also held a 39.9 per cent stake in an Indian textile producer. Tootal, a British firm taken over by Coats Viyella in 1991, also had large Asian interests, including joint venture spinning mills in China (Payne 1992: 59).

Japanese textile capital penetrated into most corners of the globe. An early foray was made into the USA in 1965, when Tsuzuki opened a cotton spinning mill, in order to exploit its superiority over the Americans in cotton blending (Tsurumi 1976: 120). Although Japanese investments in the USA were substantial, they did not become overwhelming and, in 1990, Britain, Canada and Germany all had larger stakes than Japan in the ownership of the American textile industry (Howenstine and Zeile 1994: 39). In tropical Africa, Mitsui established the Kenya Toray synthetic fibre mill, a project in which the Kenyan Industrial and Commercial Development Corporation held a minority interest (Swainson 1980: 237, 248). In England, in 1989, Toray bought Samuel Courtauld & Co., the oldest part of the Courtaulds empire, for £25 million, an acquisition of great symbolic value, since it showed how the balance of power in textiles had shifted from Europe to Asia during the twentieth century (Blackburn 1993: 254).

Making international comparisons between firms conducting FDI is difficult, although some evidence is available. Dunning and Pearce (1985) gathered data on the world's largest industrial enterprises of 1982. Estimates were made of the overseas production ratios (sales of overseas affiliates and associates, net of goods imported from the parent for resale, as a percentage of total group sales) of nineteen major firms engaged in the manufacture of textiles, apparel and leather goods. The British firms in the group had an overseas production ratio of 49 per cent, the US firms 11.8 per cent and the Japanese firms 9.3 per cent (ibid.: 143). Stopford and Dunning (1983) examined the overseas activities of large multinationals in 1981. Some of their findings are given in Table 5.3. The two British multinationals were more heavily committed to their overseas activities than either the American or Japanese firms. Presumably, the pressure on large British firms to cut costs by moving overseas was even more intense than that faced by the Japanese and the Americans. By the early 1990s, Coats Viyella, the successor of Coats Paton, was manufacturing in thirty-five countries (Ritchie 1992: 356).

Latin America and the Caribbean have become increasingly important locations for FDI. A survey of investment plans among American apparel producers, in 1985, showed that the Caribbean and Central America were the most popular destinations for FDI (Mody and Wheeler 1987: 1280). Possessing abundant labour, the Caribbean basin is close to the American market and most of this region is under the informal sway of Washington. In 1993, Cone Mills announced a plan to build a large new denim plant in Mexico with the assistance of Cipsa, Mexico's largest denim producer (Reingold 1993: 20). Burlington regarded the prospect of free trade with Mexico as a signal to transfer production facilities south of the border (Taub 1993: 12). But the extent of American FDI in Latin America should not be exaggerated. The quaintly named Lovable de Honduras S.A., a manufacturer of underwear, with modest sales of $6 million in 1990, was the largest local

Table 5.3 The contribution of overseas subsidiaries to the sales and assets of selected textile and clothing multinationals, 1981

	Sales of overseas subsidiaries (as % of total world-wide sales)	Foreign assets (as % of total assets)
Coats Paton (UK)	68[a]	71[b]
Courtaulds (UK)	37[a]	41[b]
Levi Strauss (USA)	33	31
Blue Bell (USA)	28	31
Burlington (USA)	12	17
Toray (Japan)	5[a]	12
Teijin (Japan)	5	9

Source: Stopford and Dunning (1983: 116, 118)

Notes: a Excludes all exports: any intra-group exports are therefore included with direct exports
b Capital employed

affiliate of the American textile and clothing sector in Honduras. The total stock of FDI from all countries in textiles, leather and clothing in El Salvador in 1990 was $26.3 million, and in the Dominican Republic it was a mere $3.5 million (UNCTAD, Division of Transnational Corporations and Investment 1994: 244, 277, 282). European firms have not failed to exploit the opportunities for investing in developing countries. Gruppo Finanziario Tessile of Turin, established a joint venture, Gruppo Industriale Interamericano, in Mexico in 1969. The Italian parent had a 40 per cent stake in this firm and its objectives were to reduce the labour cost of making clothing and gain a base from which to assault the American market (Schieppati and Viesti 1988: 168–9). French firms often went to former colonies in Africa, such as the Ivory Coast (Mytelka 1985: 83–101). German textile and apparel manufacturers, in the 1960s and 1970s, favoured locations in Tunisia, Greece and Malta (Fröbel, Heinrichs and Kreye 1980: 111–31). In 1979, developing countries hosted 26 per cent of the stock of German FDI in textiles and 16 per cent of that in clothing (Schatz and Wolter 1987: 46).

One of the most significant developments in textile and apparel FDI since the 1960s has been the readiness of countries outside the OECD to engage in overseas investment. Hong Kong firms established plants in Singapore in the early and mid-1960s. Hong Kong textile and apparel manufacturers wanted to find a way around British import quotas, and Singapore was not subjected to quotas by the UK until 1965, or by the USA until 1966 (Luey 1969). Taiwanese firms also treated Singapore as a launching pad for entry into Western markets (Ting and Schive 1981). Hong Kong companies, sometimes in collaboration with Japanese and local partners, ventured into Indonesia, Malaysia and Taiwan in the 1960s and 1970s, as well as Nigeria and Ghana (L. T. Wells 1978; Chen 1981). Rising domestic labour costs became an increasingly important reason for firms based in Hong Kong, South Korea and Taiwan to engage in FDI (Khanna 1993). China is considered an attractive location, due to its abundance of cheap labour (Glasse 1995: 185–251). South Korean groups had invested $5 million in nine textile and clothing plants in China by the end of 1990, and planned a further $7 million (Hong, Yim and Park 1991: 73). Hong Kong firms have undertaken a number of FDI projects in China's Pearl River delta (Sit and Wong 1989: 219–30). Large Indian industrial groups also invested abroad, ambitiously claiming that their entrepreneurial prowess gave them a competitive advantage over firms in host countries. Birla opened joint venture textile plants in Thailand, Uganda, Indonesia and the Dominican Republic in the 1970s (Lall 1982). Malaysian firms have recently sought overseas production facilities, and one company has made direct investments in Puerto Rico and Vietnam (O'Connor 1993: 271). Facing rising wages at home, appreciating exchange rates and protectionism abroad, Asian firms even opened facilities in the USA in the 1980s. Textile Alliance of Hong Kong bought a yarn mill in North Carolina from Burlington, and Saha Union purchased an empty mill in

116

Georgia for one-quarter of the cost of a new factory in Thailand (Velasco 1990: 104).

Many FDI projects were relatively ephemeral. An Anglo-German mill opened in Kenya in 1976 went into liquidation within one year, allegedly because of competition from cheap imports (Swainson 1980: 279). Half of the Japanese textile firms which had established plants in Hong Kong after 1960 had withdrawn by 1988, as had one-quarter of those with plants in Indonesia (Horaguchi 1993: 43–9). Depending on the local circumstances, withdrawal could be a reaction to rising wages, the expiry of government assistance, or increasing competition. Firms often relocated in countries offering grants and cheaper labour. In the 1980s, Liz Claiborne, an American garment producer with production facilities in Hong Kong, decided to move some lines back to New York, even though costs were higher in the USA, because quality was more assured and turnaround faster (Velasco 1990: 103).

Offshore processing is an alternative to FDI, involving a lower level of commitment. A strategy of offshore processing necessitates the integration of operations at the international level. Its drawback, however, is that the amount of supervision which can be exercised over formally independent establishments is more limited. International subcontracting is a modern version of the putting-out system, under which textile merchants distributed fibre and yarn for processing by cottage workers (Wadsworth and Mann 1931). Japanese and Western firms discovered in the 1960s that they could reduce costs by sending fabric to developing countries to be made up into garments, either for re-importation or export to third countries. In 1975, about 14 per cent of West Germany's textile exports and 6 per cent of its clothing exports were destined for subcontractors, overwhelmingly in Eastern Europe, and especially in Yugoslavia. Offshore processing was complementary to FDI and helped to sustain the competitive advantage of German firms, despite their high domestic costs (Fröbel, Heinrichs and Kreye 1980: 106–10; Schatz and Wolter 1987: 112–13). Offshore processing continued to grow in importance and, in 1992, accounted for one-third of German clothing imports. As Eastern and Western Europe become more closely integrated, German outward processing in former communist countries is likely to expand, possibly to the detriment of arrangements with firms in advanced Asian economies such as Hong Kong. The Germans aim to control quality by helping their foreign affiliates to train personnel and to maintain their machinery. Some machines are actually provided by the Germans in payment for work done. With the gradual phasing out of the MFA, German firms are expected to offer more work to producers in the less-advanced Asian countries, such as Vietnam, in lower-quality clothing. Italian groups, possibly as a result of Italy's stricter interpretation of the EU's outward processing regulations, have been slow to follow Germany down this path, and this omission has improved Germany's relative performance (Spinanger and Piatti 1994; Spinanger 1995).

Under section 807 of the US tariff regime, American firms which export textiles for making up, pay tariffs only on the value added abroad when they re-import completed garments. Latin America has become a favourite location for American textile firms seeking subcontracting arrangements. In Colombia, the Talleres Rurales del Valle (TRV) programme was set up by the coffee industry to find work for the families of subsistence coffee producers during the off-season, in the hope of reducing the rate of migration to the cities. TRV officials opened apparel workshops and negotiated subcontracting agreements for sewing work with foreign companies, including Levi Strauss (Truelove 1987). Jamaica is another significant offshore processor under section 807 (Steele 1987).

From the point of view of a joint venture partner or offshore affiliate, cooperating with a firm from a technically advanced country may be a useful strategy for obtaining markets, management expertise, capital and technical knowledge. Sometimes, as in Thailand and South Korea, the strategy of local entrepreneurs and their contacts in the government has been to squeeze out foreign partners as soon as it is believed that their assistance is no longer required (Tran 1988; Hewinson 1989: 168–73). At Thai Melon Polyester, in 1982, it is reported that the French synthetics producer Rhone Poulenc was forced to sell up to its partner Thai Blanket Industries after French nationals had received threats (Doner and Ramsay 1993: 695–6). But relations between Hong Kong firms and their Japanese joint venture partners appear to have been smoother and beneficial to both partners (L. T. Wells 1978).

The degree to which overseas subsidiaries, joint ventures and offshore processing partners are integrated into a global strategy differs from case to case. A study of the overseas subsidiaries of American textile multinationals in 1975 indicated that the majority concentrated on supplying the host country's market (Kirkpatrick and Yamin 1981). Statistics for the USA in 1977 show that there was a high degree of intra-industry trade in textiles and clothing between the USA and a handful of developing countries, such as Mexico, the Philippines, Haiti and Ireland. About two-thirds of US clothing imports from Mexico were from related parties (Helleiner 1981: 70). The industrial activities of Coats Viyella in 1990 in Britain, Germany, Italy, Portugal, Spain, Turkey, the USA, Canada, South America and Asia were virtually identical, suggesting that host countries were treated as separate markets (Payne 1992: 56–9). Tootal appears to have followed a more global strategy, closing many of its factories in the UK in the 1980s and expanding production in Asia, for importing into Britain (Chapman 1991: 185–6; Payne 1992: 62–4, 73). Where the decision to invest abroad is made for reasons of tariff avoidance, rather than the minimization of production costs, the objective is clearly to defend markets in the host country. Smith & Nephew's investments in textile plants in South Africa and Australia in the 1950s took place against a background of tight import controls and import substitution policies in these countries (Foreman-Peck 1995: 189–96). Although the trend, since the 1960s, has been for Western and Japanese producers to relocate their more labour-intensive activities in low wage countries, the extent of globalization remains partial. In most cases, the revealed strategy of firms involves a compromise between treating overseas subsidiaries as separate facilities for meeting local demand and integrating them into a global production and distribution network. To some extent, this state of affairs reflects the assets which have been inherited from a previous era.

NATIONAL STRATEGIES

National strategies in textiles and clothing are constantly evolving. Distinctive strategies can be identified in textile history, such as Lancashire's export strategy of the nineteenth century, Japan's early involvement in multinational production, the newly industrializing countries' emulation of Lancashire in the 1960s, Courtaulds' mass-production debacle, modern Italy's penchant for high-quality clothing produced and distributed by networks of small firms, and Germany's enthusiasm for offshore processing. These are distinctive national strategies, but they are not permanent ones. National strategies are influenced by the level of development of the country, and the position of its textile and clothing sector on the life cycle. The classic Lancashire strategy, involving small firms and exports of unsophisticated products, is a common one in the early stages of development. At a later stage, there is a tendency for firms to invest in more capital-intensive machinery, establish overseas subsidiaries and diversify. Later still, offshore processing, or a concentration on small batches of high value added products, enable some firms based in high-cost locations to survive and prosper. From Vietnam to Germany, the national strategy of the textiles and clothing sector at any particular moment is related to the country's position on this ladder, give or take a few rungs. Global strategies are appropriate for substantial firms in established textile-producing nations and also, indirectly, for their joint venture and outward processing affiliates in less-developed areas. The main difference between Lancashire in 1800 and Vietnam today is that Vietnam operates in an international trading framework which has already been partially globalized.

6

FIRM STRUCTURE AND NATIONAL RIVALRY

The ways in which firms are organized and managed, and the degree of competition between them, are important factors influencing the success or failure of an industry (Porter 1990: 107). Porter's analysis of the structure of firms is more impressionistic than those of Chandler (1962; 1977; 1990) and Lazonick (1990; 1991; 1992). For Chandler and Lazonick, organizational structure is crucial to the firm's prospects. They subordinate other aspects of the diamond to strategy and structure. Chandler emphasizes the superiority of the multidivisional (M-form) structure in mass-production industries, but has little to say about textiles, accepting that it is not a mass-production industry. Lazonick, however, argues that large hierarchical firms are necessary for sustained competitive advantage in textiles. Porter does not outline an ideal organizational structure. Conditions in the industry, and national characteristics, including the preference of some cultures for family firms, influence the choice of an appropriate structure (Porter 1990: 108). Goals and behaviour vary across national boundaries. The implication of this eclecticism is that we should not be surprised to find that each organizational structure generates both successes and failures.

The first section establishes that small- or medium-sized firms have continued to play a major role in textiles and clothing until the present day. Family businesses have proved that they are capable of competing successfully with the managerial corporation. There is no tendency for either type of firm to gain a permanent ascendancy. Subsequent sections examine the development of organizational structure in the UK, USA, Japan and developing Asia.

FAMILY FIRMS AND MANAGERIAL CORPORATIONS

Textile and clothing firms of all shapes and sizes have coexisted throughout the nineteenth and twentieth centuries. Although massive textile corporations have emerged in a number of countries, it is inconceivable that the small firm will be eradicated, and many have shown themselves to be highly competitive.

Family firms are numerous in textiles and clothing, distinguishing this sector from others, including motor vehicles, arms production and aerospace, where family businesses are generally relegated to the role of component suppliers. Family businesses occupy a controversial place in the literature on organizational structure. Chandler and Lazonick regard the survival of personal capitalism, marked by small- and medium-sized family enterprises, as the principal cause of the relative decline of British industry in the twentieth century. They argue that family enterprises rarely develop the multidivisional structure which is necessary for long-term success, because of their reluctance to promote outsiders to positions of leadership and thereby risk the loss of family control. Families cannot provide a sufficient number of qualified managers to run a multidivisional firm (Chandler 1990: chs 7–9; Lazonick 1992: 3–139, 218–84). Lazonick directs much of his fire on family businesses in the British cotton industry. He concludes that the fierce independence of family firms militated against mergers between spinners, weavers and merchants. Vertical integration of spinning and weaving would have facilitated the coordination of investment decisions, leading to the speedier adoption of the complementary technologies of ring spinning and automatic loom weaving. Vertical integration of manufacturing and marketing would have encouraged longer production runs and better planning (Lazonick 1992: 21–82).

Porter is restrained in his comments on family enterprise. In an otherwise scathing indictment of post-war British business, he does not mention the family firm as a problem (Porter 1990: 482–507). Nevertheless, in the light of the widespread interest in this subject, this chapter gives full weight to the question of family enterprise. The historical performance of family firms is vigorously defended in the October 1993 issue of *Business History*. Contributions to this symposium demonstrate the capacity of family businesses to grow, and to sustain their profitability, over several generations. Detailed examples are given from the textile industries of Philadelphia and northern France (Chadeau 1993; Church 1993; Scranton 1993: 115–34).

Chandler portrays the development of large, professionally managed corporations in the USA as a response to new technologies offering substantial economies of scale and scope. Family firms found it difficult to mobilize the capital required to operate on a large scale. They also lacked adequate supervisory resources. Textiles and apparel, however, have not been dominated by high throughput technologies. Using British data of the 1960s, Pratten (1971: 226–38) found that the minimum efficient scale (MES) of cotton spinning mills was no more than 60,000 spindles, while the MES of cotton weaving mills was under 1,000 looms. In both cases, this represented under 2 per cent of the UK market. From an engineering perspective, there was room for over fifty efficient spinning mills, and the same number of weaving mills. The same study found no conclusive evidence to suggest that multi-plant firms were more efficiently managed than single plant firms, although it was commonly believed that multi-plant firms had greater bargaining power with suppliers and customers, and the capacity to hire specialist managers. Pratten (ibid.: 239–45) found similar results in hosiery. An American study, employing 1967 data, confirmed that technical economies of scale were slight in weaving, where the MES was 0.2 per cent of US demand. Multi-plant firms had a modest advantage, particularly if they integrated forward into finishing. But the gains of the multi-plant firm were exhausted once it supplied 1 per cent of the market. Given that the three largest weavers were able to meet 30 per cent of US demand, it seems that size may have been desired for its own sake (Scherer and Ross 1990: 115, 140). Empirical work conducted in the 1980s on European data produced similar results. Manufacturing was divided into twenty sectors, ranked in order of technical economies of scale. Motor vehicles, other transportation and chemicals occupied the three leading places, while textiles ranked seventeenth, and footwear and clothing nineteenth (Emerson *et al.* 1988: 129–30). Current developments may reduce the MES. Computer-aided design (CAD), computer-aided manufacturing (CAM) and associated innovations permit small orders to be processed more economically (Jaikumar and Upton 1993).

Porter stresses the region as the geographical focus of competitive advantage (Porter 1990: 154–9). Small firms benefit from the existence of industrial districts. In Victorian Lancashire, the close proximity of hundreds of small textile firms generated external economies, including a pool of experienced labour and skilled technicians, efficient ancillary industries, rapid information flows and sophisticated markets for intermediate and finished goods. Transactions costs were low because information was plentiful, and firms were anxious to maintain a good reputation, since they needed to make sequential contracts with suppliers and customers (Marshall 1919: 599–603; Farnie 1979; Sunley 1992). Other industrial districts with a strong emphasis on textiles existed in late nineteenth-century Philadelphia, Connecticut and Japan (Abe and Saito 1988; Scranton 1989; B. Smith 1991; Abe 1992).

Since the 1970s there has been a revival of interest in the industrial district and its business networks, partly as a result of developments in Italy, where the unexpected success of these arrangements has thrown into question mid-twentieth-century assumptions about the superiority of the corporation. Carpi and Modena in knitwear, and Prato and Biella in wool textiles, have attracted the most interest (Piore and Sabel 1984: 213–16; Buxton 1988; Camagni and Rabellotti 1992; Bigarelli and Crestanello 1994). Equivalent cases are found in the textile and clothing sectors of west Jutland in Denmark, the Lyons area of France and, in lower-quality goods, Tiruppur in India (Bull, Pitt and Szarka 1991; Illeris 1992; Cawthorne 1995). Around Prato, in 1970, a struggling textile industry was populated by vertically integrated mills, using capital-intensive machinery. Unit fixed costs soared, since it was difficult to obtain full order books due to competition from other Italian firms and imports. The solution, for some mills, was to split themselves into small business units renting space in the factory. These new firms were partly owned by their workers and partly by the original mill proprietors. Vertical integration was abandoned. Cooperation between firms at different stages in the production and distribution chain proved to be an efficient alternative to vertical integration. More flexible types of machinery were gradually introduced and firms accepted smaller orders for higher-quality products. Organizational innovation was not confined to the old mills, and additional firms sprang up around the district, taking advantage of local reservoirs of talent in design and manufacturing. Attractive designs, frequent changes of product and improved marketing procedures became the basis of Prato's recovering competitive advantage. Prato's textile and clothing sector employed 60,000 workers in 2,000 industrial enterprises in 1987. These firms both competed and collaborated with each other. Brokers called *impanatori*, a title with medieval origins, managed this network. Much depended on the use of information technology to coordinate production and marketing. Artisan and peasant traditions had not disappeared in the Prato region, in contrast to some larger industrial regions, where the masses had been proletarianized over several centuries. Local traditions of self-reliance and independence, which may have been smothered in Lancashire, were an asset in Italy (Buxton 1988; Jaikumar and Upton 1993).

Alliances have often developed between small and large firms in this sector, although their consequences are the subject of conflicting assessments. At Tiruppur, the more substantial knitwear producers admit that one reason for putting out work to smaller businesses is to avoid investment in additional plant and machinery. Cawthorne (1995: 47–8), however, concludes that the exploitation of subcontractors in Tiruppur has not prevented the growth of these small businesses. Benetton's rapid development during the 1980s was facilitated by the use of smaller enterprises to manufacture its products. The expansion of Benetton and the transformation of the Italian textile and clothing sector were complementary. But the stranglehold of British retail chains over domestic apparel suppliers has attracted criticism. British retailers demanded long runs of standardized garments from captive manufacturers. According to one interpretation, suppliers became so dependent on one large store that they never learned how to contract with other customers or how to develop independent design skills (Steedman and Wagner 1989: 43; Bull, Pitt and Szarka 1991: 94). Defenders of the retailers argue that, on the contrary, retailers encouraged suppliers to upgrade their products and processes (Rees 1969: 191–6). In the light of competition from Benetton, major British retailers have become more willing to cooperate with their suppliers in the design and manufacture of more fashionable lines of clothing (Zeitlin 1988). But some writers continue to take a jaundiced view of relations between networks of small apparel firms and large retailers. They suggest that flexible specialization in the USA and UK has rarely led to improvements in quality. Flexibility is necessitated by pressure from retailers for quick response and shorter production runs, and it is achieved by increasing the exploitation of the work-force (Taplin 1994; Taplin and Winterton 1995). Small suppliers cooperating with larger customers undoubtedly face dilemmas, but if they keep costs down, improve quality and retain the freedom to contract with other customers, there is no reason why they should not be competitive with larger rivals.

A further aspect of small business activity is the revival of backstreet sweatshops and homeworking in decaying quarters of many European and American cities. Firms in this segment aim to compete in price and delivery with low-quality imports. They have access to large pools of unemployed labour, including illegal immigrants. Labour regulations are ignored because workers are afraid to complain (Chisolm *et al.* 1986; Mitter 1986; Morovokvasic, Waldinger and Phizacklea 1990). A recent attempt to predict the impact of free trade between the USA and Mexico concludes that small textile and clothing firms in California, employing immigrant labour, have the brightest prospects of exporting to Mexico (Henderson 1993). Even in the realm of the sweatshop, beauty is in the eye of the beholder, and Waldinger (1984) commends small-scale entrepreneurs from the Dominican Republic for helping to revitalize the New York clothing industry.

The fact that many small businesses have succeeded does not mean that they are inherently more efficient than managerial enterprises. Lancashire's external economies did not save its cotton industry from extinction in the twentieth century. What is beyond question is that family businesses can compete successfully with bigger rivals, for extended periods, in a variety of national settings. Large textile businesses also have a long history. Three textile enterprises qualified for membership of the world's ninety-eight largest industrial companies in 1912. Ranked by market capitalization of equity, J. & P. Coats, the British sewing thread producer, valued at $300.8 million, was the third largest industrial firm in the world. US Steel ranked first ($757.2 million) and Standard Oil of New Jersey was second ($389.5 million). The other leading textile corporations, in 1912, were American Woolen (63rd, $39.6 million) and the Britain's Fine Cotton Spinners and Doublers' Association (72nd, $34.4 million) (Schmitz 1995). J. & P. Coats's position was all the more remarkable because the Coats family continued to play a significant part in its direction (Cairncross and Hunter 1987; Kim 1994).

Table 6.1 shows the numbers of textile and apparel firms among the 200 largest industrial businesses in each of four leading countries between the First World War and 1973. The proportion of textile firms in the top 200 has fallen in each country, suggesting that opportunities for rapid growth, and the exploitation of economies of scale and scope, have been relatively modest in this sector.

Based on information extracted from *Fortune*, Table 6.2 lists the world's leading textile and apparel companies, by sales, in 1960 and 1992. Several aspects of this table invite comment. The apparent survival of J. & P. Coats

Table 6.1 Number of textile and clothing firms among the 200 largest industrial enterprises measured by employment in each of four countries, *c.* First World War to 1973

	1917[a]	*1930*[b]	*1948*[c]	*1973*
United States	8	3	6	3
United Kingdom	27	27	19	10
Germany	13	15	19	4
Japan	56	64	24	11

Source: Chandler (1986: 411–14)
Notes: a Britain 1919, Germany 1913, Japan 1918
      b Germany 1928
      c Germany 1953, Japan 1954

Table 6.2 World's largest textile and clothing firms, 1960, 1992

1960	Global 275 rank	Sales US$ mil.	1992	Global 500 rank	Sales US$ mil.
Burlington (USA)	58	913	Toray (Japan)	192	7,862
J. P. Stevens (USA)	130	513	Hyosung (South Korea)	236	6,335
Courtaulds (UK)	141	481	Haci Omer Sabanchi (Turkey)	249	6,083
UM&M (USA)	147	468	Levi Strauss (USA)	274	5,570
AKU (The Netherlands)	154	447	Kanebo (Japan)	284	5,303
J. & P. Coats (UK)	199	371	Teijin (Japan)	314	4,753
Toray (Japan)	237	310	VF (USA)	371	3,865
Snia Viscosa (Italy)	273	272	Coats Viyella (UK)	381	3,747

Sources: Extracted from *Fortune* July 1961: 168–72; August 1961: 130–1; 26 July 1993: 71
Notes: Rankings refer to industrial companies. 1960 rankings are derived by combining the US 500 and foreign 100 tables

is misleading. Coats merged in 1960 with the woollen spinners, Patons & Baldwins, and was taken over by Vantona in 1986; hence it would be dangerous to treat the J. & P. Coats of 1912 and the Coats Viyella of 1992 as the same company. While six textile and clothing firms ranked among the global top 200 in 1960, only Toray was clinging on to a top 200 spot in 1992. There was a high turnover among the leading textile and clothing businesses. The presence of South Korean and Turkish firms in 1992 demonstrates the growing scale of business organization outside the established industrial countries. The American textile companies on the 1960 list, Burlington, J. P. Stevens and United Merchants & Manufacturers, had been relegated by 1992. Burlington's fall from grace during the 1980s was dramatic. It had accumulated debts of $1.8 billion by 1992. Recovery seemed to be under way in the mid-1990s, and it will be interesting to see whether Burlington can regain its earlier exalted position in world textiles (Schusteff 1992a; Taub 1993). Two American apparel manufacturers, Levi Strauss and VF, substituted for the missing US textile companies in 1992. Perhaps the impressive growth of Levi Strauss and VF presents a brighter picture of the overall performance of large US firms than is really warranted. A study by Dunning and Pearce (1985: 53, 56) identified the 483 leading global corporations, by sales, in 1962 and 1982. Twenty-four of these firms, in 1962, were textile, clothing or leather manufacturers: fifteen were American, five Japanese, two British, one Italian and one Dutch. Just twelve firms represented textiles and clothing in 1982: five Japanese, four American, one British, one Turkish and one South Korean. Large American textile and clothing businesses found it more difficult than their Japanese rivals to maintain leading global positions. Coleman (1994: 18) hints that anti-trust legislation made it harder for American firms to become vertically integrated multi-fibre groups. It should not be assumed that the largest firms are the most competitive. The fact that there has been a rapid turnover at the top suggests that the competitive advantage of major textile corporations is fragile. Size is partly a measure of the propensity to engage in mergers, a trait which may have little bearing on competitiveness.

It is possible that some large textile and clothing enterprises are successful for reasons unrelated to high throughput, standardization and the elimination of family control. Major textile corporations are agglomerations of smaller businesses, and the overall success of the group depends on the performance of its constituent parts. South Carolina's Milliken & Co., a group with 15,000 employees and overall sales of $2,000 million in 1992, owes some of its recent success to the excellent results of its European division. These European factories, in the UK, France, Belgium and Denmark, employed a total of 1,000 people and produced industrial textiles and carpets for export to eighty countries. Small factories, short production runs and an emphasis on quality and customer satisfaction brought profitability to this collection of modest businesses. Milliken is an intriguing company for another reason. The Milliken family, despite squabbling, maintained control over the business into the 1990s. Roger Milliken, the chairman (and grandson of the founder), was converted to the application of Japanese approaches to quality assurance and to the fostering of better relationships between the business and its workers and customers. Although Milliken's leadership was not without its critics, the company prospered. In 1993, *Textile World* judged Milliken as the most successful US textile company over the previous twenty-five years, taking into account financial performance, management and innovation (Jacobson 1992; Isaacs 1993; Caulkin 1994; Jeanes 1995). The trouble with Milliken, and many other successful businesses, is that they do not fit into the textbook categories.

The existence of such diversity ensures that national rivalry is strong. Grand totals of 4,982 textile and 21,301 apparel businesses were identified by the 1987 US Census of Manufactures. Dozens or hundreds of firms existed in each subsection of these industries. Tyre cord, where nine companies were identified, was the branch with the fewest competitors, and thread came next with forty-nine competitors (United States, Department of Commerce 1992: 6.4, 6.11). Even nine is sufficient to facilitate strong competition, if the Japanese automobile industry is any guide (Porter 1990: 118). In the UK, in 1993, there were 4,569 legal units in textiles and 9,732 in footwear and clothing, establishing a high level of domestic rivalry. Plenty of firms were engaged in all the main processes (United Kingdom, Central Statistical Office 1993: 47–8). Collusion has never been sustainable, except in niches such as calico printing, simply because of the profusion of businesses (Kirby 1974; Singleton 1991: 191–208). Rivalry should encourage higher-quality standards. If it results in the elimination of marginal firms, the survivors may be freed to adopt new strategies based on product differentiation.

THE UNITED KINGDOM

Between 1750 and 1850, cotton textiles was the UK's most dynamic industry, and the woollen industry also made large strides forward (Farnie 1979; Jenkins and Ponting 1982). The organizational structure of the textile industry, and especially of its cotton branch, has attracted interest from those who seek to understand Britain's industrial supremacy in the mid-nineteenth century, and its subsequent relative decline.

At the height of its powers, Lancashire's cotton industry was extremely atomistic. According to the 1841 factory inspector's report, there were 1,105 firms in the cotton industry, excluding the finishing processes, and 806 of these businesses had less than 200 employees. The smallest firms rented room and power in multi-unit mills, anticipating modern arrangements in some factories in Prato. Given the instability of demand, most concerns were short-lived and were lucky to survive one recession (Gatrell 1977: 98). Early firms were organized as family businesses or partnerships, of which only a handful grew to a substantial size (Boyson 1970; Rose 1986; Fitton 1989). The typical business remained on a small scale in the second half of the nineteenth century. Moreover, there was a steady retreat from the vertical integration of spinning and weaving, in favour of specialization in one process. No alarm was excited by these developments. The technically optimum size of a mill was constrained by the power of the steam engine. Specialization by process was regarded as a strength because each firm could develop a narrow expertise. Efficient regional markets linked firms at different stages of the production and distribution chain, acting as an alternative to vertical integration (Jewkes and Jewkes 1966; Farnie 1979: 301–23).

Large firms, whilst uncommon, were not absent from the cotton industry. The Peels had fourteen cotton mills in 1803, plus a number of printing works (Chapman and Chassagne 1981: 62). In the 1880s, Rylands & Sons, the largest firm in the industry, owned seventeen mills, including capacity in spinning, weaving and finishing. Rylands was even more unusual because it occupied a leading position in the merchanting section (Farnie 1993a: 42–3). Although some owner-managers minimized their supervision problems by confining themselves to a single mill, enterprises such as Peels and Rylands had no option but to employ salaried managers, drawn from the ranks of skilled workers, technicians and office staff. Rylands, although dominated by the founder's son, was a partially vertically integrated textile group (Chapman and Chassagne 1981: 70–7; Farnie 1993a: 51–2). J. & P. Coats, the world's largest textile firm in 1912, also showed a readiness to appoint outside managers. One of these, Otto Philippi, a German with experience as a bank clerk, cotton broker and thread salesman, was appointed director in 1890, and became the firm's key strategist. But neither Philippi's involvement nor the introduction of intricate management structures led to the elimination of family influence. A recent historian of J. & P. Coats has difficulty pigeonholing the company as a family or managerial firm because, like Milliken, it was a mixture of both (Kim 1994).

Horizontal mergers were a feature of the British cotton industry in the late 1890s, the post-war boom of 1918–20 and the depressed late 1920s. Some of the resulting firms were huge. The Fine Spinners and Doublers' Association controlled 2,789,236 spindles in 1913, making it the largest cotton spinning company in the world, at a time when the entire Japanese cotton industry could muster only 3,199,200 spindles (Farnie and Yonekawa 1988: 174, 180). Combines like the Fine Spinners and Doublers' Association, the Calico Printers' Association and the Bleachers' Association were no longer family concerns. They resembled holding companies and were distinguished in their early years by weak central direction. The Bleachers' Association, formed in 1900 by the amalgamation of fifty-three firms, had an unwieldy board of forty-nine directors, representing the parochial interests of individual bleachworks. A managerial hierarchy was introduced, but it included jobs for cantankerous relatives of the previous owners. At one point, in the 1900s, there were six managing directors attempting to coordinate the Bleachers' Association's activities, and it is hardly surprising that its financial performance was poor (Jeremy 1993: 163–85). As the cotton industry reeled from the loss of overseas markets in the 1920s, pressure from the banking system for the financial reorganization of the industry led to further mergers. The most notable occurred in 1929 and involved the formation of the 10 million-spindle Lancashire Cotton Corporation (LCC) out of the ruins of ninety-six businesses. At first the LCC also suffered from parochial resistance to central direction, but under the leadership of its second chairman, Frank Platt, the company made a faltering recovery and closed some of its most decrepit mills (Kirby 1974; Bamberg 1988). Horizontal mergers ensured that, by 1938, the five largest spinners controlled 31 per cent of productive capacity in the UK, compared with just 11 per cent in the USA. A lengthy tail of small firms remained in both countries (Farnie and Yonekawa 1988: 180). It may be observed that horizontal reorganization in spinning was not accompanied by greater vertical integration. In 1939 only 23 per cent of spindles and 24 per cent of looms in Britain were controlled by combined spinning and weaving firms (Jewkes and Jewkes 1966: 122).

The formation of large, vertically integrated multi-fibre textile groups did not take place until the mid-1960s, when the man-made fibre producer Courtaulds and its rival Imperial Chemical Industries (ICI) intervened in the ailing textile industries of Lancashire, Yorkshire and the Midlands in an attempt to prevent the collapse of this important market for man-made fibres. By 1968, Courtaulds had acquired 30 per cent of Lancashire's spindles and 12 per cent of its looms, together with a number of knitting, finishing and merchanting companies. ICI preferred to finance acquisitions made by its allies, Viyella International and Carrington & Dewhurst. After a series of painful episodes, in 1982, ICI sold its 35 per cent share in what had become Carrington Viyella for a bargain price. The purchaser was Vantona, the vehicle of Sir David Alliance, who had built up a textile empire by the judicious acquisition of medium-sized businesses, in part with the assistance of public sector reorganization loans. Vantona Viyella soon took over Coats Patons and renamed itself Coats Viyella. In 1991, Coats Viyella absorbed Tootal. Coats Viyella and Courtaulds Textiles reign supreme over the wreckage of the traditional British textile industry. Courtaulds and Coats Viyella have performed a similar role to that of marine salvagers, by rescuing and cannibalizing the viable parts of smaller businesses and closing down the rest. But thirty years of wheeling and dealing have done little to restore the industry's competitiveness (Coleman 1980: 270–88; Singleton 1991: ch. 10; Ritchie 1992; Blackburn 1993). A small number of innovative firms from the old textiles sector, such as Shiloh Spinners, have managed to escape the clutches of the big corporations, suggesting that size is not the principal guarantor of success in this industry (Millington 1995).

The organizational structure of major British textile firms in 1969–70 was examined in Channon's study of British business hierarchies. Carrington & Dewhurst and Coats Patons were holding companies; Viyella International was multidivisional; and Courtaulds and Tootal (then called English Calico) were a mixture of the holding company and multidivisional forms. Such labels tell only half of the story. Viyella International, despite its apparently impressive adoption of the M-form, was a shambles. Viyella divisions were in receipt of little strategic assistance from head office and the company stumbled through a series of worsening crises, culminating in its merger with Carrington & Dewhurst in 1970 (I. C. Hill 1969; Channon 1973: 61–2, 173–8). Smith & Nephew adopted the M-form between the wars, as befitted the diversity of its product range (Foreman-Peck 1995: 80–1). The M-form would have been pointless in a coarse spinning combine such as the LCC, but its potential value increased as the largest firms became more diversified. Sir Frank Kearton, the chairman of Courtaulds, professed a wish to model the company and its management structures on the best international practice. Given this laudable aim, it was odd that Courtaulds should have immersed itself in the quagmire of Lancashire, but Kearton believed that a vertically integrated textile group could succeed in this unpromising environment. Courtaulds' managerial resources, although considerable by British standards, were inadequate to its daunting task. According to one of its most senior figures, Sir Arthur Knight, Courtaulds failed to introduce a coherent multidivisional structure during its period of rapid growth between 1962 and 1972. Despite making public speeches in favour of a multidivisional organization, in private Kearton was reluctant to act. Improvisation was one of his specialities, and a considerable degree of central control was retained (A. Knight 1974: 69–93). Following Kearton's departure in the late 1970s the new regime of Chris Hogg reorganized Courtaulds into 200 profit centres and eight divisions: clothing, fabrics, spinning, plastics, films, paints, woodpulp and fibres. Reorganization was accompanied by a dramatic improvement in rates of return. In 1985, the clothing, fabrics and spinning divisions were put under a separate Courtaulds Textile board, and this group separated from the rest of Courtaulds in 1991. Some observers wondered whether decentralization had gone too far in the early 1980s and viewed the creation of Courtaulds Textiles as a timely attempt to introduce greater cohesion into strategy-making (Goold and Campbell 1987: 87, 102–3). The distinction between personal and managerial capitalism in British textiles is still blurred. Kearton's personal power at Courtaulds in the 1960s was immense. Sir David Alliance, at Vantona and Coats Viyella, also exhibited a strongly individual style of leadership during the 1970s and 1980s. One suspects that Kearton and Alliance would have felt at home during the Industrial Revolution.

Britain's textile industry was most successful in the nineteenth century, when small firms were not perceived as liabilities. Since economies of scale are few, except in man-made fibre production, the major firms in the industry have arisen as a result of mergers, most of which can be interpreted as a response to unfavourable market conditions. Few of these combines have been effectively managed, although we must reserve judgement on the two major corporations which have survived into the mid-1990s. The rather awkward British emphasis on size, in the 1960s and thereafter, makes for an instructive comparison with the more flexible Italian attitude towards industrial structure. Close cooperation between spinners and weavers did exist in Britain in the 1950s, but these arrangements failed to develop into innovative networks in the Italian style (Higgins 1993). Many small innovative firms have made progress in recent years, but they have yet to make as large an impact in the UK as their counterparts have done in Italy (H. Hall 1994).

THE UNITED STATES

The origins of the modern US textile industry can be traced back to the late eighteenth and early nineteenth centuries. An English immigrant, Samuel Slater, who had been the assistant of a leading British cotton manufacturer Jedediah Strutt, established America's first mill in Rhode Island in 1790. Slater went into partnership with members of the Brown family of Boston. This family of merchants and investors provided Slater with capital for his mill ventures. A relatively small network of financiers was responsible for the development of factory production in New England. Individual mills tended to be run as separate joint stock companies, but they drew on a common pool of capital. Since the Boston financiers had no understanding of either textile processes or factory management, they delegated day-to-day management to mill agents and overseers drawn from the ranks of technicians and skilled workers. Marketing was normally conducted through independent sales agents (Zevin 1971; Chandler 1977: 67–73; Tucker 1981; Cohen 1990: 122–3; Gross 1993).

Unlike its British rival, the textile sector in America had no doubts about the advantages of vertical integration. Temin (1988) argues that vertical integration was forced upon US firms by the geographically scattered nature of industrial activity. Spinning mills preferred to weave their own cloth because the market for yarn was thin and uncertain. Vertical integration brought greater stability to the production process. If American firms had been concentrated in a close-knit industrial district, such as Lancashire, the benefits of vertical integration would have been greatly reduced. German cotton mills faced identical problems to those of the Americans and also solved them by vertical integration (J. C. Brown 1992). After the Civil War, Southern mills found a further justification for vertical integration. Parents were reluctant to allow their daughters to live away from home near the spinning mills. Integrated mills offered a wider variety of jobs and attracted whole families to the vicinity of the factories (G. Wright 1986: 145). An impressive 84 per cent of American cotton spindles and 96 per cent of American looms were located in integrated mills in 1899 (Jewkes and Jewkes 1966: 119). Vertical integration also extended into marketing, especially in the early twentieth century, in order to reduce the sometimes exorbitant exactions of selling agents or merchants and to make certain that the mill's product was pushed with sufficient vigour in periods of weak demand (Scranton 1989: 393–4; Gross 1993: 29, 163–4; French 1994).

Until recently, the integrated cotton and woollen mills of New England and the South were regarded as the backbone of American textiles in the nineteenth and early twentieth centuries. These substantial firms, producing standardized goods, were among the earliest businesses to employ specialist managers, and hence they occupy a place in the history of modern management. Detailed work on Philadelphia, however, has brought to light an intricate web of textile and clothing production, in which personal and family capitalism were to the forefront until the Second World War. In Philadelphia, ownership and management overlapped, and barriers to entry were very low, ensuring intense competition. Philadelphia textiles were much more varied than the products of the New England mills, and they were produced in smaller batches (Scranton 1983; 1989). Even parts of the New England textile industry became more flexible, and began to incline towards the production of shorter runs of higher-quality cloth, in the early twentieth century, in response to Southern competition (French 1994). Perhaps the more adaptable New England firms were emulating those in Philadelphia rather than vice versa.

As in Britain, the 1890s and 1900s saw an amalgamation movement in American textiles, as well as in many other sectors of the economy. Some new combines, such as the New England Cotton Yarn Company and the Cotton Duck Consolidation, were loosely structured attempts to reduce competitive pressure in an industry suffering from financial instability. Their managerial problems were similar to those of the Bleachers' Association (Dewing 1914: chs 12–14). The interwar period saw some quite far-reaching changes in the structure of the US textile industry, which confirmed the transfer of power from the old industrial regions of the north-east to the South. At Manchester, New Hampshire, in 1936, Amoskeag, once the largest mill in the world, closed down after an unsuccessful struggle against Southern competition. So much for the organizational efficiency of New England textiles. After the First World War, the Amoskeag directors appeared to have given up on cotton. Instead of spending money on new machinery, they siphoned off capital to invest in other industries (Sweezy 1938; Harevan and Langenbach 1978: 75; Farnie and Yonekawa 1988: 188–9). Another leading New England firm, Appleton, moved to South Carolina, and several directors of the Boott company acquired stakes in their Southern competitors (Gross 1993: 165, 167). Burlington Mills of North Carolina, established in 1923, showed what could be achieved by Southern firms during this era. During the depression, Burlington added to its capacity by purchasing and modernizing bankrupt mills. This firm integrated forwards into marketing on a large scale. In 1962, Burlington became the first textile corporation to exceed $1 billion in annual sales. Like many of the firms discussed in this chapter, Burlington combined elements of personal and managerial capitalism. Its founder, Spencer Love,

himself a Harvard graduate, had a policy of recruiting graduates for managerial positions (A. C. Wright 1995). The difference between Burlington and
Amoskeag, where the senior manager during the 1920s was an office boy who
had risen through the ranks, was striking.

After the Second World War, large American textile and clothing firms
tended to adopt the multidivisional structure (Rumelt 1974: appendix C). As
these corporations diversified their operations, they discovered that the M-
form offered greater flexibility. Top executives were freed from the minutiae
of business, and could now devote themselves to strategic matters. Burlington replaced its functional structure, which had comprised manufacturing
and sales departments, by an M-form structure in 1954, following diversification into apparel and the weaving of cotton, wool and polyester fibres (A. C.
Wright 1995: 71–6). Personal or family control continued to be a powerful
factor in some major companies. While Spencer Love did not create a dyn-
asty, the Stevens family continued to dominate J. P. Stevens in the 1960s.
Although the family held only 4.4 per cent of J. P. Stevens's voting stock in
1970, four Stevenses were directors, of whom one was president, and family
members occupied other prominent positions in the group (Kotz 1978: 184).
Springs Mills, based in South Carolina, did not appoint a non-family president until 1969, and its first non-family chairman was elected in 1983. In
1993, 75 per cent of the voting shares of Springs Industries were owned by
the Close family. This group has continued to produce good financial results
(Ring 1992; Ozanian 1993).

Widespread restructuring has taken place in the US textile and apparel
sector since the 1960s. Conglomerates, including US Industries, purchased
numerous medium-sized textile and apparel companies in the 1960s and
1970s. The results of this intervention were mixed, as was often the case with
conglomerates. Many American textile firms, like their British counterparts,
were in a state of decline. Defensive mergers were followed by the closure of
the least viable plants, thereby potentially improving the financial performance of the group. Takeover activity increased during the 1980s and was in
part fuelled by a broad speculative movement associated with the invention
of the junk bond. Finnie (1990: 70) identifies four types of takeover in the
US textile industry in the 1980s. First, there were takeovers of one textile
company by another textile company: for instance, Springs Industries
acquired M. Lowenstein in 1985. Second, some firms changed hands
through an employee stock ownership plan (ESOP). Burlington Industries,
in 1990, underwent an ESOP, in order to protect itself from an unwelcome
leveraged buyout by Asher Edelman and Dominion Textiles. Third, outsiders
could mount a leveraged buyout (LBO) in which the takeover was financed
by the issue of bonds backed by the assets of the target company. The
Wickes Company bought Collins & Aikman, and William Farley bought the
underwear producer, Fruit of the Loom, along with West Point–Pepperell
through the LBO technique. Fourth, some companies were taken over by

Table 6.3 Leading US textile and apparel firms by sales, 1960, 1992

1960	US industrial 500 sales rank	Sales US$ mil.	1992	US industrial 500 sales rank	Sales US$ mil.
Burlington	48	913	Levi Strauss	99	5,570
J.P. Steven	90	513	VF	127	3,865
UM&M	98	468	Collins & Aikman	208	2,227
Celanese	179	264	Burlington	216	2,066
Lowenstein	190	253	Springs Industries	219	1,976
American Viscose	231	207	Fruit of the Loom	232	1,855
Cannon Mills	232	203	Shaw Industries	241	1,751
Cone Mills	248	189	West Point–Pepperell	272	1,500
Springs Mills	250	188	DWG	301	1,279
Dan River Mills	271	163	Amoskeag[a]	307	1,248

Sources: Extracted from *Fortune* July 1961: 168–76: 19 April 1993: 131–2, 146
Note: a This is not the original Amoskeag company

individual financiers with some experience in textiles: for instance, Joseph Lanier Jr. bought Dan River in 1989. As well as mergers, there were break-ups. In 1988, J. P. Stevens was dismembered: its household textiles division was sold to West Point–Pepperell; the Bibb Co. acquired some sheet manu-facturing facilities; and outside investors carved two new groups from the rump of the company, calling them JPS Textile Group and Forstmann & Co. The component elements of the US textile and apparel complex were shuf-fled and reshuffled like a pack of cards. Companies tried to strengthen their position by disposing of less profitable divisions, acquiring and eliminating smaller competitors, and purchasing apparel manufacturers in a desperate attempt to stabilize demand for their core products (Anon 1986; Finnie 1994b: 46–51). These financial transactions were a distraction from the real issues affecting competitiveness, and it is unlikely that they have done much to improve the long-term performance of the industry.

Table 6.3 shows the position that had been reached among the major US firms by 1992. Turnover among the ranks of the leading firms had been considerable since 1960. An important omission from these tables is the privately owned Milliken & Co., with sales of around $2,000 million in the early 1990s. The rise to prominence of Levi Strauss and VF was facilitated by changing lifestyles, which favoured jeans producers, during the 1960s and 1970s. Although this particular market is no longer as attractive, both firms have reached out into other areas of the apparel industry. VF, originally called Vanity Fair, acquired Blue Bell, the makers of Wrangler jeans, in 1986, and this manoeuvre confirmed the group's position as a major force (Rourke 1992; Schusteff 1992b). Restructuring has not, however, resulted in the dis-appearance of the small firm. Table 6.4 shows concentration levels in the

Table 6.4 Concentration ratios in US textile and apparel industries, 1987

	Number of firms	n-Firm concentration ratios 4	8	20	50	Herfindahl–Hirschman index (top 50)
Textiles	4,982	15	25	38	52	113
Apparel	21,301	10	14	20	29	36

Source: United States, Department of Commerce (1992: 4)
Note: Figures refer to value of shipments

textile and apparel industries in 1987. In neither case did oligopolistic firms dominate the industry. There still appears to be a place for small- and medium-sized firms in the USA. Mention has already been made of the sweatshops in the major cities, but there is also scope for cooperation between medium-sized firms and the textile majors. Milliken and the apparel producer Seminole Manufacturing of Mississippi collaborate in the production of slacks for Wal-Mart. This alliance between textile producer, garment manufacturer and retailer is a product of the quick response movement (Hammond 1993: 132–3).

Studies which focus on New England cotton mills give a misleading picture of the organizational evolution of the US textile and clothing sector. Vertical integration and the separation of ownership from management did not save New England in the 1920s and 1930s. Several of the most successful textile and clothing groups in the twentieth century have been under family or personal leadership, including Burlington during the reign of its founder, Spencer Love, and Milliken. Moreover, small firms have survived and still constitute the vast majority of enterprises in this sector. Firm size, managerial control and organizational structure cannot fully explain the success or failure of individual enterprises.

JAPAN

Japan's first steam-powered cotton spinning mill was established in 1867 by the Satsuma clan. Early Japanese mills, many of which were water-powered, were too small to be profitable. Osaka Boseki opened the first commercially viable cotton spinning mill in 1883. Osaka Boseki was formed as a company in the Western sense. Its founder, Eiichi Shibusawa, was an established entrepreneur and banker. Capital was tapped from various sources, including the aristocracy and merchant community (Yamamura 1978: 219–20; Minami 1987: 207–11). The years 1887–9 witnessed a great flotation boom of limited liability cotton spinning companies in Japan (Yonekawa 1987: 574–9).

Generally speaking, the *zaibatsu* groups did not take a strong interest in textiles. *Zaibatsu* were not prepared to take the risk of sinking large sums of money into spinning mills, although they were willing to acquire modest shareholdings in mill companies. The exception to this rule was Mitsui. Following a financial crisis in 1890, Kanegafuchi Boseki was bailed out by Mitsui Bank and taken into Mitsui. Kanegafuchi achieved rapid growth, with the assistance of injections of capital and trained managerial talent from Mitsui. Sanji Muto, a graduate of Keio University, was transferred to Kanegafuchi from Mitsui Bank, in 1893, and became the firm's managing director. By 1914, Kanegafuchi had fifteen cotton mills plus several silk factories, and it had integrated spinning and weaving. Despite its rapid expansion, however, Kanegafuchi's financial performance was unexceptional (Yonekawa 1984: 210–14; Morikawa 1992: 27; Abe 1993).

Early Japanese textile firms had a simple management structure. Companies owning several mills usually ran them from an office at the most important mill, instead of from a separate headquarters. When the largest firms, Kanegafuchi (Kanebo) and Toyo Boseki (Toyobo), did establish separate head offices, in the early twentieth century, these were comparatively small, and most administrative workers continued to be based at the mill level. Considerable autonomy was also retained by the managers of mills taken over by bigger groups (Suzuki 1985; Fruin 1992: 116–18). These modest organizational arrangements were similar to those of contemporary American and British textile producers. Managerial hierarchies in Japanese textiles became somewhat more elaborate during the 1920s and 1930s, and a few firms established regional headquarters below their national head offices (Fruin 1992: 147). Japanese cotton spinners differed from most of their Western rivals in the area of graduate recruitment. Graduate scientists and social scientists were employed in large numbers. As early as 1914, Kanegafuchi employed 269 graduates and Toyo Boseki employed 136. Nearly all of Kanegafuchi's plants were managed by graduates (Yonekawa 1984: 196, 211–12). Kanegafuchi, which was becoming increasingly diversified, had adopted the multidivisional structure by 1940. But Kanegafuchi was exceptional (Suzuki 1985: 272). Generally speaking, the impact of formal organizational structures should not be exaggerated. Much still depended on traditional frameworks of authority, especially the paternalistic relations between top executives and their protégés among the plant managers. Fruin (1992: 147) concludes that there was no clear separation between operational and strategic decision-making in large Japanese firms. Mass and Lazonick (1991: 37–50) praise Japanese textile companies for their excellent management, appropriate choice of technology and superior marketing. But it is not at all obvious, given the evidence presented here, that Japanese management structures were in practice more sophisticated than those of the British or Americans.

Japan's textile industry was split into a large-scale sector, producing for export, and a small-scale sector, supplying the domestic market. In the export sector, a few vertically integrated corporations were dominant, but in the domestic sector the hold of the family firm was unshakeable. The largest Japanese textile businesses were very substantial even by Western standards. In 1928, Toyo Boseki and Dai Nippon Boseki ranked fourth and fifth in the world in terms of spindleage. The five largest firms possessed 58 per cent of Japan's cotton spindles in 1913. Their share declined to 47 per cent in 1938, reflecting the faster growth of firms of medium size (Allen 1980: 65; Farnie and Yonekawa 1988: 174, 180; Abe 1994). Between the wars, collections of independent weaving mills, equipped with 100 or 200 power-looms, sprang up in a number of localities. Some of these small- to medium-sized firms were not afraid to venture into the export market. The MES for weaving plants was so low that these firms were not at a competitive disadvantage. The smallest firms constituted the largest cohort in the population. In 1933, businesses with under five employees made up 91 per cent of the establishments in the Japanese cotton industry (Abe 1992).

On the distribution side, the Japanese textile industry had some distinctive characteristics. Cloth merchants varied in size from those resembling minor British export merchants to the giant Mitsui Bussan, which was the trading arm of the Mitsui *zaibatsu*. Mitsui Bussan's role in the textile industry was originally that of an importer of raw cotton and machinery. By 1907–10, however, it was in control of 40–50 per cent of Japanese cotton cloth exports. Mitsui Bussan acted on behalf of the export cartels of large integrated firms in the Korean and Manchurian markets. A subsidiary called Toyo Menka was established by Mitsui Bussan in 1920 to specialize in serving the cotton industry. Before the Second World War, most traders in textiles were specialists. Two of the largest were C. Itoh in the cotton industry and Marubeni in the silk industry (Yoshihara 1982: 24–5, 52–5; Sugiyama 1988b). In Osaka, in the 1920s, dozens of merchants specialized in the wide cloths which were suitable for export. Obitani Shoten, an independent weaver, exported a substantial amount of cloth through the Osaka merchant firm Yagi Shoten (Abe 1994: 18–19). Textile exports to particular markets were coordinated, to ensure that Japanese mills competed against foreigners rather than each other. This contrasts with the lack of coordination among British merchants, many of whom were indifferent as to whether they sold British or foreign textiles (Shimizu 1986; Mass and Lazonick 1991: 44–5). Cooperation between manufacturers and merchants was an acceptable substitute for formal vertical integration. Some reorganization of this system occurred after the Second World War. New firms came to prominence and existing firms, like Toyo Menka and C. Itoh, became general trading companies (or *sogo shosha*), and expanded their stakes in industrial activities. The role of large-scale traders has remained an important one in textiles. In 1975, three-fifths of textile exports from Japan were handled by the ten general trading companies (Young 1979: 27).

Major Japanese textile firms struggled to find an enduring management structure after 1945. Toyobo introduced a multidivisional structure in 1948, but the motive for this reform was a curious one. Toyobo mistakenly believed that the Allied occupation authorities would divide the company into smaller businesses and thought that the disruption would be minimized if the firm had already been decentralized. The multidivisional structure at Toyobo was abandoned in 1963, when top management decided that greater centralization was needed to hold the firm together in a period of dramatic change, which involved diversification into synthetic fibres and a number of mergers. Toyobo reverted to a multidivisional organization in 1974. Kanebo abandoned its short-lived multidivisional structure after the war, when it withdrew from a number of non-textile businesses. The M-form was re-adopted in 1958, when Kanebo decided to enter nylon production and to rebuild its position in cosmetics and food in response to growing competition from chemical fibre companies. Kanebo continued to make adjustments to its divisional structure in the 1960s and 1970s, a period marked by considerable diversification (Suzuki 1991: 109–13). These shifts in direction cannot have been entirely misguided. As Table 6.2 shows, Kanebo was still the fifth largest textile and clothing group in the world in 1992. It is interesting that these two firms responded to apparent crises, in the years around 1960, in opposite ways. Toyobo opted for greater centralization while Kanebo chose increased decentralization. Both reacted to a perceived crisis by overhauling their organizational structure. Perhaps the direction of change mattered less than the perception that decisive action was being taken.

Rayon and synthetic fibre producers, such as Toray, Teijin and Kuraray have integrated forwards into textiles since the 1950s, while textile producers, such as Toyobo, Kanegafuchi and Dai Nippon, have increasingly integrated backwards into the manufacture of man-made fibres. Widespread merger activity has assisted the related processes of integration and rationalization. For instance, in 1969, the Nichibo cotton spinning company (formerly Dai Nippon) merged with Nippon Rayon to form Unitika, and subsequently formed an alliance with Kanebo to develop polyester production. The erosion of the distinction between textile and man-made fibre firms has gone further in Japan than in the USA (O'Leary 1992; Yamazaki 1992a; 1992b).

Since the 1950s, Japanese big business has been organized into *kigyo shudan* or *keiretsu*, which are alliances of leading firms in separate industries. In some cases, these were based around the members of the old *zaibatsu* groups. Of the six leading *kigyo shudan* in 1989, all but Sumitomo had a significant presence in textiles and man-made fibres. The pertinent members of these groups were Toray (Mitsui), Mitsubishi Rayon (Mitsubishi), Toho Rayon and Nisshin Spinning (Fuyo), Unitika and Teijin (Sanwa) and Asahi Chemical (Dai-Ichi Kangyo). These alliances cemented the textile industry into solid banking, insurance and trading networks, and could be called upon for help and encouragement in times of difficulty (Gerlach 1992: 82).

It would be myopic to deny the continuing existence of a small-scale sector in Japanese textiles and clothing. As late as 1990, establishments employing between four and nineteen persons produced 30 per cent of value added in the Japanese textile industry and 29 per cent of value added in the apparel industry (UNIDO 1993: 550). Cooperation agreements between large textile groups and small weaving concerns were common. Weaving workshops with twenty to thirty modern looms, operated by a boss, his wife and two or three employees, were attached by long-term contracts to a large company, such as Teijin or Nisshin, and could expect to receive a steady flow of orders if their prices and quality were satisfactory. Given that these workshops employed family and neighbourhood labour, often on a part-time basis, they were able to pay lower wages than the organized sector. Vertical *keiretsu*, linking a dominant firm with an army of subcontractors, exist in a number of industries. Without access to this relatively inexpensive source of labour, it is possible that the Japanese textile industry would have suffered even greater misfortunes at the hands of its competitors from low wage countries (Abegglen 1959: 52–4, 62–3; Dore 1986: 153–81). From a slightly different perspective, cooperation between these Japanese firms illustrates Mark Casson's (1990: 122) point that, where there is a climate of trust between firms, vertical integration is not necessary.

Once more, in the Japanese case, the diversity of organizational arrangements in the textile and clothing sector is striking. Equally striking is the cooperation between large and small firms in Japan. Mechanisms of cooperation between these different types of organization seem to have been more stable in Japan than elsewhere. Cooperation between firms in Britain, continental Europe and the USA, while not absent, has been much more patchy, at least until the last two decades. This is not to suggest that the Japanese have structured their firms and their business networks in a perfect way. Japan has lost its competitive advantage in labour-intensive processes, but in the future it may be easier for the Japanese, with their experience of cooperation, to devise new forms of inter-firm collaboration.

DEVELOPING ASIA

Although the textile and clothing industries of Asia have experienced rapid growth in recent decades, it would be difficult to attribute their success to the adoption of a particular managerial structure. Personal capitalism has been prominent in all of the countries under consideration, but it has taken a number of forms. Network relationships of various sorts have been prominent in Asian textiles and clothing. This section is inevitably highly selective. It progresses from the successful newly industrializing countries to some of the following tier, such as Indonesia and Thailand, and ends in India.

We begin with South Korea, Taiwan and Hong Kong. The organizational structures of businesses in Japan, South Korea and Taiwan since the Second

World War have been influenced by political factors. In Japan, the government favoured the development of responsible business groups with which it could cooperate, such as the *kigyo shudan*. Korean regimes were devoted to planning, and their policy was to foster enormous conglomerates led by a small group of industrial bosses who were forced to do the government's bidding. Taiwanese governments, reflecting the more individualistic Chinese culture, also encouraged industrial development, but felt less strongly inclined to choose between large and small firms (Hamilton and Biggart 1988). Singapore is left out of our discussion because textiles and apparel were not at the forefront of its drive for development (Rodan 1989: 175; Huff 1994: 323).

South Korea's decisive economic growth since the 1950s has been accompanied by the emergence of a number of very substantial textile enterprises. In 1983, 12.8 per cent of the 172 largest South Korean manufacturing firms, ranked by sales, were textile corporations. A glance at Table 6.1 shows that this proportion is similar to those obtained by textile enterprises in the top 200 industrial firms in Britain in 1917 and 1930, and Japan in 1948 (Amsden 1989: 165). Japanese firms, including Toyo Boseki, established mills in southern Korea in the 1930s (Kimura 1995: 564). After 1945, the Koreans seized these mills. This inheritance from South Korea's former colonial masters ensured that the spinning industry was highly concentrated, and eight firms controlled 85 per cent of cotton spindles in 1958 (McNamara 1992: 332–3). The *chaebol*, a Korean version of the pre-war *zaibatsu*, entered textiles at an early stage in their development. Samsung, now one of South Korea's foremost industrial groups, had its origins in trading and the sugar industry, but in 1954 it diversified into woollen manufacturing by establishing the Cheil Wool Textile Company. Aided by profits from import substitution in woollen textiles, Samsung later moved into synthetic fibres and other areas of manufacturing (Jones and Sakong 1980: 349–54). Daewoo began as an importer and exporter of textiles and apparel, branched out into textile manufacturing in the late 1960s and later expanded into heavy industry (Clifford 1994: 118–23). Major Korean companies possessed complex managerial hierarchies and employed professional middle managers, and in these respects they resembled Japanese and Western business groups. Due to the power of the *chaebol* founders and their successors, these groups also exhibited strong elements of personal capitalism. Thousands of small- and medium-sized textile and clothing businesses also sprang up in industrializing Korea. These small firms were not necessarily uncompetitive. One study found that, in the late 1960s, firms with under 100 employees enjoyed total factor productivity levels which were at least as high as those of larger enterprises in certain activities, including weaving, knitting and clothing manufacture (Ho 1980: 141–51). In contrast to Japanese practice, the larger textile corporations in South Korea tended to avoid cooperation with smaller enterprises.

The Japanese also transferred some cotton spindles to Taiwan in the 1930s. Since the early 1950s the Taiwanese textile sector has been controlled by two, often antagonistic, social groups. First, wealthy textile capitalists fled Shanghai following the communist takeover and subsequently opened new mills in Taiwan. Second, land reform in post-war Taiwan dispossessed many rural landlords. Compensation payments and other forms of aid encouraged former landlords to take up manufacturing in the 1950s. By 1976, thirty-three of Taiwan's 106 largest business groups had textiles as their core activity (Gold 1988: 188). These groups have continued to grow, although they have not attained the same scale as the *chaebol*. Taiwanese business groups are based on family ties and alliances deriving from a particular locality. Central coordination of the constituent businesses is haphazard. They are in effect clusters of semi-independent firms with partially overlapping directorates, rather like the mill companies established by the Boston merchants in the early nineteenth century (Numazaki 1986). An investigation of the history of a business group with strong textile interests from the Tainan area, concluded that *bang* or clique was the most appropriate term for its organizational structure (Numazaki 1993). When a member of the *bang* proposes a new venture, the other members have a powerful incentive to support him, since a refusal to participate would create bad feeling. This is a recipe for continuing, if sometimes random, expansion. Personal capitalism is common in the largest Taiwanese enterprises. Small firms exist in even greater profusion in Taiwan than they do in Korea, mainly because the Taiwanese government has not been biased in favour of huge conglomerates. Modestly sized textile and clothing enterprises frequently take on work as subcontractors when the big factories are overbooked (Silin 1976: 28, 104; Lam and Lee 1992: 109–12).

Hong Kong's modern textile industry is of recent provenance. During the 1940s and early 1950s, Shanghai textile capitalists fled nationalist and communist persecution to reside in the British colony (Wong 1988). They invested in modern mills and, as a result, cotton spinning became the core of the Hong Kong textile and clothing complex. By 1978, there were thirty-two spinning mills in Hong Kong, twenty-five of which were owned by Shanghainese interests. Sixteen mills were owned by families and most of the remaining sixteen were effectively under family control. A degree of vertical integration was introduced by the more successful of these firms. For example, by the late 1970s, the Winsor Industrial Corporation possessed four cotton spinning and four woollen spinning mills, four knitwear and four garment-making works, and two finishing works (ibid.: 56, 148). But the large spinners comprised only a tiny proportion of the total number of firms in the industry. In 1989, the Hong Kong textile industry possessed 5,118 establishments, only seventy-five of which employed more than 200 workers, while the apparel industry consisted of 9,757 establishments (UNIDO 1993: 540). Over 90 per cent of garment manufacturers were owner-managed.

Subcontracting for larger local or overseas firms was common, and small businesses were organized in networks, in which kinship ties were an important consideration (Sit and Wong 1989; Redding 1994: 74–8). Managerial corporations are unlikely to replace the family business in Hong Kong because people are unwilling to commit themselves to impersonal organizations. But family firms are difficult to sustain for long periods of time, since brothers and children of the founder would rather set up their own businesses, thereby extending the network of firms, than tolerate a subordinate position (Redding 1993). This state of affairs makes it difficult for Hong Kong to develop large textile corporations. Even so, two Hong Kong firms ranked among the lower regions of the world's 100 largest textile firms, by sales, in 1977 (Clairmonte and Cavanagh 1981: 173).

Indonesia's textile and clothing sector is well documented. In 1987, there were ninety-four firms employing 66,586 workers in spinning, and 1,030 firms employing 155,025 workers in mechanized weaving, plus thousands of small garment workshops. Forty-nine per cent of spindleage was owned by Indonesian firms, 27 per cent by joint ventures between local capitalists and foreign investors, and 26 per cent by state enterprises (MacIntyre 1990: 69; H. Hill 1991). A handloom weaving sector has also managed to survive (Hardjono 1990). A number of textile factories were established in the Netherlands East Indies between the two world wars. After independence in 1949, the Indonesian government tried to encourage industrialization. The regime's *dirigiste* attitude, its policy of discriminating against ethnic Chinese capitalists and a persistent balance of payments crisis meant that the textile industry was tightly regulated. Licences were needed to import raw materials and textile machinery. Control of these licences fell into the hands of a small number of magnates who enjoyed friendly relations with the administration (Palmer 1972; Robison 1986). Thus, a few fortunate capitalists enjoyed high rewards. They were able to develop large, if somewhat ramshackle, conglomerates. Meanwhile, the majority of small textile producers were pushed into a subordinate position by their dependence on large firms for access to crucial inputs (Yoshihara 1988: 175–6, 224–34). Indonesian *chaebol*, if we may use the term, are far more primitive in their organizational structure, and far less disciplined, than their South Korean counterparts.

Thailand exhibits many similarities with Indonesia in terms of the structure of its textile and clothing businesses. A select group of textile corporations emerged amid a sea of small producers. The dominant firms were Thai Blanket Industry and Saha Union, and their leaders forged close personal ties with senior government and army personnel in the 1950s and 1960s. In countries such as Thailand, Indonesia and formerly South Korea, where the cultivation of politicians was the key to profitability for large firms, it is difficult to generalize about the relationship between organizational structure and economic efficiency. The most that can be said is that large textile firms reaped substantial political economies of scale, and a few individuals made fortunes. Chaos often reigned in the large corporations, and the hidden activities of numerous small businesses deserve a substantial share of the credit for the generation of competitive advantage (Yoshihara 1988: 105–6, 192, 194; Suphachalasai 1992; Doner and Ramsay 1993).

India's factory textile industry has had a chequered history. The first operational steam-powered cotton spinning mill in Asia was opened at Bombay in 1856. Ahmedabad and Bombay became the leading cotton textile districts in the factory sector before the First World War (S. D. Mehta 1954; Yonekawa 1987; Tomlinson 1993: 109). British capitalists played a secondary role to that of Indian textile traders in the development of the cotton industry. The British were much more prominent in the jute industry of Bengal. Cotton and jute mills were administered under the managing agency system. Capital and managerial talent were scarce in India. Managing agencies helped to finance new mills, drawing upon capital from Indian merchants or the UK. These agencies also managed the mills, and were able to obtain very favourable terms for their services. It was virtually impossible for a mill to dismiss its managing agents. Since the agents were paid on the basis of the mill's revenue rather than its profits, they had no direct incentive to maximize efficiency. Managing agencies extended their tentacles throughout the industrial sector (Bagchi 1972: 219–90). In 1959, Birla Brothers managed six cotton, one rayon and two jute mills, together with twelve other businesses in the tea, motor vehicle, bicycle, textile machinery, paper, plastic and wholesale distribution industries (M. M. Mehta 1961: 284; Ghosh 1975). Although the managing agency system was abolished in 1969, by this time most agency firms had relaunched themselves as diversified industrial corporations and they were not seriously inconvenienced (Sengupta 1974).

After independence, in 1947, a policy of forced industrialization in steel and engineering meant that little capital was available for modernizing the textile mill sector. A further justification for neglecting the textile factories was found in Gandhi's call for the encouragement of cottage industry and the preservation of rural employment and lifestyles (Mazumdar 1984). Indian governments imposed tough restrictions on factory weaving, promoted handloom weaving and permitted the development of a large number of small workshops using power-looms. Handloom weavers produced approximately 30 per cent of India's cloth output in the early 1980s (Leadbeater 1993: 214). Vertically integrated mills were forbidden to increase their weaving capacity. Some mills supplied old machinery to former employees who opened power-loom weaving workshops and became subcontractors (Mazumdar 1991; Leadbeater 1993: 216–18). These circumstances were far from conducive to the development of efficient business organizations in the mill sector. Mills which went bankrupt were taken over by the state and kept in operation in order to save jobs. State mills could undercut private mills because their losses were covered by subsidies (Anubhai 1988). Since

1985 there has been a gradual liberalization of the Indian economy and the arrangements governing the textile industry (Bhagwati 1993). These new economic conditions have led to the rapid growth of small businesses in districts such as Tiruppur (Cawthorne 1995). In the medium term the Indian textile industry could benefit from its rather painful reintroduction to market forces.

Chandlerian organizational structures have not been prominent in the textile and clothing sectors of Asian countries. Family enterprise, networks of small firms, sprawling conglomerates or managing agencies occupied centre stage. Political interference moulded the organizational structure of many large textile and clothing businesses. In the absence of political intervention, it is doubtful whether many of the *chaebol*, or large Indonesian or Thai textile producers, would have appeared. Freely functioning markets would have resulted in the replication of the family business structure prevailing in Hong Kong. In the light of these considerations, it is all the more interesting that many Asian textile and garment industries have been so successful. The connection between organizational structure and expansion has been tenuous. Low costs, especially of labour, played a much more important role in generating competitive advantage.

CONCLUSION

Handloom weavers, and even hand spinners, exist in many countries today. At the other end of the scale, large volumes of textiles are produced by giant corporations, such as Kanebo and Coats Viyella. Thriving family businesses in Hong Kong and Italy may be compared with those which failed in Britain. In Japan, the largest synthetic fibre producers are not too proud to cooperate with small rural weaving enterprises. This diversity demonstrates that it is possible for several organizational structures to coexist, and even to prosper, in the textile and clothing sector. Under conditions of unregulated free trade, many firms would not survive, but it is difficult to believe that the small family firm would be eliminated. Family firms have shown great adaptability in a variety of environments, including Victorian Lancashire, colonial Hong Kong and modern Italy. Although it may be difficult for family businesses to operate on a large scale, the records of Benetton and Milliken show that it can be done.

Due to the lack of economies of scale in textiles and clothing, small- and medium-sized firms should be able to obtain a minimum efficient scale of production. Big firms do not have substantial advantages over more modest firms, but neither do they have serious disadvantages. A firm with ten integrated textile factories, or even one with ten single-process factories, is fundamentally an aggregate of ten business units. Large firms often believe that they have the edge over smaller competitors, but belief and reality do not always coincide. Courtaulds, in the 1970s, was no doubt organizationally superior to a typical Lancashire mill company, but this was not a relevant yardstick, since its most threatening competitors were elsewhere. Despite the complexity of its organizational structure, Courtaulds was at a competitive disadvantage in relation to family businesses, such as the Hong Kong spinners and the members of the Italian textile and clothing networks. The emergence of large firms in the twentieth century was in the main a response to the competitive decline of the textile industries in the advanced industrial nations. Mergers encouraged rationalization and gave producers some respite from local, but rarely from international, competition.

7

CHANCE

A provocative article by a leading shipping historian purports to show that the rise of the Philipps brothers, in the City of London and the shipping trade, before the First World War, owed much to a freak occurrence in 1876 (P. N. Davies 1981). In that year a canal barge carrying gunpowder blew up in London, resulting in a series of individual tragedies, including two suicides and the unexpected inheritance of a fortune by Leonora, John Philipps's future wife. Although the Philipps brothers possessed considerable business talent, their ascent would have been far less certain in the absence of help from the hand of fate. More topically, and less gruesomely, Krugman (1994: 469–70, 478–9) illustrates how chance moulded the development of the American carpet industry. In 1895, Catherine Evans, a teenager living in Dalton, Georgia, made a bedspread as a wedding gift. This present attracted attention because it was tufted, a technique which was no longer in common use. Catherine was encouraged by this response and soon devised an improved method of tufting. Inspired by Catherine's example, other people in the area took up tufting as a hobby and Dalton gradually became the centre of a handicraft industry making tufted bedspreads and sweaters. When a carpet-tufting machine was invented shortly before the Second World War, the people of Dalton capitalized on their expertise and opened a number of small factories. Tufted carpets were now cheaper than woven ones. Ancillary industries were attracted to Dalton, and carpet manufacturers from other regions moved into this area, where they could find reserves of skilled labour. By the 1990s, six of the top twenty carpet producers in the USA had factories in Dalton, and a further thirteen had plants nearby. A chance event in 1895 had set off a cumulative process of change, like a snowball rolling downhill, and Dalton had become the centre of the American carpet industry.

By including chance among the determinants of competitive advantage, Porter (1990: 124–7) explicitly recognizes the uncertain nature of the business environment. He refers to seven principal categories of chance event: pure inventions, major technological discontinuities (such as the emergence of biotechnology or microelectronics), sudden alterations in the cost of inputs, major shifts in world financial markets or exchange rates, sudden changes in demand, political actions by foreign governments, and wars. Geography could also affect a state's competitive advantage. A recent study of the economic history of Singapore concludes that it obtained a head start over many of its competitors as a result of its advantageous location on international trading routes (Huff 1994: 7–8, 370). A change in any of these exogenous variables is liable to affect the pattern of competitive advantage, at least in the short term, and possibly also in the long term. For instance, a technological breakthrough shifts the balance of competitive advantage in favour of the country making the breakthrough.

Porter is not discussing completely random events. The causes of fluctuations in exchange rates, and the timing and location of inventions, are amenable to logical investigation, although the results may not be conclusive. Economists understand the general causes of variations in exchange rates, but they are unable to predict the details of these disturbances. Historians of science understand that, in a given era, radical technological discontinuities are more likely to occur in some countries than in others, but greater precision may be impossible. From the perspective of an individual firm, or industry, such occurrences are surprising and call into question existing strategies. Elsewhere, Porter (1985: 445–81) discusses the advantages of making contingency plans for such crises. A firm should consider how it would respond to various unexpected events. It would be easier to develop a contingency plan for a change in the exchange rate than it would for the appearance of a major new invention. The unexpected cannot be eradicated from the business environment, despite the most elaborate efforts. As F. H. Knight (1971: 231–50) indicates, most decisions in business are taken in situations which are so complicated that it is impossible to assign probabilities to the possible outcomes. Choices are made with inadequate data and, especially in industries with high fixed costs, often entail commitments which could prove disastrous in the event of an error (Ghemawat 1991: 33–51). Thus, we would expect mistakes to be more costly in textiles than in apparel manufacturing.

Porter adopts a moderate position in relation to the role of chance in business success and failure. Landes (1994), a prominent economic historian, is reluctant to give chance any credit for influencing the historical process. The resort to explanations based on probability is categorized as a form of defeatism. Since Landes focuses on major historical developments, such as the rise of the West and the Industrial Revolution, his strictures may be less telling at the level of the firm or industry. Chance events affecting individual firms could cancel each other out at a higher level of aggregation. Kaufman (1985), however, assigns an important role to chance in accounting for the survival of businesses, on the grounds that other explanations are inadequate. Kaufman also doubts whether flexibility enables firms to escape from the tyranny of unexpected changes in the environment. Flexibility is expensive, and it could foster indecision and weakness. Porter is more optimistic: a firm or region with a favourable diamond should be in a good position to adapt to chance events. Effective systems for gathering and processing information should help it to anticipate and respond to exogenous events, such as shifts in tastes, changes in the prices of raw materials, turning-points in the economic cycle and the emergence of new technologies (Porter and Millar 1985; Fransman 1994).

The following sections examine the implications for the textile sector of various types of chance event, starting with technological breakthroughs, continuing with economic events and concluding with political changes.

PURE INVENTIONS AND TECHNOLOGICAL BREAKTHROUGHS

A pure invention is the fashioning of a prototype of a device or process with a specific application, whilst a technological breakthrough is a more general scientific revolution which could have implications for several industries. The first mechanically powered loom would fit into the former category. The latter category would include the emergence of steam power. Inventions may not lead to successful innovations, if, for example, the original design is flawed or if there is a failure to recognize its potential. The Chinese invented a hemp spinning machine in the fourteenth century. Drawings of this machine show that it had many similarities to Western inventions of the eighteenth century. For an unknown reason this Chinese machine was not brought into production, although the historian of this episode wonders whether the Europeans gained some inkling of what the Chinese had achieved and incorporated it into their own technical thinking (Elvin 1973: 194–9).

While chance plays a part in determining the distribution of major inventions (Crafts 1995: 756–7), it is not suggested that they occur at random. Even before the introduction of systematic R&D programmes, amateur technologists directed their efforts towards the solution of pressing industrial problems, in the hope that their labours would be well rewarded (Schmookler 1966; Rosenberg 1976). In the eighteenth century, an era of technological revolution in textiles, good fortune played a significant role. But it would be impossible to weigh the contribution of chance against those of other relevant factors. John Kay's flying shuttle of 1733 is usually regarded as the invention which initiated the technical revolution in the English cotton textile industry, although it was originally developed with wool in mind. The flying shuttle made it possible for a handloom to be operated by one person instead of two, and it came into widespread use in the 1760s. Rising demand for cotton goods, and the intensification of the bottleneck in handspinning, due to the introduction of the flying shuttle, encouraged people to search for a method of revolutionizing the archaic

148

spinning process. Lewis and Paul were the pioneers of mechanical spinning in the 1730s. But Hargreaves's spinning jenny (1766), Arkwright's water frame (1769) and Crompton's mule (1779) represented the most practical answers to the yarn shortage. Higher spinning productivity, arising from the use of these machines, created pressure for further improvements in weaving. A power-loom was devised by Cartwright in 1785, but the general adoption of this machine was delayed until the mid-nineteenth century, first by technical problems and then by a new influx of labour, including returned servicemen, which led to falling wages in handloom weaving after the Napoleonic Wars. Shifting disequilibria between the spinning and weaving processes encouraged inventive activity, but did not guarantee its successful outcome. The vastly improved spinning machines of the late 1760s were the product of thirty years of trial and error. Technological change in the cotton industry was far from a smooth, scientifically planned exercise (Farnie 1979: 277–84; Chapman 1987: 17–25; O'Brien, Griffiths and Hunt 1991; Hills 1994; von Tunzelmann 1995). Furthermore, these technical advances would have counted for nothing if British entrepreneurs and their financial backers had not been willing and able to take advantage of them. The response of the British textile industry to the eighteenth-century inventions was vigorous and a commanding competitive advantage was established. Other countries, such as the USA, were soon confronted by the same textile inventions. These inventions were even more unexpected, seen from the perspective of the USA and continental Europe, than they were to people in Britain. The reaction of the USA and Europe was to emulate the UK in the efficient deployment of the new technology.

It is curious that the great textile inventions were bunched in one country. Could England's primacy have been influenced by good fortune, as well as by more systematic factors? Crafts (1977) suggests that the UK's emerging industrial supremacy at the end of the eighteenth century was not inevitable. Luck may have played some part in England's establishment of an industrial lead over France, which was a close rival for many years. Perhaps the French were held back by the disruptive effects of revolution and war. Speculation of this nature is strenuously resisted by Landes (1994), who argues that the duty of historians is to supply logical explanations of events, and thereby to diminish uncertainty. It is doubtful whether these philosophical issues can be resolved. If we choose to admit chance as a contributory factor, we must conclude that either England or France could have become the first country to develop modern textile machinery, even if we accept that England was the country most likely to succeed because of its more favourable underlying conditions for development.

During the nineteenth century, the most important inventions in the textile sector occurred in the USA. Both ring spinning and automatic (or weft-replenishing) loom weaving originated in the USA (Sandberg 1974; Mass 1989). By the mid-nineteenth century, the USA had achieved a rough technological parity with Western Europe. Hence there was a rising, although immeasurable, probability that further important inventions in textiles and other industries would now take place in the USA. It would be unreasonable to suggest that only the Americans could have invented either ring spinning or the automatic loom. Ecuador would have been an unlikely location for these inventions, but Britain or France would not. These two inventions led to an improvement in the competitive position of American textile producers, even though it was not a sufficient one to give them an advantage over English textile firms in most export markets. Textile regions in other countries reacted to the invention of rings and automatic looms in various ways, depending upon the suitability of the new technologies to their circumstances (Saxonhouse and Wright 1984b).

Systematic R&D became more widespread in the twentieth century, and it is tempting to believe that this restricted the stochastic element in the process of invention. Although most prospective inventors now required a formal scientific education, the role of chance was by no means eliminated in the location of significant inventions. Rudolf Rossman, who patented the first shuttleless loom in 1928, was a qualified textile engineer in Europe. He turned to the Swiss engineering company, Sulzer Brothers, for assistance with the development and production of his shuttleless loom (Mass 1990). If Rossman had lived in either the USA or Britain, it is probable that a firm in one of these countries would have pioneered the shuttleless loom. If Sulzer Brothers had not been interested in branching out into textile engineering, perhaps Rossman would have had to look further afield for a manufacturer. The Swiss and their German neighbours successfully exploited their initial lead in shuttleless loom technology. American firms, such as Drapers, failed to catch up with them. Although this episode tended to strengthen the European textile cluster relative to that of the USA, it would be going too far to suggest that it had a major impact on their relative performance. Textile firms in the USA could import superior machines from Switzerland, so that the relative backwardness of American loom manufacturers was not a serious problem. Open-end rotor spinning, another key twentieth-century advance, was invented in Czechoslovakia in the 1960s. It is not surprising that open-end rotor spinning was invented in a country with a modern engineering industry, as opposed to say Cyprus or Vietnam. But it is harder to account for the fact that the most important invention in spinning in the twentieth century should have occurred in Czechoslovakia rather than in, say, Britain, the USA or Japan. Czechoslovakia's pioneering role in open-end rotor spinning gave it some advantage in the incremental development of this technology, although West Germany and Japan also made great strides forward (Antonelli 1989; Lücke 1993). Open-end rotor spinning did not give the Czechoslovakian spinning industry a dominant position in the world market, in marked contrast to the effect of mule spinning on the fortunes of the British cotton industry in an earlier era. Either the Czechoslovakians

Table 7.1 Major technical changes in textile production

	Eighteenth century	*Nineteenth century*	*Twentieth century*
Spinning	Crompton's mule (UK)	Ring spinning (USA)	Open-end rotor (Czechoslovakia)
Weaving	Power-loom (UK)	Automatic loom (USA)	Shuttleless loom (Switzerland)

were less capable entrepreneurs, which would not be surprising under communist rule, or else the open-end rotor system was a less decisive technical advance than the mule. Table 7.1 shows the distribution of major inventions over the last 200 years. It is interesting to note that only the eighteenth-century inventions conferred a decisive competitive advantage on the textile industry of the initiating country.

Some more general technological breakthroughs have had a major impact on the textile and apparel industries. The centrifugal governor, first used in conjunction with waterwheels and windmills in the early eighteenth century, was a crucial development enabling the speed of machinery to be regulated (von Tunzelmann 1978: 164). Early steam engines were designed for pumping unwanted water out of mines. Steam power began to be applied to textile machinery in the late eighteenth century. At first, reciprocating engines were used at some mills to pump water to operate the waterwheel. Then Watt's rotary engine of 1782 made it possible for steam to drive textile machinery directly. Steam did not replace water power immediately, but by 1835 steam provided three times as much horsepower as water power in the cotton mills of Britain (ibid.; Chapman 1987: 19). American mills were slower to adopt steam, and Temin (1971: 234) estimates that steam provided only about 15 per cent of the power of US textile mills in 1838, although its eventual victory was irresistible. Without steam, textile mills would have been restricted to areas of fast-flowing water, thereby imposing an awkward constraint on the industry until the advent of electric power. The good fortune to have ready access to steam technology enhanced the competitive advantage of textile producers in Europe and North America in the nineteenth century. Steam's application to transportation, especially to shipping, in association with the transition from wooden to iron and steel vessels, had a further positive effect on the textile industries of the Western world, by reducing the shipping costs of imported raw materials and consignments of exports (Harley 1971; 1988). In the twentieth century, however, low transport costs assisted developing countries to invade the domestic textile markets of Britain, the USA and Europe.

The case of man-made fibres is more difficult to assess. Did their appearance, like that of the steam engine, constitute a lucky break for the textile industry or was it the result of systematic research by textile producers themselves? Courtaulds was at the forefront of the development of a commercially viable form of rayon in the 1900s. But Courtaulds cannot be given the credit for the initial discoveries in this area. Courtaulds' achievement was principally in the area of strategy. The company had the wit and good fortune to identify a promising new technology, and was sufficiently flexible to take full advantage of this opportunity (Coleman 1969b). Nylon was developed outside the traditional textile complex by Du Pont, and thus it represented an unexpected gain to user firms (Hounshell and Smith 1988). Later, Terylene was discovered by researchers in the laboratory of a textile company. Thus, the record is mixed. Generally speaking, in the early and mid-twentieth centuries, the emergence of man-made fibres boosted the competitive advantage of textile and apparel firms in the economically advanced countries, and helped them to resist competition from the developing countries. In recent decades, the production of man-made fibres has spread to many developing nations, and the first movers have lost their temporary advantage. Man-made fibres did not affect all segments of the textile industry in the same way. Some firms were actually harmed by their introduction. For instance, the growing popularity of nylon stockings had unpleasant consequences for the Japanese silk-reeling industry. Silk shipments to American hosiery mills failed to recover after the Second World War due to the popularity of nylon (Allen 1958: 80).

Advances in electronics had a significant effect on textile and apparel producers during and after the 1960s, especially those in OECD countries and the high-performance Asian economies. Computer-aided design and, to a lesser extent, computer-aided manufacturing were introduced in the clothing industry. Electronics are now used in sophisticated machinery in all areas of textile production (Hoffman and Rush 1988; Mody and Wheeler 1990). Electronic information systems are used in textile and clothing marketing, linking retailers and producers, and speeding up the response of suppliers to adjustments in demand (Rullani and Zanfei 1988a; 1988b; Camagni and Rabellotti 1992). Computers were not originally designed for the benefit of textile producers, and therefore the exogeneity of this breakthrough is not in question. The earliest applications of the computer were in military and scientific establishments. Only later were computers adopted by the business world. Computer technology has presented the textile complex with many opportunities. Like man-made fibres, computers have tilted the distribution of competitive advantage in favour of countries with a strong technological base. But it is possible that, as a result of the rapid diffusion of computer technology, this gain will prove transitory.

Genetic engineering is the most recent exogenous scientific revolution with major implications for textile producers. Pioneers in the use of genetic engineering in the design of natural fibres have amassed great power. Patenting and the costs of licensing restrict the ability of cultivators, especially in poor countries, to introduce genetically engineered strains of cotton. Textile firms which rely on cotton grown in areas lacking access to this new technology could find themselves at a disadvantage. Agracetus, founded in 1981, a subsidiary of the American conglomerate W. R. Grace, is the global leader in cotton gene research. Gene guns fire DNA into the cells of cotton plants. The aim is to improve the quality of cotton by making it more resistant to tearing, for example. A controversial decision by the American patenting authorities in 1992 granted Agracetus a complete monopoly of genetically engineered cotton products until 2008. Agracetus licensed Monsanto and Calgene to develop new products based upon this technology. Calgene duly engineered a variety of cotton which was less vulnerable to the herbicide bromoxynil, hopefully enabling farmers to use more herbicide without damaging the cotton. Agracetus has been criticized by those who fear that its patent will inhibit research by other scientists and result in high prices for new varieties of cotton. Attempts were made to challenge Agracetus's patent and, in 1994, India revoked it on the grounds that wider access to genetically engineered cotton was in the public interest (Shulman 1994; Thayer 1994; Anon 1995). In the long term, the benefits, and any unforeseen costs, of genetic research into natural fibres will become more widespread, but in the short and medium terms large rents could be extracted by the patent holders, at the expense of cultivators and fibre-using industries. The role of chance has been prominent in these scientific and legal developments.

Technological revolutions cannot be made to order. From the perspective of the textile sector as a whole, and of its constituent firms, most radical technical changes are exogenous. Steam power, computers and genetic engineering fall into this category, as do some key inventions in man-made fibre technology and textile machinery. Textile and apparel manufacturers located in the vicinity of the original inventions usually reap the greatest initial benefits, although these are later diffused over a wider area. Since major technological advances take place in relatively advanced economies, the textile sectors of these countries are in a privileged position, which partially offsets their relatively high cost structures.

EXOGENOUS ECONOMIC FACTORS

Much of the environment of the firm is beyond its control. To a lesser extent, the same is true for a regional industrial cluster. For example, a supply of cheap labour is crucial during the initial growth of a modern textile industry, but textile firms have no control over demographic trends and little over the general level of wages in the economy.

In the analysis of chance events, it is often difficult to make a clear distinction between economic and political factors. A sudden fall in deliveries of wool to manufacturers looks like an economic factor, but this shortage may be the result of a political decision, such as the imposition of a blockade. Nevertheless, it is convenient to try to distinguish between largely economic and largely political influences. Doubt may also exist about the duration of the impact of exogenous factors on the industrial environment. A downturn in the trade cycle is likely to have a transitory effect on the textile industry as a whole, although it could be more serious for individual firms. But a phenomenon such as global warming, which is the outcome of several centuries of industrial activity, may have long-term implications for the textile sector. Predicting the consequences of global warming (should it exist) is an exercise fraught with difficulty (Cline 1992). Its possible effects are numerous. For instance, an increase in average temperatures would reduce the trade of many ski resorts, to the detriment of manufacturers of skiwear. On the other hand, warmer weather in such places as Alaska and Scandinavia would generate an increase in demand for golfing apparel and more fashionable summer clothing. Hundreds of other implications could be imagined and it is impossible to state the net effects, either on global textile demand or on the competitive advantage of particular regions.

Changes in preferences introduce a large element of uncertainty into business. The market for some types of apparel may be destroyed by chance revolutions in taste. The late-Victorian rebellion against melodramatic mourning rituals resulted in the collapse of the market for black mourning crape (Coleman 1969a: 165–6). During the 1950s, traditional menswear manufacturers and retailers were caught unawares by the beginnings of a cultural revolution which swept aside formality in attire (Mort and Thompson 1994). Changes in fashion are more frequent and more pronounced in wealthy societies. In the poorest countries, families produce more of their own clothing, and consumers value cheapness and durability rather than style. As economies develop and living standards rise, apparel becomes a focus of conspicuous consumption. Textile and apparel producers in countries undergoing economic development must show increasing flexibility in their responses to shifts in demand. In wealthy economies, electronic communications enable producers to react more speedily to changes in tastes. But, if there are simultaneous improvements in the quantity and quality of information available to consumers, shifts in preferences may occur more often, and manufacturers will be back at their starting-point.

Fluctuations in raw material prices, caused by variations in agricultural conditions, may have significant effects on textile and apparel producers. A serious disease among silkworms is credited with much of the responsibility for the decline of the Chinese silk industry during the first half of the twentieth century (L. M. Li 1981: 23). Overstocking and resultant environmental damage constrained the size of the Chinese wool crop during the economic reforms of the 1980s (Findlay 1992). The oil price increases of the 1970s had a discouraging effect on the manufacturers and users of synthetic fibres (Shaw and Shaw 1983). Movements in the prices of raw materials have more impact at early stages of the production process: spinners feel the effects of rising input prices more than weavers. Finishers and clothing manufacturers are the least affected by changes in raw material costs. Taking a standard cotton fabric of the 1920s, raw cotton comprised 73 per cent of the cost of the yarn, 55 per cent of the cost of the grey cloth and 43 per cent of the total cost after finishing, packing and shipping (Committee on Industry and Trade 1928: 136). Raw material costs are relatively less important in the case of a designer sweater of the 1990s. Materials account for 13 per cent of the retail price and manufacturing accounts for 33 per cent. The remaining 54 per cent stems from distribution and sales costs. Even a substantial rise in the price of raw materials would not wreak havoc in this segment of the industry (Kay 1993: 293). Regions which produce fashionable textiles and clothing should enjoy a measure of insulation from the consequences of fluctuations in materials costs.

Economic cycles present textile and apparel producers with a number of problems. The turning-points and amplitude of cycles are difficult to predict, so that the cycle appears to incorporate a substantial element of chance. During the early nineteenth century, firms in the British textile industry had a short life expectancy because crises were sharp and small firms lacked financial reserves (Gatrell 1977). A high level of instability in demand militates against investment in new plant and equipment, and may lead to falling competitiveness in the long term. Exporters are affected by foreign economic cycles, which may or may not coincide with those in the home economy. Cyclical fluctuations do not exert a uniform effect throughout the textile industry, especially where there is a low degree of vertical integration, as in Britain until the 1960s and Philadelphia in the early twentieth century. During a cyclical downturn, consumers economize on their purchases of clothing and shops and apparel manufacturers place smaller orders with merchants. The merchants run down their stocks of cloth and make a more than proportional cut in orders for cloth. Weavers react by using up their stocks of yarn, thereby magnifying the reduction in orders for new yarn. Shocks in demand are intensified in the section furthest from the final consumer – spinners bear the brunt of the crisis. The reverse process occurs during an upswing where the rise in orders is magnified at each stage, with the result that spinners do particularly well (Vibert 1966). A movement towards vertical integration would result in greater stability. Sometimes the cyclical process is intensified by speculative fever. During the post-war boom of 1918–20, many textile mills in England were acquired at inflated prices by speculators, using borrowed funds, in the expectation that high profits would continue. When the boom collapsed and prices and profits fell, these mills were saddled with large debts. Speculative crises damage an industry's competitive advantage by increasing its interest costs (Daniels and Jewkes 1928; Bamberg 1988: 83–7).

Since trade cycles operate in all capitalist economies, it is doubtful whether they have a strong effect on the relative competitive advantage of textile regions. Moreover, any discussion of economic cycles impinges on related themes, such as economic growth (Maddison 1991). Macroeconomic forces are exogenous when considered from the perspective of the textile sector. It is difficult to be precise about the relationship between the macroeconomy and competitive advantage. Strong domestic growth, with relatively mild cycles, appears to constitute a good foundation for the prosperity of textile and apparel businesses. But positive factors are offset by the high costs and high exchange rate which are typical of a rapidly expanding economy.

Much strike activity in textiles is linked to the general economic cycle. Workers fight for wage increases during the upswing and attempt to prevent reductions during the downswing. Attempts to reform traditional working practices also risk provoking workers into striking. The balance of power between labour and capital depends upon the relative organizational strengths and attitudes of unions and employers' associations. Some firms may be singled out as targets, while others are protected because of their cooperation with the unions. One recent study analyses labour disputes in Philadelphia's textile and apparel industries between the 1880s and the outbreak of the Second World War. Strikes reflected the economic cycle and changes in the underlying competitiveness of different trades. Although strikes were damaging to the prospects of some firms, they did not exert much control over the long-term competitiveness of Philadelphia's textile sector (Scranton 1989). The uncertainty generated by the possibility of strikes could affect the strategies of firms in several ways. It has been suggested that many British cotton textile producers were reluctant to risk conflict with the unions about labour practices during the 1920s and 1930s. This caution resulted in a slower pace of modernization in the industry (McIvor 1996: 183–210). Workers' ability to disrupt the plans of their employers increases as the national economy becomes more developed. Greater prosperity is often accompanied by the introduction of legislation to protect the rights of unions. During industrialization, textile employers in Europe and the USA attempted to insure themselves against recurring labour unrest by taking stern measures against strikers and agitators (Cohen 1990). Firms in contemporary developing countries endeavour to discourage strike activity by suppressing independent unions. For instance, during a sit-down strike for higher pay at Daewoo Apparel in South Korea in 1985, the company raised a force of security guards, who stormed the factory and restored order. In Export Processing Zones, such as Bataan in the Philippines, which contain many textile and apparel factories, strikes were outlawed by industrialists and their political allies in the 1970s, in an attempt to pre-empt any threat to the authority of management (Chisolm, Kabeer, Mitter and Howard 1986: 45–6).

Fluctuations in exchange rates may be due to a mixture of economic and political factors. Most governments take an interest in the exchange rate, even if they choose to regulate it indirectly. An overvalued currency damages industries which are highly dependent on exports. British textile exports struggled in the early 1920s because sterling was maintained at an unrealistically high level (Wolcott 1992). Those Japanese textile producers who survived the 1923 Tokyo earthquake benefited from the ensuing devaluation of the yen (Abe 1994: 16). But the gains from devaluation are usually transitory, since wages and import costs are raised. For a brief and disastrous period, in 1930–1, Japan submitted to the gold standard at an unsustainably high exchange rate. Tokyo's decision to abandon the gold standard in late 1931 led to a depreciation of the yen against sterling by 42 per cent by 1933, enabling the volume of Japanese cotton textile exports to double between 1931 and 1935 (Robertson 1991: 96–7). More recently, in the 1980s and 1990s, Japan's textile industry has been squeezed by a rising yen, intensifying an already difficult competitive environment for high-cost producers. The soaring yen contributed to the relocation of Japanese textile firms to other parts of Asia and further afield (Steven 1990). German textile producers also reacted to a strong exchange rate by transferring labour-intensive work to factories in other countries. These relocations show that some firms responded positively to the challenge of rising currencies.

Exchange rates ought not be considered in isolation from other economic variables. The level of the exchange rate reflects the overall prosperity of an economy. Countries with high exchange rates are likely to enjoy other attributes of prosperity, such as high incomes, and these conditions react upon the competitiveness of the textile and clothing sector. Strong exchange rates and high wages in Japan and Germany are the consequences of impressive records of economic growth since 1950. This success is damaging to branches of the textile sector which produce goods of low value added. Individual firms and industries are powerless to influence either the national growth rate or the level of per capita income. They must accept these variables as given and adapt their strategies accordingly.

Changing patterns in the development of the world economy are also beyond the control of firms and industries (Rostow 1978; Foreman-Peck 1983; Maddison 1991). Comparative advantage may evolve in unexpected ways. Europeans and Americans, in the mid-nineteenth century, failed to predict the rapidity with which Japan and, to a lesser extent, India and China would industrialize and become powerful competitors in Eastern textile markets. In 1950, few predicted the rise of Asian economies, such as South Korea and Indonesia, and the threat they would pose to established textile producers in the UK, the USA and Japan. These developments were exogenous, when observed from the positions of textile manufacturers in the economically advanced countries. Such firms needed to adapt to the new global conditions if they were to survive. Variations in the performance of the world economy as a whole affect the opportunities open to textile and apparel producers. Competition for orders should have been less severe during the long boom of 1951–73 than it was in the following period of slow growth and instability. On the other hand, in the absence of buoyant world economic conditions after 1950, the East Asian countries could have been frustrated in their attempts to challenge the textile sectors of older industrial nations.

The identification of a chance, or exogenous, event depends upon the perspective of the onlooker. A student of world economic history might not regard the impressive economic development of Japan since 1868 as a manifestation of chance or exogenous factors. But the rise of Japan was interpreted as a misfortune by the executives of textile companies in the USA and Europe whose markets were undermined by Japanese goods.

POLITICAL FACTORS

Political events often influence the environment in which firms and industries operate. Few industries are in a position to control the direction of national and international politics, although they may be able to affect political decisions at the margin, through lobbying for tariffs, subsidies and changes in labour laws.

The rise and fall of the European empires, especially the British empire, had profound implications for the development of the global textile industry and for the place of particular regions within this sector. Increasing commercial and political intercourse between Europeans and Asians during the sixteenth and seventeenth centuries, introduced many European consumers to new varieties of textiles and stimulated European manufacturers to imitate imported goods (Chaudhuri 1978: 237–312; Lemire 1991). Import substitution policies were successful in Europe, and most of all in the UK, where the world's first fully mechanized textile industry emerged. The dominant Western European nations, Britain and France, were involved in a global military struggle, in the mid-eighteenth century, from which the British emerged triumphant (Kennedy 1976: 1–107; Meyer 1980; Baugh 1988; Cain and Hopkins 1993). Britain became the leading power on the Indian subcontinent during the eighteenth century, but the British textile industry did not send exports to India until much later. It took some time for the British to establish a competitive advantage over Indian textiles, and it was in the interests of the East India Company to encourage Indian textile producers. The victory of the British over the French in India, in the eighteenth century, had a powerful delayed effect on the world textile economy in the nineteenth century. As the mechanized textile industry expanded in Britain during the early nineteenth century, its exports were constrained by tariff barriers in the USA and continental Europe. Alternative markets had to be found, and India became the main overseas consumer of Lancashire's cotton cloth, absorbing one-third of its exports by volume (and one-quarter by value) in the late 1870s (Farnie 1979: 117). If France, instead of Britain, had controlled India, French textiles would have dominated the Indian import market in the nineteenth century and Manchester would have been a less significant actor than Lyons in world textiles. If the French navy had controlled the sea routes, French exports would have swept other markets in Latin America, Africa and Asia. In the 1880s, the UK supplied four-fifths of the world's cotton cloth exports, a proportion which would have been inconceivable in the absence of Britain's imperial supremacy, as projected by the Royal Navy. It is not suggested that Britain built an empire in order to sell cloth. The emergence of the UK as the leading world power in the eighteenth century fortuitously bestowed upon British textile manufacturers a golden opportunity for profit. If France had been the dominant power in India, British textiles would have faced substantial tariffs in this market. Notwithstanding their competitive advantage, British exporters would have suffered in a world controlled by other nations.

Nineteenth-century Lancashire was lucky in India, but it was unlucky in North America. The conflict between the UK and the thirteen colonies, which resulted in American independence, had significant consequences for the development of the world textile industry. If the American colonies had remained within the British empire, it is unlikely that they would have built a mechanized textile industry with such determination. The US textile industry was unable to compete with its British rival, except in the coarsest wares, in the nineteenth century, and relied on tariff protection to ensure its survival (Bils 1984; Temin 1988; Harley 1992). Had it not been for the American revolution, the trend towards specialization in textiles in Lancashire and Yorkshire would have been even more pronounced. While the American revolution was not a dispute about textiles, the right of Americans to control their own economic policy was a key issue. What matters is that American independence created a nationalistic environment which was conducive to the growth of a large and heavily protected textile industry during the nineteenth century (Pincus 1977). The lack of a substantial US overseas empire was a disadvantage for the American textile industry. US manufactures were admitted to the Philippines free of duty, under a preferential tariff agreement signed in 1909 (Stifel 1963: 60); but America had no equivalent of India. Although the Chinese market was of considerable value to American producers, it was not under their political control. Access to large captive markets abroad would have increased the size of the US textile industry, but if this empire had crumbled American firms would have faced severe problems. Export-oriented, imperial textile industries are destined to be unstable in the long term.

The examples of India and Ireland show that the British were not prepared to tolerate competition in textiles from subordinate parts of their empire during the classical period of the Industrial Revolution. British tariffs against Indian textiles were increased on a number of occasions between 1797 and 1819 (Farnie 1979: 96), but the Indians were denied the power to protect their own textile producers from British exports. In Ireland, the

British manipulated tariffs in order to suppress the fledgling mechanized textile industry and to secure the Irish market for English manufactures. Free trade between Britain and Ireland was not introduced until 1801, by which time the English cotton industry had established its competitive advantage. Prior to 1801 the English were not prepared to risk open competition with Ireland (O'Hearn 1994). Had Ireland obtained independence at the end of the eighteenth century, it is unlikely that it would have acquiesced in British attempts to destroy its cotton industry. These cases reveal the extent to which the geography of the world textile industry was influenced by exogenous political and military factors. The superior efficiency of the British textile industry was not a sufficient cause of its leadership in world markets. Overseas markets had to be opened and kept open, if necessary by force, while potentially troublesome competitors were denied access to the British domestic market until the British felt completely secure. Mercantilist policies were as important in Britain as they were in the USA or France. Britain did not abolish tariffs on imports of textiles until the 1840s.

Japan's rise to prominence in textiles in the early twentieth century threatened the dominance of existing exporters, especially the UK. Compared with other Asian countries, Japan was fortunate in that it possessed sufficient resilience to maintain its political independence and the initiative to emulate Western industrial development. By the early 1900s, Japan was an imperial state, with colonies in Korea and Taiwan and a naval treaty with the UK. British naval forces were inadequate to provide complete protection for British interests against potential European aggressors in the Far East, and an alliance with Japan was considered to be a cheap solution to this problem. Japan was also fortunate in so far as it was not regarded as a major threat to Western interests until after its victory in the Russo-Japanese war of 1904–5. A new power was emerging, over which Britain and the USA could exert no control and relatively little influence once the unequal commercial treaties had lapsed in 1911 (Kennedy 1976: 205–37; B. L. Reynolds 1986; Minami 1987: 197–256; Sugiyama 1988a: 1–76). The First World War gave Japanese textile producers a considerable boost. Japanese firms took advantage of the shipping shortages, which disrupted the exports of the leading belligerents, in order to undermine the markets for British and European textiles in Asia and Latin America (Kirk and Simmons 1981). Although the war did not create Japan's competitive advantage, it was responsible for accelerating Japan's drive into export markets. Restrictions were placed on imports of Japanese textiles by many countries, including the USA and British colonies, in the 1930s, but these measures were not designed to eliminate the Japanese challenge. Western textile industrialists simply had to accept that their governments would not risk a serious confrontation with Japan over a secondary matter such as textiles when wider strategic issues were at stake (Kennedy 1976: 267–98; Dupree 1990; Wurm 1993: 193–287). In the political climate of the 1830s or the 1880s, the Western response could have been rather different. The Second World War had disastrous effects on Japanese textiles and the industry failed to regain its pre-war level of output until the late 1950s. Captive markets were lost in Taiwan and Korea, but the most serious blow was the disappearance of the market on the Chinese mainland. It was difficult for Japan, which was short of foreign exchange, to obtain good-quality raw materials in the 1950s. Newly independent Asian countries followed import substitution policies, and American political pressure deterred Japan from reconstructing its trading relations with China (Allen 1958). But Japan's new role as an ally of the USA and UK in the cold war against communism ensured that its textile interests were not totally disregarded. Japanese prosperity and loyalty to the alliance were thought to depend on the provision of adequate export opportunities. Falling trade barriers during the 1950s helped Japan to find new markets, in the British Commonwealth, for example. Japan actually increased its share of world textile exports relative to its major rival, the UK, during the 1950s (S. J. Wells 1964). World political events had a mixture of effects on the Japanese textile industry. The First World War was a boon for Japanese producers; the Second World War constituted a major setback; while the cold war facilitated the partial rehabilitation of Japan into the international trading community (Hunsberger 1964; Shiraishi 1989; Choucri, North and Yamakage 1992).

The growth of Japanese power between 1890 and 1940 was accompanied by a decline in the global economic and political position of the UK. In Asian markets, these developments were closely related. During the interwar period, Britain was losing its hold over the Indian subcontinent. The protection of Indian industries was tolerated by the UK, although Lancashire remained sufficiently influential to ensure that tariff levels were moderated and that British textiles received a preference over imports from Japan (Dewey 1978; Chatterji 1992). War against Japan, between 1941 and 1945, and the stimulus which this gave to the Indian, and later Malayan, independence movements, destroyed any remaining political hold which the British had over Asian textile markets. Britain no longer had the power to force open its traditional Asian markets for textiles. If Britain's imperial authority had been preserved after 1945, its textile firms would have continued to find easy markets within the empire, irrespective of their declining competitiveness.

One of the most important developments in the world textile economy after 1945 was the emergence of new Asian producing and exporting countries. Political circumstances contributed to the success of these countries. If Japan had either won the Second World War or fought its opponents to a stalemate, it would have retained an empire in North-east Asia, together with some or all of the territories conquered from the Europeans in 1941–2. Under the Japanese imperial system, the main functions of colonies were to buy Japanese manufactures and to supply the imperial centre with primary products (Myers and Peattie 1984). Some mechanized textile production was undertaken under Japanese rule in Taiwan and Korea in the 1930s, but it is unlikely that the Japanese would have allowed colonial textile production to reach the stage at which it posed a challenge to the dominance of Osaka. Exports from the Japanese empire to the rest of the world would have been held back by continuing international tensions. In the 1950s and 1960s, the perceived communist threat to Western interests in Asia was sufficiently alarming for the Americans to take an active role in supporting more or less any non-communist government in the area. Taiwan and South Korea, in particular, received large doses of American aid, including cheap raw materials and capital for industrial development. US aid to South Korea included grants of $176 million worth of raw cotton. American and United Nations grants were provided for the purchase of modern textile plant and machinery. For example, Keumsong Spinning received a US grant of $102,000 for new equipment in October 1958 (McNamara 1992). Taking the South Korean economy as a whole, between 1953 and 1961 US assistance financed 70 per cent of total imports and 75 per cent of total fixed capital formation (Haggard, Kim and Moon 1991: 852). American markets were kept open for Taiwanese and South Korean textiles and apparel because it was deemed important to strengthen the economic and political systems of these countries.

Asian countries enjoyed several other strokes of good fortune. Adverse political conditions in China in the 1940s induced a number of textile capital-ists to migrate to Hong Kong and Taiwan, where they helped to build up competitive industrial sectors (Wong 1988). Britain's desire for good rela-tions with Asian Commonwealth countries resulted in a continuation of their preferential terms of access to the UK market in the 1950s and con-tributed to the laxity of the quantitative restrictions which were imposed on Commonwealth textiles and clothing in the 1960s (Singleton 1991: 114–40). Textile producers in Asian countries gained as a result of the uneasy balance of power in their region. Neither the Western powers nor the communists were absolutely dominant. The communist countries were not strong enough to overrun the majority of Asian countries, but the communist threat was serious enough to dissuade the Americans and their allies from withdrawing their patronage from states such as Taiwan and South Korea.

The insular economic attitudes of Asia's most populous countries, China and India, served to lessen the competition encountered by other Asian textile and clothing exporters. If the People's Republic of China had pursued a vigorous export-oriented policy earlier, in the 1960s and 1970s, the smaller exporters of the region would have faced stiff competition in export mar-kets. Rising Chinese textile and garment exports, during the current era of reform, pose a formidable threat to the trade of other nations, simply because Chinese wages are so low. Hong Kong, however, has gained from the expansion of the Chinese export sector, as a result of its role as an entrepôt and the opportunities which have arisen for cooperation with Chi-nese producers in coastal areas near the colony (Sung 1991; Anderson and

Park 1992). India also chose a form of semi-autarky after 1947, in which the interests of its textile mills were subordinated to those of village handicraft workers. With different policies, India could have become a far more potent force in world textile markets (Mazumdar 1991; Leadbeater 1993). Furthermore, unfavourable political conditions in some other Asian states helped to pave the way for Hong Kong, South Korea and Taiwan. Countries such as Malaysia and Indonesia, which were riven by racial jealousies, experienced a slower rate of economic development and did not achieve competitiveness on world textile and apparel markets until the 1980s. If these internal divisions had been overcome, Malaysia and Indonesia could have followed the North-east Asian growth path in the 1960s. Considering the impressive performance of Hong Kong, South Korea and Taiwan, a strong case can be made for suggesting that they were in the right place at the right time.

It has been demonstrated that the outcome of wars, and the ensuing peace settlements, define the international environment within which textile industries compete. But the direct effects of war are usually less traumatic. For instance, during the First World War, a large portion of the French textile industry was occupied by the Germans, but post-war recovery was relatively swift (Aftalion 1923). Some textile firms actually profited from war. Raw material shortages, between 1914 and 1918, led to a fall in textile production in the UK. Many firms found that rising prices, especially on government contracts, more than compensated them for declining activity and rising costs. Large profits were made (Singleton 1994). The Second World War had a similarly benign impact on the UK textile industry (Lacey 1947). Between 1941 and 1945 the Japanese textile industry suffered much more serious losses from bombing, but labour productivity had recovered to the pre-war level by 1950 and the main constraints on the industry's revival were Allied restrictions on industrial activity and the dislocation of traditional export markets (Allen 1958: 90–1).

Political developments have helped to mould the evolution of the world textile economy. Exogenous political and military events were parts of the process of allocating export markets. Britain's textile industry was sustained by naval power in the nineteenth century, while Japan's position as a strong regional power underpinned its textile industry's success before the Second World War. After 1950, certain East Asian political entities took advantage of American aid and protection and established competitive textile and garment industries.

CONCLUSION

This chapter has illustrated the impact of chance (or exogenous) events on the development of a major world industry. Perhaps chance is an unfortunate description for the phenomena investigated in this chapter. Chance implies randomness, but meteorologists, macroeconomists and scientific and military historians have convincing explanations for many of these 'chance' events. A sense of perspective is crucial to our understanding of the role of exogenous forces in the development of the textile sector. Seen from the perspective of the firm or the industry, fluctuations in the business cycle, technical progress, global warming, developments in the world economy and changes in global political arrangements are exogenous influences. The timing and effects of these phenomena are difficult to predict with any accuracy. Events unfold in ways which emphasize the contingency of the business environment. A firm which adapts its strategy to take into account changes in its environment has a better chance of survival. Successful adaptation also involves an element of chance because firms must interpret their environment on the basis of partial information. Making the right choice requires a mixture of skill and good fortune. Perhaps more skill and more good fortune are needed by businesses in the complex environments of the advanced industrial countries than they are in the simpler conditions prevailing in the developing world. Where adaptation necessitates upgrading, the opportunities for error are greater. The alacrity with which textile and apparel businesses in certain parts of Asia have responded to favourable economic and political conditions since the 1950s suggests that their dilemmas are less challenging.

8

GOVERNMENT

Government policy is an important aspect of the business environment, and it may have either positive or negative effects on competitive advantage. Many of the links between government policy and the fortunes of a particular industry are indirect. For instance, the government affects the quality of human inputs by its education strategy. Excessive taxes and unproductive government spending are likely to damage the prospects of many industries. The reciprocal negotiation of tariff reductions will benefit those exporters who have the capability to compete internationally (Porter 1990: 617–82). More directly, regional policies, such as the provision of industrial parks, research facilities and consultancy services, may strengthen existing industrial clusters. Subsidies of various kinds may assist manufacturers to upgrade their plant and machinery. The most common form of direct interference in the textile sector is the granting of protection against imports. Porter argues that the temporary protection of infant industries in developing countries may be justified under three conditions. First, there should be enough firms to generate strong domestic rivalry. Second, the industry should have a realistic prospect of becoming competitive. Third, protection must be strictly limited in duration. Porter denies that there are grounds for giving mature industries a temporary respite from international competition in order to facilitate modernization. Industries are unlikely to regain their competitive advantage if they are shielded from their rivals (ibid.: 665–6). Government policy may be influenced by lobbying. Textile lobbyists tend to emphasize tariffs and import controls. This distinguishes textiles from such sectors as aircraft and armaments, where lobbying often focuses on subsidies and state procurement.

It is easy to understand the reasons for intervention in strategic industries. Engineering, electronics and aircraft industries may be deemed important for the preservation of national security. But textiles and clothing are not strategic industries. A politically convincing rationale for intervening in textiles must be sought elsewhere. Textile and apparel factories absorb surplus labour during industrialization with its attendant population growth. Since the textile and clothing industries are labour-intensive, they also employ large work-forces in mature economies, many of whom may be voters. Unless overall unemployment is negligible, governments are reluctant to see hordes of textile workers thrown out of work.

The first section considers the development of state policies towards textile industries in the eighteenth, nineteenth and early twentieth centuries. In the second section, we examine the policies of developing countries since 1945. The third section analyses the textile strategies of advanced industrial countries since 1945.

THE STATE AND TEXTILES BEFORE 1939

Government policies encouraged the early development of factory textile industries in Europe and North America. Europe's mercantilist states, in the seventeenth and eighteenth centuries, had no compunction about protecting their textile producers from foreign competition.

Indian cotton goods, imported by trading giants such as the East India Company, began to challenge the wool, linen and silk textile industries of Europe in the seventeenth century (Chaudhuri 1978). Reacting to pressure from powerful established textile interests and their political representatives, in 1701 the English Parliament banned imports of painted, dyed, printed and stained Indian cotton cloth, except for re-export. High tariffs were imposed on imports of plain Indian cotton cloth, and in 1721 it was made an offence to wear any garment of painted, stained or dyed cotton, thereby terminating the importation of plain fabrics for finishing in English plants. English consumers, however, retained their taste for cottons. Fustian, which was a mixture of cotton and linen, was produced in England as a substitute for pure cotton cloth. Manufacturers responded to new consumer tastes by improving, and eventually mechanizing, their methods of spinning and weaving cotton. The ratio of cotton to linen in fustian rose, until pure cotton fabrics were being made. The progress made by the English cotton industry was acknowledged in 1774, when the ban on the use of cotton fabrics was lifted (Lemire 1991; O'Brien, Griffiths and Hunt 1991). Indian competition, fostered by the East India Company, was now seen as a threat to both the cotton and woollen industries. Parliament increased tariffs against Indian textiles on twelve separate occasions between 1797 and 1819, and did not begin to reduce them until 1826, by which time Lancashire's mechanized cotton industry had established a strong competitive advantage. Tariff policy was also manipulated to the detriment of the fragile, but potentially threatening, Irish cotton industry (O'Hearn 1994). Lancashire textiles were later forced upon India. The East India Company, as the Western distributor of Indian textiles, sought to protect Indian manufacturers by restricting imports from Britain. But Parliament abolished the East India Company's monopoly of trade in 1813, because it was anxious to encourage British exports and reduce domestic unemployment and unrest (Webster 1990). Once Lanca-

166

shire had gained free entry to large markets in India, its yarn and cloth exports enjoyed increasing success. The subcontinent soon became Lancashire's premier outlet. Britain's own duties on imported cotton textiles were finally withdrawn in 1846 and were not reimposed until 1932, when Lancashire's competitive advantage was waning. Infant industry protection, and the forcible opening of overseas markets, assisted the British cotton industry to establish itself as a world leader.

Following the abrogation of the Eden trade treaty with England in 1793, French industry received generous protection. A study of the cotton and hosiery industries in Troyes and the Aube describes how spinning was mechanized behind the tariff wall (Heywood 1981; 1994). Factory spindleage in the Aube rose from 7,950 in 1806 to 85,500 in the early 1840s. Annual output of yarn per worker increased from 196kg in 1806 to 706kg in the early 1840s. The number of hosiery frames also rose from 1,000 in 1791 to 12,000 in 1860. When tariffs were reduced in 1860, the textile industry survived, despite the pessimistic expectations of employers, and Troyes remained competitive in some specialities. Since tariff cuts did not ruin Troyes, perhaps they should have occurred earlier, in line with the recommendation of leading French economists (Ratcliffe 1978: 71–4). During the nineteenth century, the government of Saxony subsidized the production of worsted yarn and specialized worsted spinning equipment. British competition in these areas was comparatively weak, and Saxony developed a lucrative niche (Sabel, Herrigel, Deeg and Kazis 1989: 386).

State intervention helped the early growth of the American textile industry. American markets were flooded with Indian textiles in 1816, after the conclusion of the wars between Britain and France, and Britain and the USA. American textile interests lobbied the legislature for protection. Francis Cabot Lowell, a prominent Boston cotton mill promoter, mounted a successful campaign for the introduction of a fixed duty of 6.25 cents on all imported cotton fabrics priced below 25 cents per yard, and a 25 per cent *ad valorem* tariff on more expensive fabrics. The 1816 tariff gave most protection to Massachusetts, where the mills of Lowell and his associates produced the coarse fabrics which were most vulnerable to Indian competition. A more liberal attitude was shown towards imports of fine British cloth made from cotton grown in the South, in order to safeguard the interests of American plantation owners. Moreover, the Rhode Island mills which produced finer textiles, were owned by rival investors, and Lowell was not inclined to press their case (Temin 1988: 897–8). Further tariffs, in 1824 and 1828, made it even more costly to import coarse fabrics. Their protective effect was magnified by falling prices. The negotiation of tariffs in the early nineteenth century involved a complex trade-off between different interest groups and their friends in Congress (Pincus 1977). But growth did not lead to competitiveness. Taussig (1931: 136) argued that infant-industry tariffs should have been scrapped by the mid-1820s or, at the latest, the mid-1830s.

David (1975: 95–173) went further, and maintained that the selective subsidization of model mills would have been a better policy. Tariffs damaged the welfare of consumers, but model mills would have encouraged local entrepreneurs by showing them how to operate modern technology and manage a factory. Both Taussig and David appear to have believed that competitiveness was within the grasp of American cotton mills. A less optimistic conclusion is reached by Bils (1984), who estimates that the New England cotton industry would have been devastated by repeal of the tariff in the 1830s. A comparison of the prices of US textiles and imports from England (net of tariff and shipping charges) suggests that free trade would have wiped out most US mills as late as 1860. In Canada, where British and US cotton textiles faced identical tariffs, American firms failed to make much headway in the 1850s, and supplied a mere 12 per cent of the import market in 1860. Despite half a century of protection, the US cotton industry remained uncompetitive (Harley 1992). The US textile industry continued to hide behind tariff barriers during the late nineteenth and early twentieth centuries (Hawke 1975; J. C. Brown 1995: 504).

A resort to massive protectionism was more difficult for Japan. Under the commercial treaties imposed on Japan by the USA and Britain in 1858, import duties on cotton and wool textiles could not be raised above 5 per cent *ad valorem*. The Americans were prepared to tolerate 20 per cent tariffs, but the British persuaded them to insist upon more stringent terms. Japan did not regain complete tariff autonomy until 1911 (Sugiyama 1988a: 34–6, 236). Otsuka, Ranis and Saxonhouse (1988: 70, 226–7) argue that even the limited tariffs permitted in Japan offered a significant level of effective protection to cotton mills in the 1890s. But central and local authorities were forced to search for additional methods of stimulating industrialization. Under the Meiji government's development programme, the state established two model silk-reeling plants in 1870 and 1873 and equipped them with machinery brought from continental Europe. Although the earliest cotton spinning mills, Kagoshima in 1867 and Sakai in 1870, were built by the Satsuma clan, between 1879 and 1885 the government constructed and operated the Aichi and Hiroshima spinning mills and subsidized fifteen new private mills. These became known as the 2,000 spindle mills. The state provided interest-free credit and advice to entrepreneurs wishing to import English textile machinery. Equipment was also imported by the government for resale on easy terms to textile masters. The 2,000 spindle mills were financial failures, but they exerted a useful demonstration effect, teaching the Japanese about Western textile technology and factory organization. Japan's investment in education, including the universities, also contributed to its industrial success (T. C. Smith 1955: 54–66; Seki 1956: 14–18; Yonekawa 1984; Minami 1987: 181–2, 207–9). The private sector soon made good progress and Japan became a large net exporter of cotton yarn by 1900. Of course, the textile industry would have grown without the help of the state.

Japanese society was highly sophisticated and found it relatively easy to assimilate Western methods (E. L. Jones 1988). It also possessed plenty of cheap labour. But the state accelerated the process of development by creating a favourable environment and providing limited protection and subsidies. Perhaps more heavy-handed methods would have been less conducive to the growth of enterprise.

India's story is somewhat different. Before the First World War, Indian textile producers received no protection against imports (Otsuka, Ranis and Saxonhouse 1988: 224–5). The British authorities adopted a policy of *laissez-faire* and had no inclination to favour Indian mills over those in Lancashire (Harnetty 1972). The main contributions of the Raj to the growth of the textile industry were the provision of a stable environment for investors and the integration of India into the multilateral trading system. Regardless of official neglect, a large and efficient mill sector emerged in the second half of the nineteenth century, taking advantage of low wages. By 1906, India supplied 77 per cent of China's yarn imports. It had won this market from British mills (B. L. Reynolds 1986: 143). Rising government expenditure during the First World War necessitated the imposition of a cotton textile tariff in 1917. Further substantial tariff rises occurred in the 1920s, much to the satisfaction of Indian capitalists. Cloth production in Indian cotton mills more than doubled between the eve of the First World War and 1930, while imports of cotton cloth fell by more than half (Sandberg 1974: 185; Dewey 1978; Chatterji 1992). Although protection assisted the Indian industry to expand between the wars, it did not improve its competitiveness. Productivity levels were now improving much faster in Japan than in India. A recent study argues that the Indian mills would not have been able to compete with the Japanese in the 1920s and 1930s in the absence of protection. Indian workers obstructed the introduction of new technology and the implementation of more efficient staffing methods, in order to protect their jobs (Wolcott 1994).

What conclusions can be reached about the state's role in fostering textile industrialization? Britain experienced high levels of protection in the eighteenth century, followed by the vigorous promotion of exports by the builders of empire, and enjoyed an astonishingly successful transformation in its textile sector. Eventually, the British were able to dismantle protection without damaging their competitive position. Since the British were first to industrialize, perhaps they were most in need of infant industry protection, even though it was introduced for reasons unrelated to the needs of potential cotton manufacturers. America's case was different. Here protection led to the growth of a large but internationally uncompetitive textile sector. Labour costs were high and therefore the USA lacked a comparative advantage in textiles. Infant industry protection of US textiles did not improve the welfare of the nation. India and Japan made good progress in modernizing their textile sectors before 1914, despite their open trade policies. Both countries had cheap labour and easy access to imported technology, and these factors were crucial. The Japanese government's use of limited measures for stimulating industrialization probably accelerated the growth of the mill sector, and may have helped it to overtake the Indian industry. Governments could not generate competitive advantage where the underlying conditions were unfavourable, as in the USA, but they could give industry a helping hand, as happened in Japan.

DEVELOPING COUNTRIES SINCE 1945

Labour-intensive techniques are capable of competing with advanced, capital-intensive methods in the textile sector. Developing countries are aware of this fact, and consequently the establishment of a modern textile industry is often an early objective of industrial policy. This section concentrates on Asia, where textile-based industrialization has had its greatest successes. The British pattern, starting with import substitution and leading to an export drive, has been replicated in many Asian countries. It is doubtful, however, whether government policies were the critical factor in the development of textile industries in Asia. Market forces would have ensured similar outcomes, and the success of government policies was more apparent than real.

The South Korean government, assisted by the American aid administration, adopted a vigorously interventionist policy in the 1950s (McNamara 1992). An officially sponsored cartel was formed among the fifteen or so leading textile producers. This Spinners and Weavers' Association of Korea worked closely with the authorities. Textile imports were strictly controlled in order to give local firms a free run of the domestic market. Firms which made generous contributions to the coffers of the ruling party could expect to obtain the capital which they needed for modernization. They received grants and subsidized investment loans through the aid system and the government banks, and were provided with licences to import textile machinery. As a result of protection, high profits were made, and these were either reinvested in additional plant or siphoned off to buy further political favours. Foreign direct investment was generally discouraged because the government, resentful of Korea's previous colonial status, wished to limit outside ownership of the economy. Labour was kept in check by harsh measures against agitators. South Korea became self-sufficient in textiles in 1957. The government proceeded to prohibit imports on the grounds that they were now unnecessary (Amsden 1989: 65). Export subsidies were available to counteract the overvaluation of the won, but Korean textiles and clothing could not attain a competitive advantage in world markets during the 1950s.

An export-oriented policy was adopted by South Korea in the 1960s. The won was devalued by 50 per cent in 1961. This led to protests from the textile industry concerning the rising costs of imported raw cotton and machinery. Imported inputs were vital to the textile sector and, since exports remained underdeveloped, a fall in the exchange rate was regarded as deleterious to the industry's profitability. Hence, new subsidy programmes were introduced to compensate firms for their rising costs. From 1965 onwards, the Park government linked the distribution of subsidies to past export performance. Export targets were not wistful aspirations. They were commands to be obeyed, whether or not they could be fulfilled profitably. If companies failed to meet their targets, they risked losing favour and missing out in the next round of subsidies and import licences. It has been estimated that, in the absence of export subsidies and tax relief, Korean cotton cloth exports would have cost 27 per cent more in 1967 and knitted goods 10 per cent more (G. Brown 1973: 150). Considered on their own terms, these policies were highly successful. Korean textile exports, as a share of the industry's output, rose from 4.8 per cent in 1963 to 47.2 per cent in 1973 (Amsden 1989: 67). But Korean citizens had to pay more for clothes and faced higher taxes. Competitive advantage was bought at the expense of local consumers and taxpayers. In view of Korea's potential comparative advantage in textiles, and the example of Hong Kong, the elaborate industrial policies of the authorities in Seoul were largely unnecessary.

The switch from import substitution to export orientation was not part of a master plan. Political upheavals led to changes of government in 1960, 1961 and 1964. South Korea was under persistent pressure from Washington to end its economic isolation. Whereas the South Korean regime of the 1950s was unimaginative, those of the 1960s were technocratic (Haggard, Kim and Moon 1991). By the 1970s, Korean planners were focusing on the next wave of industries, including heavy engineering and shipbuilding, so that textiles were given a lower priority. When the heavy industries ran into difficulties in the late 1970s, textiles temporarily returned to favour. A Textile Industry Modernization Act was passed in 1979. This sought to promote vertical integration, diversification, re-equipment, R&D and improved methods of marketing. A Fund for Textile Industry Modernization was established in 1980 to finance these objectives (Moon 1989: 200–1). The measures taken to assist the textile industry in the 1980s were modest by earlier standards, amounting to 2 per cent of the industry's value added in 1986–8 (Hamilton and Kim 1990: 172–3). Suffering from rising labour costs and a high won, the Korean textile industry has found it difficult to maintain its competitive advantage. The 1979 modernization legislation and subsequent initiatives are reminiscent of policies adopted by European countries to aid their declining textile industries.

Taiwan's textile policy passed through similar stages. Textile entrepreneurs, who fled from Shanghai to Taiwan in the late 1940s and early 1950s, were given a head start in the industry, as a reward for their loyalty. The state provided them with cotton, credit and markets, and for a time they were insulated from risk (Gold 1988: 188). Compulsory trade associations, such as the Cotton Textile Manufacturers' Association, were established. These bodies regulated prices and competition, and coordinated the policies of different firms and sections. Several mills were owned by, and run for the benefit of, the ruling Nationalist Party and other worthy causes, including the veterans' association (Silin 1976: 21–2). Import substitution was the policy regime in the 1950s. Textiles and apparel were deemed spearhead industries in the First Four Year Plan of 1953. According to one investigation, in 1965 the textile industry as a whole enjoyed an effective rate of protection of 250 per cent (Sun 1969: 114). Opportunities for further import substitution diminished in the 1960s. Substantial improvements had been achieved in technical efficiency, and the government turned its attention to export promotion by means of various incentives. Exports as a share of the output of the textile and apparel sector rose from 20 per cent in 1961 to 39 per cent in 1969 (Ho 1978: 201). Export processing zones were established to attract foreign, and especially Japanese, capital. Trade associations monitored the behaviour of exporters to make sure that they did not undercut one another. But, by the late 1970s, Taiwan faced problems of faltering competitiveness which were similar to those of South Korea. A Ten Year Textile Industry Revitalization Plan was introduced in 1980. It aimed to encourage vertical integration, the upgrading of product lines, higher R&D and the installation of new machinery. Small firms objected to the government's plans for mergers, as they had done in Lancashire in the 1940s, and this proved a serious constraint on the government's ability to implement the Ten Year Plan (Moon 1989: 203).

Indonesian textile policy in the 1950s and 1960s reflected the state's socialist inclinations and its determination to favour indigenous entrepreneurs over the Chinese. Many of the decisions taken in those decades retarded the development of the textile industry (Palmer 1972). Acting through the state-owned Bank Industri Negara, the government built and operated a number of mills in the 1950s. Plans to transfer them to private, or joint public and private, ownership were quietly forgotten. But socialized industry was not a great success. Indonesia's state-owned weaving mills lagged behind private mills in technical efficiency. Many of the state mills were incompetently managed (H. Hill 1982). State policies in relation to private sector textile production were equally unsatisfactory. Under the Benteng programme of 1950, the right to import raw materials was put into the hands of a clique of indigenous traders, who made the most of this opportunity to exploit their customers. When the Benteng policy was abandoned in 1957, the government established a Federation of Homogeneous Enterprises to oversee textiles and related industries. Although the nominal purpose of this body was to facilitate development, it was in reality a scheme to enable politicians and officials to collect bribes in return for raw materials allocations (Robison 1986: 81). Behind a facade of planning, the Sukarno regime used industrial policy to extract rent, reward its friends and punish its enemies.

The Soeharto regime, installed in 1966, began to dismantle some of the restrictions on the textile industry and showed greater willingness to accept inward foreign direct investment. Production of textiles and clothing expanded rapidly in the 1970s, and Indonesia's exports became more competitive. New representative organizations were created, including the Indonesian Textile Association. These associations worked closely with the Department of Trade. In the 1980s, business groups sought, and sometimes achieved, greater autonomy from the state. When ten prominent leaders of the Indonesian Textile Association were granted a monopoly over the distribution of raw cotton and synthetic fibre in 1986, disgruntled spinners formed a rival organization to protest against favouritism. Amid widespread surprise, the government revoked the monopoly. This signified that the state was beginning to loosen its grip over business and that it was prepared to allow real competition (MacIntyre 1990: 66–141). Government interference in Indonesia delayed the achievement of competitive advantage until the 1980s.

Thailand's strategy in the 1950s and 1960s was apparently more liberal. Protection was relatively modest. Japanese firms were welcomed into Thailand in the 1960s. Joint ventures with local entrepreneurs were given tax holidays and duty-free access to imported raw materials and machinery. Then, in the 1970s, the introduction of tighter laws on foreign ownership enabled the Thai partners to gain control over these joint mills. Fearing excess capacity in the textile sector, and wanting to assist their business cronies, the government increased the level of protection and granted new export subsidies. Thailand's textile and clothing industries enjoyed considerable success in international markets in the 1980s. But much of this improvement was due to the activities of smaller firms, and some of the larger firms and former joint ventures struggled to assimilate their imported technology. Thai strategy was far from consistent, but at least the state left sufficient freedom for comparative advantage to assert itself (Hewinson 1989: 168–73; Suphachalasai 1992; Doner and Ramsay 1993).

The textile strategy of independent India militated against the success of the factory sector. Indian mills were caught in a vice between the advocates of village industry and those of socialist heavy industrialization. Official policy involved placing restrictions on the activities of textile mills in order to preserve employment for handicraft workers. Indian mills also suffered because priority was given to investment in the capital goods industries. Cloth manufactured in the mills was taxed to raise revenue for the subsidization of handicraft producers. Textile mills had no option but to buy Indian cotton, even though it was of poor quality. Consequently, Indian textiles were relatively shoddy, limiting their prospects on world markets. The production of certain types of cloth was officially reserved for handicraft workers. Quota restrictions were put on the export of yarn spun in the mills, ensuring that handloom weavers never ran out of supplies. The use of synthetic fibres was artificially curtailed for the benefit of Indian cotton growers. Textile imports were severely restricted, partly to conserve foreign exchange and partly to protect village weavers. Protection failed to compensate the mill sector for losses due to other government policies. Small power-loom sheds, although not officially encouraged, were allowed to increase their presence at the expense of the organized sector. Hardly surprisingly, India's strategy resulted in the financial collapse of many mills (Nayyar 1976: 35–86; Anubhai 1988; Mazumdar 1991; Leadbeater 1993). During the 1960s, the government began to pay more attention to overseas markets, and successful exporters were allowed to use foreign exchange for the purchase of machinery, cotton and chemicals (Bhagwati and Desai 1970: 417–22). But, in a decade marked by growing competition from other Asian countries and new import restrictions in the British market, such measures were barely adequate to enable Indian exporters to hold their own. Another way of boosting flagging exports was to negotiate bilateral deals with Soviet bloc countries. For instance, the Kandla Free Trade Zone, containing thirteen garment processing firms, did the vast majority of its trade with the USSR and Eastern Europe in the early 1980s (R. Kumar 1989: 129). Given that the Indian government's objective was to restrain the development of the modern textile sector, its efforts must be judged a glowing success. As the textile sector, and the rest of the Indian economy, moved deeper into crisis, there was a change of heart in the mid-1980s, leading to the introduction of policies designed to give market forces a greater role. The new textile policy of 1985 did not abolish discrimination in favour of handicrafts, but it did endeavour to weaken some of the constraints binding the mill sector. Planning mechanisms were cut back, barriers to entry and exit were reduced, and action was taken to liberalize access to raw materials, synthetic fibres and imported machinery at reasonable prices (Anubhai 1988; Bhagwati 1993). The Indian textile industry was at its most competitive under the Raj before the First World War, when it was largely ignored by the state. Perhaps current moves, however partial, in the direction of pre-1914 policy, will pay dividends.

Pakistan's textile industry was small in 1947, since most of the subcontinent's mills were on the Indian side of the border. Government policy was to establish a cotton industry to make use of the country's surplus of raw cotton. During the 1950s and 1960s the large-firm sector was given preference, in sharp contrast to the situation in India. The Bhutto regime reversed this policy between 1971 and 1977, and encouraged the growth of the domestic and workshop sector. Despite making losses during this period, the big firms clung on and regained some of their influence under the military rule of General Zia. The mill sector remained highly concentrated, with eleven industrialists owning half of its assets in 1977 (Adams and Iqbal 1983: 175–204).

Communist China, like socialist India, emphasized the development of heavy, rather than light, industry. Textiles' share of gross industrial output fell from 25 per cent in the early 1950s to 15 per cent in 1984, although in absolute terms output continued to rise. Larger factories were under the direct control of the ministry of textiles, but many smaller units were operated by collectives and local authorities. Shanghai and the coastal regions dominated the modern sector of the textile industry in the 1940s. But it was the policy of the communist government to increase regional self-sufficiency in every industry, and new textile plants were opened in the inland provinces (Sabin 1992: 229–32). The Great Leap Forward and the Cultural Revolution disrupted the development of the Chinese economy. Textiles suffered alongside other industries during these upheavals, but the overall trend was one of steady technical progress. Between 1955 and 1981, total factor productivity in Chinese textiles rose by 95.4 per cent, which was better than the improvements in coal mining and machine-making, but less than those in chemicals and electricity (Tidrick 1986: 12). After 1978 the regime introduced a number of economic reforms. Instead of supplying all of their output to state distribution authorities, firms were allowed to dispose of a proportion of their production as they saw fit. More leeway was given to factories to pay incentive bonuses, and a share of the profits could be retained for the unit's own use (Sabin 1992; J. Woo 1992: Glasse 1995: 63–70). Permission was given for the instigation of new textile and clothing enterprises, some of which were run by village communities and others by private entrepreneurs. These new rural production units were less capital-intensive and paid lower wages than the state mills. The rural sector was less subject to official interference, but it lacked privileged access to credit and raw materials. In the mid-1980s, state factories had higher levels of technical efficiency than the rural workshops, although this gap may have been narrowing (Wu 1993). Chinese textile and clothing exports rose rapidly in the 1980s, mainly because of their cheapness. In terms of quality, design and delivery dates, the Chinese performed exceedingly badly, due to the domination of the export sector by official foreign trade corporations (Crowley, Findlay and Gibbs 1992: 136–9).

Most Asian governments pursued strongly interventionist textile policies. The glaring exception to this rule is Hong Kong, where the colonial government adopted a *laissez-faire* stance. Hong Kong's policy was to welcome immigrant entrepreneurs, maintain order, keep taxes and labour regulations to a minimum and provide some industrial training. Infant industry protection was not on the agenda in this nirvana of free enterprise (Wong 1988: Sit and Wong 1989; Redding 1994). Hong Kong's textile and clothing sector was highly successful in world markets. Hong Kong had advantages which were denied to some other countries, including a ready-made cadre of entrepreneurs and preferential terms of entry into the British market, but its free market policies certainly fostered growth and competitiveness. Perhaps the textile and clothing industries of other Asian countries would have achieved faster growth, had their governments been less anxious either to plan or extract rent from them. Indonesia and India are obvious examples of disastrous state policies. But it could be argued that even South Korea and Taiwan were excessively *dirigiste* and too slow to adopt export-oriented strategies.

ADJUSTMENT IN THE ADVANCED COUNTRIES SINCE 1945

Developed countries which encounter rising competition from Asian textile and clothing producers have three options. First, their governments could do nothing, and allow the competitive process to take its course. Second, they could subsidize their industries, either to neutralize subsidies provided by developing countries or to encourage firms to modernize and move into higher value added niches of the market. Third, they could offer protection against so-called 'unfair' competition. Varying combinations of these strategies have been attempted, but the dominant one has been a relatively mild form of protection.

Japan was regarded in the West as a dangerous low-wage producer until the 1960s, and its exports received considerable attention from the governments of nations with ageing factory textile industries, such as the UK and the USA. Britain, with its free trade tradition, was not ready to react against rising Japanese competition during the 1920s. Following lobbying from Lancashire, and the refusal of the Japanese to exercise voluntary restraint, the British finally imposed quotas on imports of Japanese cotton textiles into the crown colonies in 1934 (Dupree 1990; Robertson 1991; Wurm 1993: 193–287). The USA imposed voluntary quotas on textile imports from Japan in 1937, although America was already highly protectionist (Hunsberger 1964: 316–17). In the depressed 1930s, import controls were treated as a legitimate weapon in the struggle to limit further redundancies in regions suffering from high unemployment. Protection was used as a form of regional policy in countries with geographically concentrated textile industries.

Japan continued to be treated as the main threat to the stability of world textile markets after 1945. The British cotton workers' unions hoped that a world authority would be established to regulate trade in cotton textiles; in particular it sought rigid controls over Japanese exports. Most British employers agreed that action must be taken against Japan. But ministers viewed plans for the weakening of the Japanese textile industry as unrealistic: unless Japan was allowed to pay its way in the world, it would become a permanent burden on the West and a source of political uncertainty (Singleton 1991: 26–7, 45–6). Restrictions on the activity of Japanese mills were abolished in 1950, notwithstanding protests from Lancashire (Seki 1956: 43). Even so, Britain and the Commonwealth continued to discriminate against Japanese textiles in the 1950s. Commonwealth tariff preferences were retained, and trade with Japan was strictly controlled under import licensing regimes. The American Cotton Manufacturers Institute (ACMI) turned its guns on Japan in 1953, in anticipation of the revival of the Japanese export trade. The ACMI pressed for the introduction of import quotas. As their campaign gathered momentum in Congress, the Japanese tried to defuse the situation by agreeing to restrain exports of certain cotton fabrics. This sign of Japanese weakness merely spurred on the ACMI, and in 1957 it persuaded the US government to impose ceilings on imports of Japanese cotton textiles (Aggarwal and Haggard 1983: 270–4).

Hong Kong was regarded as the next problem. The colony's exports of textiles and apparel rose dramatically in the 1950s, especially to the UK, where they enjoyed duty-free entry under the Commonwealth preference rules. British cotton textile producers campaigned for controls over imports from their Commonwealth rivals in India, Pakistan and Hong Kong. At first, the government ignored their complaints, arguing that sales of British machinery in the Commonwealth depended on keeping an open door to imports of textiles. In 1959, for electoral purposes, the Macmillan government relented and imposed ceilings on imports of cotton cloth from Hong Kong, India and Pakistan, in what was euphemistically referred to as a 'voluntary agreement'. However, these ceilings could be circumvented by the substitution of other types of textiles (Dupree 1991: 120–3; Singleton 1991: 136–7). American imports of cotton manufactures from Hong Kong rose from $0.7 million in 1956 to $45.8 million in 1959. In 1959, the USA and Hong Kong held trade negotiations with the objective of introducing voluntary restraints on exports of apparel, but American textile producers vetoed the draft settlement on the grounds that it was far too liberal. The American textile and apparel sector and its workers were becoming increasingly vocal in their calls for comprehensive measures of protection, as opposed to the half-measures which the British had introduced. Pressure from the US textile interest, which was particularly strong in such states as North and South Carolina, ultimately forced the government to take action, although Washington would have preferred not to antagonize its Asian clients (Aggarwal and Haggard 1983: 275–6). Protectionist sentiments on both sides of the Atlantic were given a veneer of respectability by the apparently plausible claim that a breathing space was required to facilitate modernization. A breathing space would always be required.

During the Dillon round of GATT talks, the Americans recommended the adoption of a coordinated programme of measures to control textile imports into North America and Western Europe from low-wage Asian countries. Japan's inclusion under this heading was a little anachronistic, except from the rather biased viewpoint of Western manufacturers. This initiative was portrayed as an emergency measure to deal with current market disruption. The Europeans, who were also suffering from Asian competition, agreed to the American proposal. When GATT had endorsed the principle that the cotton textile industry (like agriculture) was a special case, the temporary controls gradually took on a more permanent air. The Short Term

Arrangement (1961) and Long Term Arrangement (1962) established rules for Western countries seeking to place voluntary export restraints on their cotton textile suppliers. Quotas were to be negotiated bilaterally. The objective was to moderate the rise in imports from Asia, in order to give Western producers time to modernize before they were overrun. Provision was made for imports to grow by 5 per cent per annum in volume terms (Aggarwal 1985: 77–94). Japan and other adversely affected countries responded by switching their exports from cotton textiles to fabrics and garments produced from wool and man-made fibres. This strategy led to a serious bilateral clash between Japan and the USA at the end of the 1960s. Richard Nixon won the support of voters in the Southern textile states at the 1968 Presidential Election by promising further tough measures against Asian imports. He attempted to link the ensuing textile negotiations with Japan to the question of the return of Okinawa, despite the fact that this was bound to annoy Tokyo. Eventually the Japanese gave way, and in 1971 they consented to the introduction of controls over exports of textiles made from wool and man-made fibres to the USA (Destler, Fukui and Sato 1979).

America's settlement with Japan led to the diversion of Japanese exports to Europe in the early 1970s. This fuelled European resentment against American policy. Europe and the USA reached a wary compromise in 1974, when the Multi Fibre Arrangement was introduced, extending the existing GATT controls on cotton textiles to other fibres. Controls under the MFA were generally tighter than those under the previous arrangements, reflecting the problem of high unemployment in the West in the late 1970s and the 1980s. The MFA persisted into the 1990s. As well as restraining competition from Asia and other developing regions, the MFA was the focus of intense wrangling between the USA and the EC. Whenever the USA negotiated a bilateral agreement with a supplier, exports would be redirected towards the EC, and vice versa, resulting in mutual recriminations (Keesing and Wolf 1980; Aggarwal 1985: 123–82; Cline 1990; Hamilton 1990). Agreement was finally reached in 1993, at the Uruguay round of GATT, to phase out the MFA over a ten-year period, but there is no guarantee that this timetable will be met, or that something else will not be put in its place (Islam 1993/4: 80). Japan did not use the MFA against imports from other Asian countries, notwithstanding the pleas of its textile producers. The Japanese textile sector experienced increasing difficulties in the 1970s. In 1976 the Ministry of International Trade and Industry (MITI) introduced a programme of administrative guidance, which involved asking importers to exercise restraint. South Korea, Taiwan and Pakistan were asked to moderate their deliveries to reasonable levels. Japanese import controls have been more discreet than those of the Western countries (Yamazawa 1988: 412–19).

Table 8.1 shows nominal tariff rates on textiles and apparel in the main developed regions in 1962, 1973 and 1987. Textile and apparel tariffs fell, but by less than the average fall in tariffs on manufactures, and remained at a

Table 8.1 Nominal tariff rates on textiles and apparel, 1962–87

	Thread and yarn	Fabrics	Apparel	All manufactures
USA				
1962	11.5	24.0	25.0	11.5
1973[b]	14.5	19.0	27.0	11.5
1987[c]	9.0	11.5	22.5	6.5
European Community				
1962	3.0	17.5	18.5	18.5
1973[b]	8.0	14.5	16.5	9.5
1987[c]	7.0	10.5	13.5	6.5
Japan				
1962	2.5	19.5	25.0	16.0
1973[b]	9.0	12.0	18.0	11.0
1987[c]	7.0	9.5	14.0	6.5

Source: Cline (1990: 163)
Notes: a The greater of simple and weighted averages
       b Pre-Tokyo round
       c Post-Tokyo round

relatively high level in 1987. Quantitative restrictions on textile trade, such as MFA quotas, became increasingly prevalent as tariffs were liberalized. By 1983, 44.5 per cent of the textile imports of the main developed countries (including Japan) were in categories subject to non-tariff barriers. For manufactures in general, the equivalent figure was a mere 16.1 per cent (Nogués, Olechowski and Winters 1986: 189). These non-tariff restrictions were aimed at the most feared exporters: 76.4 per cent of South Korean textile and clothing exports to the USA were in categories subject to quota in 1982, compared with only 12.1 per cent of imports from Brazil. Combining tariff and non-tariff barriers, it is estimated that the nominal tariff equivalent rate of protection granted to American fabrics fell from 30 per cent in the early 1960s to 28 per cent in the late 1980s, while that granted to apparel producers rose from 31 per cent to 56 per cent. Tens of thousands of American textile and apparel workers' jobs were saved by protection, although it should be remembered that when consumers must pay more for their clothes they have less to spend on other products (Cline 1990: 160, 167).

In assessing the overall effects of tariffs and the MFA, we enter the realm of informed guesswork. According to one econometric study, in the mid-1980s the global welfare loss resulting from the MFA was $7.3 billion per annum (Yang 1994). Another study estimated that the loss of welfare due to the MFA was $14 billion in 1986, while that due to all textile and clothing protection was $15 billion (Trela and Whalley 1990). Despite the predictably wide discrepancy between these results, we can be certain that the costs of protection were substantial. Nevertheless, it must be emphasized that exports from less-developed countries have continued to increase their global market share. This has led some economists to portray the protectionist regime in this sector as reasonably moderate (Hughes and Krueger 1984: 413). Many Asian exporters, not least those in Hong Kong, adapted to quotas by upgrading their products, switching to different fibres and setting up factories in locations with unfilled quotas. Where quotas result in higher prices, they generate increased profits for some suppliers (K. W. Li 1991). Politicians in the developed countries sought to balance the interests of textile lobbyists, home consumers and overseas trading partners. The effect was to slow down, but not to reverse, the relative contraction of the textile sector in the OECD and its expansion in the developing countries.

Developed countries also assist their textile and clothing sectors by offering various forms of inducements to firms to improve their technical efficiency, such as investment grants and assistance with research funding. Subsidy programmes have often been linked to government pressure on companies to scrap excess capacity and merge into larger, supposedly more competitive, groups. Interventionist policies of this sort have been common in Japan and France. But American governments possessed few alternatives to protection, due to the political unacceptability of other forms of intervention. The AMTEX Partnership, launched in 1993, was viewed as a radical departure for the USA for this very reason. Under the AMTEX programme, textile and apparel companies, the universities and government research laboratories were to collaborate in research into improved products and processes (Finnie 1994b: 44–5). British governments followed an intermediate strategy, which became less interventionist over time. Italy and West Germany increasingly emphasized a third approach, based upon action at the local as opposed to the national level. Intervention has occurred for a number of reasons, including pure electioneering. The distinction between policies aimed at restructuring, but essentially preserving, existing textile specialisms and those designed to help firms to refocus on higher value added activities, is rarely clear-cut. Mixed motives are unavoidable, since governments must appeal to several different constituencies, ranging from workers desperate to keep their jobs to technocrats anxious to improve the competitive advantage of the nation (Shepherd 1983).

Japan's textile and clothing policies have been designed to bring about structural adjustment, modernizaton and the prevention of excessive competition. One of MITI's functions was to monitor events in the textile industry and provide firms with advice and leadership. Cooperation between the private sector and the state was regarded as essential to the industry's long-term prosperity. During the world textile recession of 1952–3, for instance, MITI and the Japanese cotton industry worked together to restrict production and cope with the excess supply of goods (Seki 1956: 44). Since raw cotton imports were licensed in the 1950s, the government could influence the spinners by regulating their access to supplies. A new law in 1952 required the registration of weaving and knitting machines. Similar legislation necessitated the registration of spinning equipment in 1956, giving the state further reserve powers over the industry. A bill of Temporary Measures for Textile Industry Equipment was passed in 1956, under which the state subsidized the scrapping of old machinery and the installation of new equipment. Further measures of a similar nature were taken at frequent intervals during the following three decades. Generally speaking, state grants were used to subsidize the elimination of excess capacity, while investment in new equipment was assisted by loans from the official Long Term Credit Bank and the Japan Development Bank. Assistance was not confined to the larger enterprises. Small firms received subsidies and low-interest loans through the Small Business Promotion Corporation. Between 1966 and 1981, the government spent ¥380 billion in order to eliminate one-third of the looms and two-fifths of the spindles in the textile industry. Structural improvement policies, beginning in 1967, tried to encourage smaller firms to amalgamate into larger groups and either engage in vertical integration or form networks and alliances with their neighbours. Suitable funding was made available to assist these programmes (Ike 1980; Yamazawa 1980; 1988: 397–412). The assumption underlying these measures was that unfettered market forces would not secure the best outcome. In the absence of state guidance, surplus capacity would act as a drag on profits, investment expenditure would be inadequate and full employment would be threatened. These points are debatable. But one thing is clear: the aid provided by the Japanese government to the textile industry has not prevented its relative decline. The fact that many Japanese firms still chose to transfer production overseas, with the aim of cutting costs, suggests that government intervention had no more than a marginal impact on competitiveness.

Under Gaullist rule in the 1960s and 1970s, the French adopted a strongly corporatist strategy. French textile policy was thrashed out between the Union des Industries Textiles (UIT), the nationalized banks, the Ministry of Finance and the Ministry of Industry. The UIT was an employers' group dominated by the big firms, such as Agache Willot and Dollfus–Mieg. Smaller enterprises and the trade unions had little voice in the formulation of national policy. In 1966, the French established the Comité Interprofessionel de Renovation des Structures Industrielles et Commerciales de l'Industrie Textile. This joint public–private sector body provided finance to encourage restructuring and the absorption of smaller firms by their bigger rivals. A further organization, the Comité Interministeriel pour l'Aménagement des Structures Industrielles (CIASI), was created in 1974, through which large firms and the government allocated state loans to finance restructuring and modernization: between 1975 and 1978 almost 600 million francs, or 55 per cent of all loans made by CIASI, went to the textile sector. The French policy of forging close links between the state and major firms was unproductive. Government assistance did not improve the industry's competitive advantage, and it must be doubted whether it was wise for the French to discriminate so blatantly against small businesses. By the end of the 1970s, the big French textile firms were in a poor state as they struggled to meet foreign competition (Mytelka 1982; Mahon and Mytelka 1983). During the mid-twentieth century it was often simply assumed that the formation of larger businesses was the first step to industrial revitalization. Policy-makers in France and elsewhere forgot that the appropriate organizational structure depends on the context.

Britain's post-war policy on textiles has been rather inconsistent. The socialist government of 1945–51 favoured economic planning and offered cotton spinning firms a 25 per cent re-equipment grant, on condition that they amalgamated into larger groups and introduced more efficient labour practices. Relatively few firms claimed this subsidy, partly because they placed a high value on an independent existence and partly because they were afraid to invest in new machinery until tougher measures were taken against Japanese competition (Singleton 1991: 106–8; Dupree 1992: 154–7). More generally, the 1945–51 government could not persuade firms to accept its philosophy of joint industrial planning by employers, unions and the state. Tripartism, as it was called, had similarities with the MITI regime in Japan. But British cotton textile firms were reluctant to cooperate with the government, in part because they feared that it was plotting their nationalization (Singleton 1995: 222–9). Conservative governments ruled Britain from 1951 until 1964. The Conservatives initially argued that market forces should determine the fate of the textile industry. But, facing a difficult General Election in 1959, they passed legislation to make grants available to cotton mills which scrapped old machinery and bought new equipment. As before, firms did not claim all of this subsidy because what they really wanted was more protection (Miles 1968; Singleton 1991: 154–60). The subsidy offered in 1959 was estimated to be the equivalent of a nominal tariff of a mere 5 per cent over two years (Miles 1976: 206). The political system in the UK did not favour the development of long-term strategies of industrial intervention. Some would see this as a disadvantage, and it undoubtedly was in some industries. Seen from a distance, the British government's almost deliberate neglect of the cotton industry after 1950 may have benefited the wider economy. Resources freed by Lancashire's decline were reallocated by market forces into growing industries. During the 1980s, initiatives were taken at the regional level to encourage smaller producers of textiles and clothing, but British policy in this area has been modest in comparison with the efforts of German and Italian regional authorities (Zeitlin 1988: 227–33; Zeitlin and Totterdill 1989).

Although West Germany was ideologically in favour of submitting its manufacturing industries to the rigours of international competition, the textile lobby could not be ignored. German textile and clothing firms received subsidies under the Marshall Plan and its successor schemes. Further aid was distributed by provincial governments. Bavaria's policy, for instance, was to provide assistance to small firms to improve their capital stock and to help them increase their exports (de la Torre and Bacchetta 1980: 109–10; Shepherd 1981: 32–3). Considerable assistance was also given to the textile machinery industry at the regional level, in the form of state-sponsored technology parks, technical consultancy services and technical education (Sabel *et al.* 1989). Help for the textile machinery industry indirectly strengthened the textile cluster as a whole. In the aggregate, however, the degree of subsidization remained quite low in West Germany. Textile producers received subsidies equivalent to 1.2 per cent of their industry's value added in 1980–1. Subsidies to clothing firms were worth 1.5 per cent of value added. These figures compare with an average of 2.5 per cent throughout German industry. Subsidies per employee, in 1980–1, were 390 DM in textiles, 390 DM in clothing and 1,100 DM in all manufacturing (Donges and Glisman 1987: 70). The success of the German textile and clothing sector relative to that of France seems to indicate that, within the confines of the European MFA laager, modest policies to encourage small firms are superior to grandiose strategies for shoring-up major enterprises.

Italy's experience is even more instructive. Between the mid-1950s and mid-1970s, the Italian government took into public ownership dozens of ailing mills, and in 1975 these establishments employed about 20,000 textile and clothing workers. These lame ducks were rescued to preserve jobs. As was the case in India, the state ownership of mills did not solve their underlying problems, and in 1977 the public sector of the Italian textile industry had losses equal to 52 per cent of its labour costs (de la Torre and Bacchetta 1980: 110–12). While the public sector propped up these hopeless cases, however, it was also trying to stimulate small businesses. Weiss (1988) argues that the Christian Democrats regarded small firms, and the sturdy values that they inculcated, as essential to the well-being of the Italian nation. There was no official dogma in Italy to the effect that small-scale enterprise was outdated. A tolerant view was taken of the evasion of social security and employment legislation by small textile and clothing workshops. This policy of benign neglect was supplemented by positive initiatives from some local authorities. For instance, in Emilia Romagna, the commune of Carpi joined with Ervet (a regional agency for promoting textile development) and local employers in the late 1970s to found a centre for disseminating information relating to clothing and knitwear. This facility provided 500 small firms with news about fashion trends and advice about marketing and new technology (Bigarelli and Crestanello 1994: 140). At Prato, in the 1980s, a consortium of private sector interests, the local authority and a national agency for technological development, were active in the promotion of electronic communications networks among small firms (Camagni and Rabellotti 1992: 279). Such projects have not been without teething troubles, but at least their intention has been to reinforce success rather than to reverse failure.

The EEC was dragged into textile and clothing policy in the 1970s, in the wake of deteriorating conditions in the European industry. Strict guidelines were introduced by the EEC in 1970–2, in an attempt to restrict the amount, nature and duration of aid given by member governments to their textile and other industries. Brussels condemned investment subsidies which resulted in the unwarranted expansion of capacity, the state ownership and subsidization of bankrupt enterprises, and export subsidies. The EEC endeavoured to suppress potentially open-ended schemes of aid, and ruled that assistance should be temporary, selective and as frugal as possible. Exit from the industry should be encouraged and declining textile regions should be helped to find new roles. Support from Brussels was forthcoming for R&D projects. The objective of the EEC was to substitute a smaller but more efficient European textile sector for a large and ramshackle one. Member states did not always refrain from indulging in the practices outlawed by Brussels (de la Torre and Bacchetta 1980). A growing crisis in the European man-made fibres sector in the late 1970s led to an attempt by the EEC Commissioner, Viscount Davignon, to introduce Community subsidies to assist restructuring and investment. Germany and Denmark succeeded in blocking these proposals, on the grounds that they would create further inefficiency (Dolan 1983; S. Davies 1995: 10–11). It was easier for the EEC to agree on protection against outsiders than it was on common internal measures.

Many inhabitants of advanced developed countries have found it difficult to accept that comparative advantage is constantly evolving. Although some initiatives in the textile sector have tried to encourage focus and differentiation, the main thrust of policy has been towards the preservation of historical positions. Given the need for politicians to win elections, this bias in favour of the past is hardly surprising. Countries differ in their relative emphasis on protection and industrial policy, but the outcome is usually the same. The influence of the textile and clothing lobby has its limits. Advanced economic powers have strong political and economic reasons for maintaining good relations with developing countries and cannot afford to exclude their textiles. As a result, the principal effect of interventionism has been to slow down, but not to reverse, the growth of the developing countries' world export market share.

CONCLUSION

Government textile policies often pass through two stages. First, there are measures to encourage the growth of the infant industry. Second, there are attempts to preserve the industry when it is contracting relative to its competitors. There may be an intermediate stage of free market bliss, such as that enjoyed by the British cotton textile industry in the Victorian period. Today's newly industrializing countries may be passing along the same cycle at an accelerated pace. It could well be that South Korea and Taiwan are already entering the descent phase (Khanna 1993).

It is important to remember that textiles and clothing are industries in which it is possible to compete on the basis of simple technology and a minimum of fixed capital, if labour costs are low. This has implications for the efficacy of infant industry policies. The post-war import substitution policies of South Korea and Taiwan were largely irrelevant to the textile sector. In the absence of intervention, this sector would have reached the same level under its own steam. The examples of free market India before the First World War and Hong Kong after the Second World War support this conclusion. Infant industry protection did not succeed in the USA, which lacked a comparative advantage in labour-intensive industries. Protection may have been most useful in eighteenth-century Britain, where it helped to forge an environment which encouraged fundamental technological and organizational change. In mature economies, government intervention has generally been defensive and half-hearted in nature. Direct government intervention has rarely generated a competitive advantage in textiles, although it has had strongly negative results, in post-independence India, for example.

BIBLIOGRAPHY

Abe, T. (1992) 'The development of the producing-center cotton textile industry in Japan between the two world wars', *Japanese Yearbook on Business History* 9: 3–27.

—— (1993) 'The diversification of a Japanese cotton spinning company: the case of Kanebo' (paper presented at conference on Managerial Strategies in Declining Textile Regions, Osaka University).

—— (1994) 'Obitani Shoten: the strategy and structure of a cotton weaving firm in the Sen'nan District of Osaka Prefecture' (Osaka University Discussion Paper in Economics and Business, no. 94-06).

Abe, T. and Saito, O. (1988) 'From putting-out to the factory: a cotton-weaving district in late-Meiji Japan', *Textile History* 19, 2: 143–58.

Abegglen, J. C. (1959) *The Japanese Factory*, Bombay: Asia Publishing House.

Adams, J. and Iqbal, S. (1983) *Exports, Politics and Economic Development: Pakistan 1970–1982*, Boulder, Colo.: Westview.

Aftalion, A. (1923) 'The effect of the war upon the French textile industry', in C. Gide (ed.) *Effects of the War upon French Economic Life*, Oxford: Clarendon Press.

Aggarwal, V. K. (1985) *Liberal Protectionism: The International Politics of Organized Textile Trade*, Berkeley: University of California Press.

Aggarwal, V. K. and Haggard, S. (1983) 'The politics of protection in the U.S. textile and apparel industries', in J. Zysman and L. Tyson (eds) *American Industry in International Competition*, Ithaca, N.Y.: Cornell University Press.

Allen, G. C. (1958) *Japan's Economic Recovery*, London: Oxford University Press.

—— (1980) *Japan's Economic Policy*, London, Macmillan.

Allen, G. C. and Donnithorne, A. (1954) *Western Enterprise in Far Eastern Economic Development: China and Japan*, London: Allen & Unwin.

Amsalem, M. A. (1983) *Technology Choice in Developing Countries: The Textile and Pulp and Paper Industries*, Cambridge, Mass.: MIT Press.

Amsden, A. H. (1989) *Asia's Next Giant: South Korea and Late Industrialization*, New York: Oxford University Press.

Anderson, E. (1993) 'Asia coming on strong in polyester fibers', *Chemical and Engineering News* 71, 20: 21–2.

Anderson, K. (1992) 'The changing role of fibres, textiles and clothing as economies grow', in K. Anderson (ed.) *New Silk Roads: East Asia and World Textile Markets*, Cambridge: Cambridge University Press.

Anderson, K. and Park, Y.-I. (1992) 'Effects of China's dramatic reforms on its neighbours and on world markets', in K. Anderson (ed.) *New Silk Roads: East Asia and World Textile Markets*, Cambridge: Cambridge University Press.

Anon (1986) 'America's textile industry', *Economist* 5 April: 73–6.

—— (1988) 'E. I. Du Pont De Nemours & Company', in T. Derdak (ed.) *International Directory of Company Histories*, vol. 1, London: St James.

—— (1990) 'Bicoastal Corporation', in L. Mirabile (ed.) *International Directory of Company Histories*, vol. 2, London: St James.

—— (1993a) 'Textiles: odd job', *Economist* 31 July: 60–1.

—— (1993b) 'Education takes a top-drawer at Collins & Aikman', *Textile World* 143, 6: 42–3.

—— (1994a) 'Benetton: the next era', *Economist* 23 April: 66.

—— (1994b) 'Statistics: fibre consumption for technical textiles in the European Union', *Technical Textile Markets* 19: 95–102.

—— (1995) 'Agracetus patents breed discontent', *Managing Intellectual Property* 46: 9.

—— (1996) 'Retailing in PR China', *Quarterly Bulletin: Textiles and Clothing* 4, 4: 33–46.

Antonelli, C. (1989) 'The role of technological expectations in a mixed model of international diffusion of processes: the case of open-end spinning rotors', *Research Policy* 15, 5: 273–88.

Antonelli, C., Petit, P. and Tahar, G. (1992) *The Economics of Industrial Modernization*, London: Academic Press.

Anubhai, P. (1988) 'Sickness in Indian textile industry', *Economic and Political Weekly* 26 November: M147–M156.

Arpan, J. S., Barry, M. and Tran, V. T. (1984) 'The textile complex in the Asia-Pacific region', *Research in International Business and Finance* 4, B: 101–64.

Bagchi, A. K. (1972) *Private Investment in India 1900–1939*, Cambridge: Cambridge University Press.

Balasubramanyam, V. N. (1973) *International Transfer of Technology to India*, New York: Praeger.

Bamberg, J. H. (1988) 'The rationalization of the British cotton industry in the interwar period', *Textile History* 19, 1: 83–101.

Barlow, C., Jayasuriya, S. and Tan, C. S. (1994) *The World Rubber Industry*, London: Routledge.

Barry, M. and Dickerson, K. (1987) 'Developmental patterns of Asia's apparel industry', in W. C. Kim and P. K. Y. Young (eds) *The Pacific Challenge in International Business*, Ann Arbor, Mich.: UMI Research Press.

Barthes, R. (1983) *The Fashion System*, New York: Hill & Wang.

Baugh, D. A. (1988) 'Great Britain's 'Blue-Water' policy, 1689–1815', *International History Review* 10, 1: 33–58.

Benson, J. (1994) *The Rise of Consumer Society in Britain 1880–1980*, London: Longman.

Berg, M. and Hudson, P. (1992) 'Rehabilitating the industrial revolution', *Economic History Review* 45, 1: 24–50.

Bhagwati, J. (1993) *India in Transition*, Oxford: Clarendon Press.

Bhagwati, J. and Desai, P. (1970) *India: Planning for Industrialisation*, London: Oxford University Press.

Bigarelli, D. and Crestanello, P. (1994) 'An analysis of changes in the knitwear/clothing district of Carpi during the 1980s', *Entrepreneurship and Regional Development* 6, 2: 127–44.

Bils, M. (1984) 'Tariff protection and production in the early U.S. cotton textile industry', *Journal of Economic History* 44, 4: 1033–45.

Blackburn, J. A. (1993) 'The British cotton textile industry since World War II: the search for a strategy', *Textile History* 24, 2: 235–58.

Blackhurst, C. (1992) 'Ernest Hall', *Management Today* June: 59–60.

Bluestone, B. and Harrison, B. (1982) *The Deindustrialization of America*, New York: Basic Books.

Boot, H. M. (1995) 'How skilled were Lancashire cotton factory workers in 1833?', *Economic History Review* 48, 2: 283–303.

Bow, J. (1993) 'Shanghai Erfangji: coming to terms with capitalism', *Asian Business* August: 16.

Boyson, R. (1970) *The Ashworth Cotton Enterprise*, Oxford: Clarendon Press.

Brown, G. (1973) *Korean Pricing Policies and Economic Development in the 1960s*, Baltimore, Md.: Johns Hopkins University Press.

Brown, J. C. (1992) 'Market organization, protection, and vertical integration: German cotton textiles before 1914', *Journal of Economic History* 52, 2: 339–51.

—— (1995) 'Imperfect competition and Anglo-German trade rivalry: markets for cotton textiles before 1914', *Journal of Economic History* 55, 3: 494–527.

Brummett, D. A. J. (1987) 'Japanese retailing strategy in fashion apparel', in W. C. Kim and P. K. Y. Young (eds) *The Pacific Challenge in International Business*, Ann Arbor, Mich.: UMI Research Press.

Buckley, P. J. and Roberts, B. R. (1982) *European Direct Investment in the U.S.A. Before World War I*, New York: St Martin's Press.

Bull, A. C., Pitt, M. and Szarka, J. (1991) 'Small firms and industrial districts: structural explanations of small firm viability in three countries', *Entrepreneurship and Regional Development* 3, 1: 83–99.

Buxton, A. (1988) 'Italy's Prato textile industry', *Textile Outlook International* 15: 8–18.

Cain, P. J. and Hopkins, A. G. (1993) *British Imperialism: Innovation and Expansion, 1688–1914*, London: Longman.

Cairncross, A. K. and Hunter, J. B. K. (1987) 'The early growth of Messrs J. & P. Coats, 1830–83', *Business History* 29, 2: 157–77.

Camagni, R. and Rabellotti, R. (1992) 'Technology and organization in the Italian textile-clothing industry', *Entrepreneurship and Regional Development* 4, 3: 271–85.

Casson, L. (1984) *Ancient Trade and Society*, Detroit: Wayne State University Press.

Casson, M. (1990) *Enterprise and Competitiveness*, Oxford: Clarendon Press.

—— (1991) *The Economics of Business Culture*, Oxford: Clarendon Press.

—— (1993) 'Entrepreneurship and business culture', in J. Brown and M. B. Rose (eds) *Entrepreneurship, Networks, and Modern Business*, Manchester: Manchester University Press.

Caulkin, S. (1994) 'The road to peerless Wigan', *Management Today* March: 28–30.

Cawthorne, P. M. (1995) 'Of networks and markets: the rise and rise of a south Indian town, the example of Tiruppur's cotton knitwear industry', *World Development* 23, 1: 43–56.

Chakrabarti, A. K. (1990) 'Innovation and productivity: an analysis of the chemical, textiles, and machine tool industries in the U.S.', *Research Policy* 19, 3: 257–69.

Chadeau, E. (1993) 'The large firm in twentieth-century France', *Business History* 35, 4: 184–205.

Chai, J. C. H. (1992) 'Consumption and living standards in China', *China Quarterly* 131: 721–49.

Chalmers, N. J. (1989) *Industrial Relations in Japan: The Peripheral Workforce*, London: Routledge.

Chandler, A. D. (1962) *Strategy and Structure*, Cambridge, Mass.: Harvard University Press.

—— (1977) *The Visible Hand*, Cambridge, Mass.: Harvard University Press.

—— (1986) 'The evolution of modern global competition', in M. E. Porter (ed.) *Competition in Global Industries*, Boston, Mass.: Harvard Business School Press.

—— (1990) *Scale and Scope*, Cambridge, Mass.: Harvard University Press.

Channon, D. F. (1973) *The Strategy and Structure of British Enterprise*, Boston: Graduate School of Business Administration, Harvard University.

Chapman, S. D. (1967) *The Early Factory Masters*, Newton Abbot: David & Charles.

—— (1987) *The Cotton Industry in the Industrial Revolution*, 2nd edn, Basingstoke: Macmillan.

—— (1991) 'The decline and rise of textile merchanting, 1880–1990', in M. B. Rose (ed.) *International Competition and Strategic Response in the Textile Industries since 1870*, London: Frank Cass.

—— (1992) *Merchant Enterprise in Britain*, Cambridge: Cambridge University Press.

—— (1993) 'The innovating entrepreneurs in the British ready-made clothing industry', *Textile History* 24, 1: 5–25.

Chapman, S. D. and Butt, J. (1988) 'The cotton industry, 1775–1850', in C. H. Feinstein and S. Pollard (eds) *Studies in Capital Formation in the United Kingdom, 1750–1920*, Oxford: Clarendon Press.

Chapman, S. D. and Chassagne, S. (1981) *European Textile Printers in the Eighteenth Century*, London: Heinemann.

Chatterji, B. (1992) *Trade, Tariffs and Empire: Lancashire and British Policy in India, 1919–1939*, Delhi: Oxford University Press.

Chaudhuri, K. N. (1978) *The Trading World of Asia and the English East India Company 1660–1760*, Cambridge: Cambridge University Press.

Chen, E. K. Y. (1981) 'Hong Kong multinationals in Asia', in K. Kumar and M. G. McLeod (eds) *Multinationals from Developing Countries*, Lexington: Lexington Books.

Chenery, H., Robinson, S. and Syrquin, M. (eds) (1986) *Industrialization and Growth*, Washington, D.C.: Oxford University Press for the World Bank.

Chisolm, N., Kabeer, N., Mitter, S. and Howard, S. (1986) *Linked by the Same Thread: The Multi-Fibre Arrangement and the Labour Movement*, London: Tower Hamlets International Solidarity.

Cho, D.-S. (1994) 'A dynamic approach to international competitiveness: the case of Korea', in R. Fitzgerald (ed.) *The Competitive Advantages of Far Eastern Business*, London: Frank Cass.

Chorley, P. (1987) 'The cloth exports of Flanders and northern France during the thirteenth century: a luxury trade?', *Economic History Review* 40, 3: 349–79.

Choucri, N., North, R. C. and Yamakage, S. (1992) *The Challenge of Japan*, London: Routledge.

Church, R. (1993) 'The family firm in industrial capitalism: international perspectives on hypotheses and history', *Business History* 35, 4: 17–43.

Clairmonte, F. and Cavanagh, J. (1981) *The World in their Web: Dynamics of Textile Multinationals*, London: Zed.

Clark, G. (1987) 'Why isn't the whole world developed? Lessons from the cotton mills', *Journal of Economic History* 47, 1: 141–73.

—— (1988) 'Can management develop the whole world? Reply to Wilkins', *Journal of Economic History* 48, 1: 143–8.

Classe, A. and Classe, O. (1991) 'Sulzer Brothers Limited', in A. Hast (ed.) *International Directory of Company Histories*, vol. 3, London: St James.

Clifford, M. L. (1994) *Troubled Tiger: Businessmen, Bureaucrats and Generals in South Korea*, Armonk, N.Y.: M. E. Sharpe.

Cline, W. R. (1990) *The Future of World Trade in Textiles and Apparel*, revised edn, Washington, D.C.: Institute for International Economics.

—— (1992) *The Economics of Global Warming*, Washington, D.C.: Institute for International Economics.

Cohen, I. (1990) *American Management and British Labor: A Comparative Study of the Cotton Spinning Industry*, New York: Greenwood.

Coker, J. (1993) 'World textile and clothing consumption: forecasts to 2002', *Textile Outlook International* 50: 10–41.

Cole, L. R. (1992) 'Literacy in the workplace', *Business and Economic Review* 39, 1: 3–6.

Coleman, D. C. (1969a) *Courtaulds*, vol. 1, Oxford: Oxford University Press.

—— (1969b) *Courtaulds*, vol. 2, Oxford: Oxford University Press.

—— (1977) *The Economy of England, 1450–1750*, Oxford: Oxford University Press.

—— (1980) *Courtaulds*, vol. 3, Oxford: Oxford University Press.

—— (1994) 'Textile growth', in D. T. Jenkins (ed.), *The Textile Industries*, Oxford: Blackwell.

Committee on Industry and Trade (1928) *Survey of Textile Industries*, London: HMSO.

Corado, C. and Gomes, J. F. (1995) 'Adjusting to trade liberalisation: the case of Portugal', in G. B. Navaretti, R. Faini and A. Silberston (eds) *Beyond the Multifibre Arrangement*, Paris: OECD.

Crafts, N. F. R. (1977) 'Industrial Revolution in England and France: some thoughts on the question, "Why was England first?"', *Economic History Review* 30, 3: 429–41.

—— (1985) *British Economic Growth during the Industrial Revolution*, Oxford: Clarendon Press.

—— (1995) 'Exogenous or endogenous growth? The Industrial Revolution reconsidered', *Journal of Economic History* 55, 4: 745–72.

Crowley, J., Findlay, C. and Gibbs, M. (1992) 'China's export marketing performance and the pressures for reform', in C. Findlay (ed.) *Challenges of Economic Reform and Industrial Growth: China's Wool War*, North Sydney: Allen & Unwin.

Dalzell, R. F. (1987) *Enterprising Elite: The Boston Associates and the World They Made*, Cambridge, Mass.: Harvard University Press.

Daniel, E. (1994) 'Willing and able to buy clothes by the label', *City Voice [Wellington]*, *Verve Fashion Supplement* 24 February: 2–3.

Daniels, G. W. and Jewkes, J. (1928) 'The post-war depression in the Lancashire cotton industry', *Journal of the Royal Statistical Society* 91: 153–92.

David, P. A. (1975) *Technical Choice, Innovation and Economic Growth*, Cambridge: Cambridge University Press.

Davies, P. N. (1981) 'Business success and the role of chance: the extraordinary Philipps brothers', *Business History* 23, 2: 208–32.

Davies, S. (1995) 'Restructuring of the west European man-made fibre industry', *Technical Textile Markets* 21: 8–32.

Davis, L. E. (1958) 'Stock ownership in the early New England textile industry', *Business History Review* 32, 2: 204–22.

Deane, P. and Cole, W. A. (1967) *British Economic Growth 1688–1959*, Cambridge: Cambridge University Press.

de la Torre, J. and Bacchetta, M. (1980) 'The uncommon market: European policies towards the clothing industry in the 1970s', *Journal of Common Market Studies* 19, 2: 95–122.

Destler, I. M., Fukui, H. and Sato, H. (1979) *The Textile Wrangle: Conflict in Japanese–American Relations, 1969–1971*, Ithaca, N.Y.: Cornell University Press.

Dewey, C. (1978) 'The end of the imperialism of free trade: the eclipse of the Lancashire lobby and the concession of fiscal autonomy to India', in C. Dewey and A. G. Hopkins (eds) *The Imperial Impact*, London: Athlone.

Dewing, A. S. (1914) *Corporate Promotions and Reorganizations*, Cambridge, Mass.: Harvard University Press.

Deyo, F. C. (1989) *Beneath the Miracle: Labor Subordination in the New Asian Industrialism*, Berkeley: University of California Press.

Diamond, N. (1979) 'Women and industry in Taiwan', *Modern China* 5, 3: 317–40.

Dickerson, K. G. (1995) *Textiles and Apparel in the Global Economy*, 2nd edn, Englewood Cliffs, N.J.: Merrill.

Dolan, M. B. (1983) 'European restructuring and import policies for a textile industry in crisis', *International Organization* 37, 4: 583–615.

Doner, R. F. and Ramsay, A. (1993) 'Postimperialism and development in Thailand', *World Development* 31, 5: 691–704.

Donges, J. B. and Glisman, H. H. (1987) 'Industrial adjustment in western Europe: retrospect and prospect' (Kiel Working Paper, no. 280).

Dore, R. P. (1986) *Flexible Rigidities: Industrial Policy and Structural Adjustment in the Japanese Economy 1970–80*, Stanford, Calif.: Stanford University Press.

Dunning, J. H. and Pearce, R. D. (1985) *The World's Largest Industrial Enterprises, 1962– 1983*, Aldershot: Gower.

Dupree, M. (1990) 'Fighting against fate: the cotton industry and the government during the 1930s', *Textile History* 21, 1: 101–17.

—— (1991) 'Struggling with destiny: the cotton industry, overseas trade policy and the Cotton Board, 1940–1959', in M. B. Rose (ed.) *International Competition and Strategic Response in the Textile Industries since 1870*, London: Frank Cass.

—— (1992) 'The cotton industry: a middle way between nationalisation and self-government', in H. Mercer, N. Rollings and J. Tomlinson (eds) *Labour Governments and Private Industry*, Edinburgh: Edinburgh University Press.

Edgerton, D. E. H. and Horrocks, S. M. (1994) 'British industrial research and development before 1945', *Economic History Review* 47, 2: 213–28.

Elvin, M. (1973) *The Pattern of the Chinese Past*, Stanford, Calif.: Stanford University Press.

—— (1991) 'Facts and problems: aspects of the transfer of western technology to China between the 1860s and the 1930s' (unpublished paper, Australian National University).

Emerson, M., Aujean, M., Catinat, M., Goybet, P. and Jaquemin, A. (1988) *The Economics of 1992*, Oxford: Oxford University Press.

Evans, I. G. and Riyait, S. (1993) 'Is the message being received? Benetton analysed', *International Journal of Advertising* 12, 4: 291–301.

Export News [New Zealand] 7 February 1994; 21 February 1994.

Faini, R. and Heimler, A. (1991) 'The quality and production of textiles and clothing and the completion of the internal market', in L. A. Winters and A. J. Venables (eds) *European Integration: Trade and Industry*, Cambridge: Cambridge University Press.

Farnie, D. A. (1979) *The English Cotton Industry and the World Market 1815–1896*, Oxford: Clarendon Press.

—— (1991) 'The textile machine-making industry and the world market, 1870–1960', in M. B. Rose (ed.) *International Competition and Strategic Response in the Textile Industries since 1870*, London: Frank Cass.

—— (1993a) 'John Rylands of Manchester', *Bulletin of the John Rylands University Library of Manchester* 75, 2: 1–103.

—— (1993b) 'The marketing strategies of Platt Bros & Co. Ltd of Oldham, 1906– 1940', *Textile History* 24, 2: 147–61.

Farnie, D. A. and Yonekawa, S. (1988) 'The emergence of the large firm in the cotton spinning industries of the world, 1883–1938', *Textile History* 19, 2: 171–210.

Feller, I. (1966) 'The Draper loom in New England textiles, 1894–1914: a study of diffusion of an innovation', *Journal of Economic History* 26, 3: 320–47.

—— (1974) 'The diffusion and location of technological change in the American cotton-textile industry, 1890–1970', *Technology and Culture* 15, 4: 569–93.

Findlay, C. (ed.) (1992) *Challenges of Economic Reform and Industrial Growth: China's Wool War*, Sydney: Allen & Unwin.

Finnie, T. A. (1990) 'Mergermania in US textiles and clothing', *Textile Outlook International* 32: 64–82.

—— (1994a) 'Profile of Sara Lee', *Textile Outlook International* 53: 10–27.

—— (1994b) 'Outlook for the US textile industry', *Textile Outlook International* 55: 33– 74.

Fitton, R. S. (1989) *The Arkwrights: Spinners of Fortune*, Manchester: Manchester University Press.

Fitzgerald, R. (ed.) (1994) *The Competitive Advantages of Far Eastern Business*, London: Frank Cass.

Foreman-Peck, J. (1983) *A History of the World Economy*, Brighton: Wheatsheaf.

—— (1995) *Smith & Nephew in the Health Care Industry*, Aldershot: Edward Elgar.

Fortune July 1961; August 1961; 19 April 1993; 26 July 1993.

Fowler, A. and Wyke, T. (eds) (1987) *The Barefoot Aristocrats: A History of the Amalgamated Association of Operative Cotton Spinners*, Littleborough: George Kelsall.

Franklin, C. (1995) 'Time for a new suit', *BBC World Asia/Pacific* September: 67–9.

Franko, L. G. (1989) 'Global corporate competition: who's winning, who's losing, and the R&D factor as one reason why', *Strategic Management Journal* 10: 449–74.

Fransman, M. (1994) 'Information, knowledge, vision and theories of the firm', *Industrial and Corporate Change* 3, 3: 713–57.

French, M. J. (1987) 'The emergence of a U.S. multinational enterprise: the Goodyear Tire and Rubber Company', *Economic History Review* 40, 1: 64–79.

—— (1994) 'Co-ordinating manufacturing and marketing: the role of the selling agent in US textiles', *Textile History* 25, 2: 227–42.

Frenkel, S. (1993) *Organized Labor in the Asia-Pacific Region*, Ithaca, N.Y.: ILR Press.

Fröbel, F., Heinrichs, J. and Kreye, O. (1980) *The New International Division of Labour*, Cambridge: Cambridge University Press.

Fruin, W. M. (1992) *The Japanese Enterprise System*, Oxford: Clarendon Press.

Gatrell, V. A. C. (1977) 'Labour, power, and the size of firms in Lancashire cotton in the second quarter of the nineteenth century', *Economic History Review* 30, 1: 95–139.

GATT (1994) *International Trade: Trends and Statistics 1994*, Geneva: GATT.

Gerlach, M. L. (1992) *Alliance Capitalism: The Social Organization of Japanese Business*, Berkeley: University of California Press.

Ghemawat, P. (1991) *Commitment: The Dynamic of Strategy*, New York: Free Press.

Ghosh, A. (1975) 'Concentration and growth of Indian industries, 1948–68', *Journal of Industrial Economics* 23, 3: 203–23.

Glasse, J. (1995) *Textiles and Clothing in China*, London: Textiles Intelligence Limited.

Glover, J. (1993) 'Benetton bucks the trend', *International Management* 48, 7: 48–9.

Gold, T. B. (1988) 'Entrepreneurs, multinationals, and the state', in E. A. Winckler and S. Greenhalgh (eds) *Contending Approaches to the Political Economy of Taiwan*, Armonk, N.Y.: M. E. Sharpe.

Golub, S. (1994) 'Comparative advantage, exchange rates and sectoral trade balances of major industrial countries', *IMF Staff Papers* 41, 2: 286–313.

Goold, M. and Campbell, A. (1987) *Strategies and Styles: The Role of the Centre in Managing Diversified Corporations*, Oxford: Blackwell.

Gort, M. (1962) *Diversification and Integration in American Industry*, Princeton, N.J.: Princeton University Press.

Goto, A. (1981) 'Statistical evidence on the diversification of Japanese large firms', *Journal of Industrial Economics* 29, 3: 271–8.

Gross, L. F. (1993) *The Course of Industrial Decline: The Boott Cotton Mills of Lowell, Massachusetts, 1835–1955*, Baltimore, Md.: Johns Hopkins University Press.

Haber, L. F. (1958) *The Chemical Industry During the Nineteenth Century*, Oxford: Clarendon Press.

—— (1971) *The Chemical Industry, 1900–1930*, Oxford: Clarendon Press.

Hadjicostandi, J. (1990) 'Façon: women's formal and informal work in the garment industry in Kavala, Greece', in K. Wood (ed.) *Women Workers and Global Restructuring*, Ithaca, N.Y.: ILR Press.

Haggard, S., Kim, B. K. and Moon, C. I. (1991) 'The transition to export-led growth in South Korea: 1954–1966', *Journal of Asian Studies* 50, 4: 850–73.

Hall, H. (1994) 'Information strategy and manufacturing industry – case studies in the Scottish textile industry', *International Journal of Information Management* 14, 4: 281–94.

Hall, J. D., Leloudis, J., Korstad, R., Murphy, M., Jones, L. A. and Daly, C. B. (1987) *Like a Family: the Making of the Southern Cotton Mill World*, Chapel Hill: University of North Carolina Press.

Hamilton, C. B. (ed.) (1990) *Textiles Trade and the Developing Countries: Eliminating the Multi-Fibre Arrangement in the 1990s*, Washington, D.C.: World Bank.

Hamilton, C. B. and Kim, S. (1990) 'Republic of Korea: rapid growth in spite of protection abroad', in C. B. Hamilton (ed.) *Textiles Trade and the Developing Countries: Eliminating the Multi-Fibre Arrangement in the 1990s*, Washington, D.C.: World Bank.

Hamilton, G. G. and Biggart, N. W. (1988) 'Market, culture, and authority: a comparative analysis of management and organization in the Far East', *American Journal of Sociology* 94: Supplement: S52–S94.

Hammond, J. H. (1993) 'Quick response in retail/manufacturing channels', in S. P. Bradley, J. A. Hausman and R. L. Nolan (eds) *Globalization, Technology, and Competition*, Boston, Mass.: Harvard Business School Press.

Hanson, J. R. (1988) 'Why isn't the whole world developed?', *Journal of Economic History* 48, 3: 668–72.

Hardjono, J. (1990) 'Small-scale industry in Majalaya, West Java', in R. C. Rice (ed.) *Indonesian Economic Development*, Clayton, Victoria: Monash University.

Harevan, T. K. and Langenbach, R. (1978) *Amoskeag*, New York: Pantheon.

Harley, C. K. (1971) 'The shift from sailing ships to steamships, 1850–1890', in D. N. McCloskey (ed.) *Essays on a Mature Economy*, London: Methuen.

—— (1988) 'Ocean freight rates and productivity, 1740–1913', *Journal of Economic History* 48, 4: 851–76.

—— (1992) 'International competitiveness of the antebellum American cotton textile industry', *Journal of Economic History* 52, 3: 559–84.

Harnetty, P. (1972) *Imperialism and Free Trade: Lancashire and India in the Mid-Nineteenth Century*, Manchester: Manchester University Press.

Harrigan, K. R. (1983) *Strategies for Vertical Integration*, Lexington, Ill.: Lexington Books.

Harvey, C. and Press, J. (1991) *William Morris: Design and Enterprise in Victorian Britain*, Manchester: Manchester University Press.

Hawke, G. R. (1975) 'The United States tariff and industrial protection in the late nineteenth century', *Economic History Review* 28, 1: 84–99.

Heertje, A. (1977) *Economics and Technical Change*, London: Weidenfeld & Nicolson.

Helleiner, G. K. (1981) *Intra-Firm Trade and the Developing Countries*, London: Macmillan.

Henderson, J. V. (1993) 'Some favourable impacts of a U.S.–Mexico Free Trade Agreement on U.S. urban employment', in P. M. Garber (ed.) *The Mexico–U.S. Free Trade Agreement*, Cambridge, Mass.: MIT Press.

Herodotus (1972) *The Histories*, Harmondsworth: Penguin.

Hess, A. (1957) *Some British Industries: their Expansion and Achievements 1936–1956*, London: Information for Industry.

Hewinson, K. (1989) *Bankers and Bureaucrats: Capital and the Role of the State in Thailand*, New Haven, Conn.: Yale University Press.

Heywood, C. (1981) 'The launching of an "infant industry"? The cotton industry of Troyes under protectionism, 1793–1860', *Journal of European Economic History* 10, 3: 553–81.

—— (1994) 'Cotton hosiery in Troyes c. 1860–1914', *Textile History* 25, 2: 167–84.

Higgins, D. M. (1993) 'Re-equipment as a strategy for survival in the Lancashire spinning industry, c. 1945–c. 1960', *Textile History* 24, 2: 211–34.

Hill, H. (1982) 'State enterprises in a competitive industry: an Indonesian case study', *World Development* 10, 11: 1015–23.

—— (1988) *Foreign Investment and Industrialization in Indonesia*, Singapore: Oxford University Press.

—— (1991) 'The emperor's clothes can now be made in Indonesia', *Bulletin of Indonesian Economic Studies* 27, 3: 89–127.

Hill, I. C. (1969) 'Management and departmental organization', in Textile Institute, *Management in the Textile Industry*, London: Longman.

Hills, R. L. (1994) 'Hargreaves, Arkwright, and Crompton: why three inventors?', in D. T. Jenkins (ed.) *The Textile Industries*, Oxford: Blackwell.

Ho, S. P. S. (1978) *Economic Development of Taiwan, 1860–1970*, New Haven, Conn.: Yale University Press.

—— (1980) 'Small-scale enterprises in Korea and Taiwan' (World Bank Staff Working Paper, no. 383).

Hoffman, K. and Rush, H. (1988) *Micro-electronics and Clothing*, New York: Praeger.

Hoffmann, W. G. (1958) *The Growth of Industrial Economies*, Manchester: Manchester University Press.

Honeyman, K. (1982) *Origins of Enterprise: Business Leadership in the Industrial Revolution*, Manchester: Manchester University Press.

Honeyman, K. and Goodman, J. (1986) *Technology and Enterprise: Isaac Holden and the Mechanization of Woolcombing in France, 1848–1914*, Aldershot: Scolar Press.

Hong, S. W., Yim, C. H. and Park, Y. C. (1991) 'The Korean experience in FDI and Sino-Korean relations', *Journal of Northeast Asian Studies* 10, 2: 66–81.

Hong, W. and Park, T.-C. (1986) 'The financing of export-oriented growth in Korea', in A. H. H. Tan and B. Kapur (eds) *Pacific Growth and Financial Interdependence*, Sydney: Allen & Unwin.

Horaguchi, H. (1993) 'Withdrawal of overseas Japanese firms from Asia: 1971–1988', *Japanese Economic Studies*, 21, 4: 25–57.

Hounshell, D. A. (1984) *From the American System to Mass Production, 1800–1932*, Baltimore, Md.: Johns Hopkins University Press.

Hounshell, D. A. and Smith, J. K. (1988) *Science and Corporate Strategy: Du Pont R&D, 1902–1980*, Cambridge: Cambridge University Press.

Houthakker, H. S. and Taylor, L. D. (1970) *Consumer Demand in the United States*, Cambridge, Mass.: Harvard University Press.

Howe, C. (1996) *The Origins of Japanese Trade Supremacy*, London: Hurst & Co.

Howenstine, N. G. and Zeile, W. J. (1994) 'Characteristics of foreign-owned U.S. manufacturing establishments', *Survey of Current Business* 74, 1: 34–59.

Hudson, P. (1986) *The Genesis of Industrial Capital: A Study of the West Riding Wool Textile Industry, c. 1750–1850*, Cambridge: Cambridge University Press.

Hufbauer, G. C. (1966) *Synthetic Materials and the Theory of International Trade*, London: Duckworth.

Huff, W. G. (1994) *The Economic Growth of Singapore*, Cambridge: Cambridge University Press.

Hughes, H. and Krueger, A. O. (1984) 'Effects of protection in developed countries on developing countries' exports of manufactures', in R. E. Baldwin and A. O. Krueger (eds) *The Structure and Evolution of Recent U.S. Trade Policy*, Chicago: University of Chicago Press.

Hunsberger, W. S. (1964) *Japan and the United States in World Trade*, New York: Harper & Row.

Ike, B. (1980) 'The Japanese textile industry: structural adjustment and government policy', *Asian Survey* 20, 5: 532–51.

Illeris, S. (1992) 'The Herning–Ikast textile industry: an industrial district in west Jutland', *Entrepreneurship and Regional Development* 4, 1: 73–84.

Inikori, J. E. (1989) 'Slavery and the revolution in cotton textile production in England', *Social Science History* 13, 4: 343–79.

Isaacs, M. (1993) 'Milliken: best of textiles' best for 25 years', *Textile World* 143, 9: 39–40.

Islam, S. (1993/4) 'Goodbye, Gatt: Asia welcomes creation of new world trade body', *Far Eastern Economic Review* 30 December/6 January: 79–80.

Jacobs, E. and Shipp, S. (1990) 'How family spending has changed in the U.S.', *Monthly Labor Review* 113, 3: 20–7.

Jacobson, R. R. (1992) 'Milliken & Co.', in A. Hast (ed.) *International Directory of Company Histories*, vol. 5, London: St James.

Jaikumar, R. and Upton, D. M. (1993) 'The coordination of global manufacturing', in S. P. Bradley, J. A. Hausman and R. L. Nolan (eds) *Globalization, Technology, and Competition*, Boston, Mass.: Harvard Business School Press.

Jeanes, C. F. (1995) 'Achieving and exceeding customer satisfaction at Milliken', *Managing Service Quality* 5, 4: 6–11.

Jenkins, D. T. and Ponting, K. G. (1982) *The British Wool Textile Industry 1770–1914*, London: Heinemann.

Jeremy, D. J. (1981) *Transatlantic Industrial Revolution: The Diffusion of Textile Technologies between Britain and America, 1790–1830s*, Oxford: Blackwell.

—— (1993) 'Survival strategies in Lancashire textiles: Bleachers' Association Ltd to Whitecroft plc, 1900–1980s', *Textile History* 24, 2: 163–209.

Jesudason, J. V. (1990) *Ethnicity and the Economy: The State, Chinese Business and Multinationals in Malaysia*, Singapore: Oxford University Press.

Jewkes, J. and Jewkes, S. (1966) 'A hundred years of change in the structure of the cotton industry', *Journal of Law and Economics* 9: 115–34.

Jones, E. L. (1988) *Growth Recurring: Economic Change in World History*, Oxford: Clarendon Press.

Jones, G. (1984) 'The growth and performance of British multinational firms before 1939: the case of Dunlop', *Economic History Review* 37, 1: 35–53.

Jones, L. P. and Sakong, I. (1980) *Government, Business, and Entrepreneurship in Economic Development: The Korean Case*, Cambridge, Mass.: Harvard University Press.

Kaufman, H. (1985) *Time, Chance, and Organizations*, Chatham: Chatham House.

Kawabe, N. (1989) 'The development of distribution systems in Japan before World War II', *Business and Economic History* 18, 33–4.

Kay, J. (1993) *Foundations of Corporate Success*, Oxford: Oxford University Press.

Keesing, D. B. and Wolf, M. (1980) *Textile Quotas Against Developing Countries*, London: Trade Policy Research Centre.

Kell, G. and Richtering, J. (1991) 'Technology and competitiveness in the textile industry' (UNCTAD Discussion Paper, no. 42).

Kenis, P. (1992) *The Social Construction of an Industry: The World of Chemical Fibres*, Frankfurt am Main: Campus Verlag.

Kennedy, P. M. (1976) *The Rise and Fall of British Naval Mastery*, New York: Charles Scribner's Sons.

Khanna, S. R. (1993) 'Structural changes in Asian textiles and clothing industries', *Textile Outlook International* 49: 11–32.

Kim, D. W. (1994) 'From a family partnership to a corporate company: J. & P. Coats, thread manufacturers', *Textile History* 25, 2: 185–226.

Kimura, M. (1995) 'The economics of Japanese imperialism in Korea, 1910–1939', *Economic History Review* 48, 3: 555–74.

King, J. (1994) 'Can America win the wardrobe wars?', *Computerworld* 24 January: 67–72.

Kirby, M. W. (1974) 'The Lancashire cotton industry in the inter-war years', *Business History* 16, 2: 145–59.

Kirk, R. and Simmons, C. (1981) 'Engineering and the First World War: a case study of the Lancashire cotton spinning machine industry', *World Development* 9, 8: 773–91.

Kirkpatrick, C. and Yamin, M. (1981) 'The determinants of export subsidiary formation of US multinationals in developing countries', *World Development* 9, 4: 373–82.

Kiyokawa, Y. (1983) 'Technical adaptations and managerial resources in India: a study of the experience of the cotton textile industry from a comparative viewpoint', *The Developing Economies* 21, 2: 97–133.

Knight, A. (1974) *Private Enterprise and Public Intervention: The Courtaulds Experience*, London: Allen & Unwin.

Knight, F. H. (1971) *Risk, Uncertainty, and Profit*, Chicago: University of Chicago Press.

Komiya, R., Okuno, M. and Suzumura, K. (eds) (1988) *Industrial Policy of Japan*, Tokyo: Academic Press.

Kono, S. (1989) 'Population structure', *Population Bulletin of the United Nations* 27: 108–24.

Korhonen, P. (1994) *Japan and the Pacific Free Trade Area*, London: Routledge.

Kotz, D. M. (1978) *Bank Control of Large Corporations in the United States*, Berkeley, Calif.: University of California Press.

Kravis, I. B. and Lipsey, R. E. (1971) *Competitiveness in World Trade*, New York: Columbia University Press.

Krugman, P. (1994) 'Location and competition: notes on economic geography', in R. P. Rumelt, D. Schendel and D. J. Teece (eds) *Fundamental Issues in Strategy*, Boston, Mass.: Harvard Business School Press.

Kudo, A. (1994) 'I.G. Farben in Japan: the transfer of technology and managerial skills', *Business History* 36, 1: 159–83.

Kumar, N. (1988) 'Foreign controlled enterprises in Indian manufacturing', *Economic and Political Weekly* 23, 48: M167–71.

Kumar, R. (1989) *India's Export Processing Zones*, Delhi: Oxford University Press.

Kuwahara, T. (1982) 'The business strategy of Japanese cotton spinners: overseas operations 1890–1931', in A. Okochi and S. Yonekawa (eds) *The Textile Industry and its Business Climate*, Tokyo: University of Tokyo Press.

—— (1989) 'The Japanese cotton spinners' direct investments into China before the Second World War', in A. Teichova, M. Lévy-Leboyer and H. Nussbaum (eds) *Historical Studies in International Corporate Business*, Cambridge: Cambridge University Press.

—— (1992) 'The local competitiveness and management of Japanese cotton spinning mills in China in the inter-war years', in D. J. Jeremy (ed.) *The Transfer of International Technology*, Aldershot: Edward Elgar.

Lacey, R. W. (1947) 'Cotton's war effort', *Manchester School* 15: 26–74.

Lach, S. and Rob, R. (1992) 'R&D, investment and industry dynamics' (National Bureau of Economic Research Working Paper, no. 4060).

Lall, S. (1982) 'The emergence of Third World multinationals: Indian joint ventures overseas', *World Development* 10, 2: 127–46.

Lam, D. K. K. and Lee, I. (1992) 'Guerilla capitalism and the limits of statist theory: comparing the Chinese NICs', in C. Clark and S. Chan (eds) *The Evolving Pacific Basin in the Global Political Economy*, Boulder, Colo.: Lynne Rienner.

Landes, D. S. (1969) *The Unbound Prometheus: Technological Change and Industrial Development in Western Europe from 1750 to the Present*, Cambridge: Cambridge University Press.

Landes, D. (1994) 'What room for accident in history? Explaining big changes by small events', *Economic History Review* 47, 4: 637–56.

Lazonick, W. (1983) 'Industrial organization and technological change: the decline of the British cotton industry', *Business History Review* 57, 2: 195–236.

—— (1990) *Competitive Advantage on the Shop Floor*, Cambridge, Mass.: Harvard University Press.

—— (1991) *Business Organization and the Myth of the Market Economy*, Cambridge, Mass.: Harvard University Press.

—— (1992) *Organization and Technology in Capitalist Development*, Aldershot: Edward Elgar.

—— (1993) 'Industry clusters versus global webs: organizational capabilities in the American economy', *Industrial and Corporate Change* 2, 1: 1–24.

Lazonick, W. and West, J. (1995) 'Organizational integration and competitive advantage: explaining strategy and performance in American industry', *Industrial and Corporate Change* 4, 1: 229–70.

Leadbeater, S. R. B. (1993) *The Politics of Textiles: The Indian Cotton-Mill Industry and the Legacy of Swadeshi 1900–1985*, New Delhi: Sage.

Lebergott, S. (1993) *Pursuing Happiness: American Consumers in the Twentieth Century*, Princeton, N.J.: Princeton University Press.

Lee, C. H. (1972) *A Cotton Enterprise 1795–1840: A History of M'Connel and Kennedy, Fine Cotton Spinners*, Manchester: Manchester University Press.

Lee, S.-M. (1989) 'Management styles of Korean chaebols', in K.-H. Chung and H.-C. Lee (eds) *Korean Managerial Dynamics*, New York: Praeger.

Lemire, B. (1991) *Fashion's Favourite: The Cotton Trade and the Consumer in Britain, 1660–1800*, Oxford: Oxford University Press.

Levine, J. (1995a) 'We have shares', *Forbes* 155, 7: 75–8.

—— (1995b) 'Wilted flowers', *Forbes* 155, 8: 94.

Levine, S. B. and Kawada, H. (1980) *Human Resources in Japanese Industrial Development*, Princeton, N.J.: Princeton University Press.

Lewis, M. (1995) 'Clothing manufacturing and distribution in France', *Textile Outlook International* 59: 32–73.

Leyland, J. (1994) 'Outlook for consumer spending on clothing in the European Union', *Textile Outlook International* 52: 96–117.

Li, K. W. (1991) 'Positive adjustment against protectionism: the case of the textile and clothing industry of Hong Kong', *The Developing Economies* 39, 3: 197–209.

Li, L. M. (1981) *China's Silk Trade*, Cambridge, Mass.: Council on East Asian Studies, Harvard University.

Lief, A. (1951) *The Firestone Story*, New York: McGraw-Hill.

Limqueco, P., McFarlane, B. and Odhnoff, J. (1989) *Labour and Industry in Asean*, Manila: Journal of Contemporary Asia Publishing.

Lloyd, P. J. (1992) 'Structural adjustments in Australia and New Zealand', in K. Anderson (ed.) *New Silk Roads: East Asia and World Textile Markets*, Cambridge: Cambridge University Press.

Lloyd-Jones, R. and Le Roux, A. A. (1980) 'The size of firms in the cotton industry: Manchester, 1815–41', *Economic History Review* 33, 1: 72–82.

Lluch, C., Powell, A. A. and Williams, R. A. (1977) *Patterns in Household Demand and Saving*, New York: Oxford University Press.

Lücke, M. (1993) 'The diffusion of process innovations in industrialized and developing countries: a case study of the world textile and steel industries', *World Development* 21, 7: 1225–38.

Luey, P. (1969) 'Hong Kong investment', in H. Hughes and P. S. You (eds) *Foreign Investment and Industrialisation in Singapore*, Canberra: ANU Press.

McCracken, G. (1988) *Culture and Consumption*, Bloomington: Indiana University Press.

McDonald, H. (1994) 'Made to order: in India's south and west, new companies proliferate', *Far Eastern Economic Review* 17 March: 50–2.

MacIntyre, A. (1990) *Business and Politics in Indonesia*, Sydney: Allen & Unwin.

McIvor, A. J. (1996) *Organised Capital: Employers' Associations and Industrial Relations in Northern England 1880–1939*, Cambridge: Cambridge University Press.

McLean, G. J. (1981) *Spinning Yarns: A Centennial History of Alliance Textiles Ltd and its Predecessors 1881–1981*, Dunedin: The Company.

McNamara, D. (1992) 'Reincorporation and the American state in South Korea: the textile industry in the 1950s', *Sociological Perspectives* 35, 2: 329–42.

Maddison, A. (1991) *Dynamic Forces in Capitalist Development*, Oxford: Oxford University Press.

Magrabi, F. M., Chung, Y. S., Chu, S. S. and Yang, S. J. (1991) *The Economics of Household Consumption*, New York: Praeger.

Mahon, R. and Mytelka, L. K. (1983) 'Industry, the state, and the new protectionism: textiles in Canada and France', *International Organization* 37, 4: 551–81.

Maizels, A. (1963) *Industrial Growth and World Trade*, Cambridge: Cambridge University Press.

Malerba, F. (1993) 'The national system of innovation: Italy', in R. R. Nelson (ed.) *National Innovation Systems*, New York: Oxford University Press.

Markham, J. W. (1952) *Competition in the Rayon Industry*, Cambridge, Mass.: Harvard University Press.

Marrison, A. J. (1975) 'Great Britain and her rivals in the Latin American cotton piece-goods market, 1880–1914', in B. M. Ratcliffe (ed.) *Great Britain and Her World, 1750–1914*, Manchester: Manchester University Press.

Marshall, A. (1921) *Industry and Trade*, London: Macmillan.

Marx, K. (1970) *Capital*, vol. I, London: Lawrence & Wishart.

Mason, J. (1987) 'Cotton spinning in the industrial revolution', in A. Fowler and T. Wyke (eds) *The Barefoot Aristocrats: A History of the Amalgamated Association of Operative Cotton Spinners*, Littleborough: George Kelsall.

Mason, R. (1981) *Conspicuous Consumption*, New York: St Martin's Press.

Mass, W. (1989) 'Mechanical and organizational innovation: the Drapers and the automatic loom', *Business History Review* 63, 4: 876–929.

—— (1990) 'The decline of a technological leader: capability, strategy, and shuttleless weaving, 1945–1974', *Business and Economic History* 19: 234–44.

Mass, W. and Lazonick, W. (1991) 'The British cotton industry and international competitive advantage: the state of the debates', in M. B. Rose (ed.) *International Competition and Strategic Response in the Textile Industries since 1870*, London: Frank Cass.

Mazumdar, D. (1984) 'The issue of small versus large in the Indian textile industry' (World Bank Staff Working Paper, no. 645).

—— (1991) 'Import-substituting industrialization and protection of the small-scale: the Indian experience in the textile industry', *World Development* 19, 9: 1197–1213.

Meacham, S. (1977) *A Life Apart: The English Working Class 1890–1914*, London: Thames & Hudson.

Mehta, M. M. (1961) *Structure of Indian Industries*, 2nd edn, Bombay: Popular Book Depot.

Mehta, S. D. (1954) *The Cotton Mills of India 1854 to 1954*, Bombay: Textile Association (India).

Meyer, J. (1980) 'The second Hundred Years' War', in D. Johnson, F. Crouzet and F. Bedarida (eds) *Britain and France: Ten Centuries*, Folkestone: Dawson.

Miles, C. (1968) *Lancashire Textiles: A Case Study in Industrial Change*, Cambridge: Cambridge University Press.

—— (1976) 'Protection of the British textile industry', in W. M. Corden and G. Fels (eds) *Public Assistance to Industry: Protection and Subsidies in Britain and Germany*, London: Macmillan.

Miller, C. (1995) 'Teens seen as the first truly global consumers', *Marketing News* 27, 7: 9.

Millington, J. (1995) 'Shiloh's survival recipe', *Textile Month* June: 25–7.

Minami, R. (1987) *Power Revolution in the Industrialization of Japan: 1885–1940*, Tokyo: Kinokuniya.

—— (1994) *The Economic Development of Japan: A Quantitative Study* 2nd edn, Basingstoke: Macmillan.

Mitter, S. (1986) 'Industrial restructuring and manufacturing homework: immigrant women in the UK clothing industry', *Capital and Class* 27, Winter: 37–80.

Miwa, Y. (1994) 'The retail market for wool products: the case of men's suits in Japan', in C. Findlay and M. Itoh (eds) *Wool in Japan*, Pymble, NSW: Harper Educational.

Mody, A. and Wheeler, D. (1987) 'Towards a vanishing middle: competition in the world garment industry', *World Development* 15, 10/11: 1269–84.

———— (1990) *Automation and World Competition*, Basingstoke: Macmillan.

Monod, P. K. (1989) *Jacobitism and the English People, 1688–1788*, Cambridge: Cambridge University Press.

Montavon, R. (1979) *The Role of Multinational Companies in Latin America*, Farnborough: Saxon House.

Moon, C. I. (1989) 'Trade friction and industrial adjustment: textiles and apparel in the Pacific basin', in S. Haggard and C. I. Moon (eds) *Pacific Dynamics: The International Politics of Industrial Change*, Boulder, Colo.: Westview.

Morikawa, H. (1992) *Zaibatsu*, Tokyo: University of Tokyo Press.

Morokvasic, M., Waldinger, R. and Phizacklea, A. (1990) 'Business on the ragged edge: immigrant and minority business in the garment industry of Paris, London, and New York', in R. Waldinger, H. Aldrich, R. Ward and Associates (eds) *Ethnic Entrepreneurs*, Newbury Park: Sage.

Morris, D. (1994) 'Interfibre competition in the 1990s', *Textile Outlook International* 56: 115–28.

Mort, F. and Thompson, P. (1994) 'Retailing, commercial culture and masculinity in 1950s Britain: the case of Montague Burton, the "Tailor of Taste"', *History Workshop Journal* 38: 106–27.

Mowery, D. C. (1984) 'Firm structure, government policy, and the organization of industrial research: Great Britain and the United States, 1900–1950', *Business History Review* 58, 4: 504–31.

Myers, R. H. and Peattie, M. R. (eds) (1984) *The Japanese Colonial Empire, 1895–1945*, Princeton, N.J.: Princeton University Press.

Mytelka, L. K. (1982) 'The French textile industry', in H. K. Jacobson and D. Sidjanski (eds) *The Emerging International Order*, Beverly Hills: Sage.

—— (1985) 'Stimulating effective technology transfer: the case of textiles in Africa', in N. Rosenberg and F. Frischtak (eds) *International Technology Transfer*, New York: Praeger.

Nakaoka, T. (1982) 'The role of domestic technical innovation in foreign technology transfer – the case of the Japanese cotton textile industry', *Osaka City University Economic Review*, 18: 45–62.

Navaretti, G. B. and Perosino, G. (1995) 'Redeployment of production, trade protection and firms' global strategies: the case of Italy', in G. B. Navaretti, R. Faini and A. Silberston (eds) *Beyond the Multifibre Arrangement*, Paris: OECD.

Nayyar, D. (1976) *India's Exports and Export Policies in the 1960s*, Cambridge: Cambridge University Press.

Nelson, R. R. and Winter, S. G. (1982) *An Evolutionary Theory of Economic Change*, Cambridge, Mass.: Harvard University Press.

Nogués, J. J., Olechowski, A. and Winters, L. A. (1986) 'The extent of nontariff barriers to industrial countries' imports', *World Bank Economic Review* 1, 1: 181–99.

Noonan, E. (1994) 'The world nonwovens industry: part 1 – the leading ten produ-cers', *Technical Textile Markets* 19: 28–47.

Numazaki, I. (1986) 'Networks of Taiwanese big business', *Modern China* 12, 4: 487–534.

—— (1993) 'The Tainanbang: the rise and growth of a banana-bunch-shaped business group in Taiwan', *The Developing Economies* 31, 4: 485–510.

O'Brien, P., Griffiths, T. and Hunt, P. (1991) 'Political components of the industrial revolution: parliament and the English cotton industry', *Economic History Review* 44, 3: 395–423.

O'Connor, D. (1993) 'Textiles and clothing', in K. S. Jomo (ed.) *Industrializing Malaysia*, London: Routledge.

O'Hearn, D. (1994) 'Innovation and the world-system hierarchy: British subjugation of the Irish cotton industry, 1780–1830', *American Journal of Sociology* 100, 3: 587–621.

Okazaki, T. (1995) 'The evolution of the financial system in post-war Japan', *Business History* 37, 2: 70–88.

O'Leary, D. H. (1992) 'Unitika Ltd.', in A. Hast (ed.) *International Directory of Company Histories*, vol. 5, London: St James.

Otsuka, K., Ranis, G. and Saxonhouse, G. (1988) *Comparative Technology Choice in Devel-opment: The Indian and Japanese Cotton Textile Industries*, Basingstoke: Macmillan.

Ozanian, M. K. (1993) 'Springs Industries: the joys of family ownership', *Financial World* 13 April: 16–17.

Ozawa, T. (1980) 'Government control over technology acquisition and firms' entry into new sectors: the experience of Japan's synthetic-fibre industry', *Cambridge Jour-nal of Economics* 4: 133–46.

Pack, H. (1977) 'The optimality of used equipment: calculations for the cotton textile industry', *Economic Development and Cultural Change* 26, 2: 307–25.

Palmer, I. (1972) *Textiles in Indonesia*, New York: Praeger.

Papanek, G. F. (1971) 'Pakistan's industrial entrepreneurs – education, occupational background, and finance', in W. P. Falcon and G. F. Papanek (eds) *Development Policy II: The Pakistan Experience*, Cambridge, Mass.: Harvard University Press.

Park, Y.-I. (1994) 'The changing role of the Korean textile industry', in C. Findlay and M. Itoh (eds) *Wool in Japan*, Pymble: Harper Educational.

Park, Y.-I. and Anderson, K. (1992) 'The experience of Japan in historical and inter-national perspective', in K. Anderson (ed.) *New Silk Roads: East Asia and World Textile Markets*, Cambridge: Cambridge University Press.

Parsonage, A. C. (1973) 'An economic and technological study of the competition between knitting and weaving in the United Kingdom textile industry' (unpublished Ph.D. thesis, University of Surrey).

Payne, M. (1992) 'Profile of Coats Viyella plc', *Textile Outlook International* 40: 53–74.

Pincus, J. J. (1977) *Pressure Groups and Politics in Antebellum Tariff*, New York: Columbia University Press.

Piore, M. J. and Sabel, C. F. (1984) *The Second Industrial Divide*, New York: Basic Books.

Pollard, S. (1965) *The Genesis of Modern Management*, London: Edward Arnold.

—— (1981) *Peaceful Conquest: The Industrialization of Europe 1760–1970*, Oxford: Oxford University Press.

Porter, M. E. (1980) *Competitive Strategy*, New York: Free Press.

—— (1985) *Competitive Advantage*, New York: Free Press.

—— (1986) 'Competition in global industries: a conceptual framework', in M. E. Porter (ed.) *Competition in Global Industries*, Boston, Mass.: Harvard Business School Press.

—— (1987) 'Changing patterns of international competition', in D. J. Teece (ed.) *The Competitive Challenge*, New York: Harper & Row.

—— (1990) *The Competitive Advantage of Nations*, London: Macmillan.

—— (1994) 'Toward a dynamic theory of strategy', in R. P. Rumelt, D. E. Schendel and D. J. Teece (eds) *Fundamental Issues in Strategy* Cambridge, Mass.: Harvard Business School Press.

Porter, M. E. and Millar, V. E. (1985) 'How information gives you competitive advantage', *Harvard Business Review* 85, 4: 149–60.

Porter, R. (1975) 'Child labour in Hong Kong and related problems: a brief review', *International Labour Review*, 111, 5: 427–39.

Power, E. (1942) *The Wool Trade in English Medieval History*, London: Oxford University Press.

Prais, S. J. (1987) 'Educating for productivity: Japanese and English schooling and vocational preparation', *National Institute Economic Review* 119: 40–56.

Pratten, C. F. (1971) *Economies of Scale in Manufacturing Industry*, Cambridge: Cambridge University Press.

Pruthi, S. P. S. (1962) 'A study of productivity problems in the cotton textile industries of the UK (Lancashire) and India (Bombay and Ahmedabad) since the Second World War' (unpublished Ph.D. thesis, London School of Economics).

Purkiss, A. (1993) 'Britain's backbone', *Director* March: 36–9.

Rasiah, R. (1993) 'Free trade zones and industrial development in Malaysia', in K. S. Jomo (ed.) *Industrializing Malaysia*, London: Routledge.

Ratcliffe, B. M. (1978) 'The tariff reform campaign in France, 1831–1836', *Journal of European Economic History* 76, 1: 61–138.

Ray, G. F. (1984) *The Diffusion of Mature Technologies*, Cambridge: Cambridge University Press.

Read, R. A. (1986) 'The synthetic fibre industry: innovation integration and market structure', in M. Casson and associates *Multinationals and World Trade*, London: Allen & Unwin.

Reader, W. J. (1970) *Imperial Chemical Industries*, vol. 1, London, Oxford University Press.

—— (1975) *Imperial Chemical Industries*, vol. 2, London, Oxford University Press.

Redding, S. G. (1993) *The Spirit of Chinese Capitalism*, Berlin: Walter de Gruyter.

—— (1994) 'Competitive advantage in the context of Hong Kong', in R. Fitzgerald (ed.) *The Competitive Advantages of Far Eastern Business*, London: Frank Cass.

Rees, G. (1969) *St Michael: A History of Marks & Spencer*, London: Weidenfeld & Nicolson.

Reich, R. B. (1991) *The Work of Nations: Preparing Ourselves for 21st-Century Capitalism*, New York: Knopf.

Reingold, J. (1993) 'Cone Mills: beautiful grunge', *Financial World* 22 June: 20.

Reynolds, B. L. (1986) 'The east Asian "textile cluster" trade, 1868–1973: a comparative-advantage approach', in E. R. May and J. F. Fairbank (eds) *America's China Trade in Historical Perspective*, Cambridge, Mass.: Council on East Asian Studies.

Reynolds, L. G. (1985) *Economic Growth in the Third World, 1850–1980*, New Haven, Conn.: Yale University Press.

Ring, T. (1992) 'Springs Industries, Inc.', in A. Hast (ed.) *International Directory of Company Histories*, vol. 5, London: St James.

Ritchie, L. A. (1992) 'Coats Viyella PLC', in A. Hast (ed.) *International Directory of Company Histories*, vol. 5, London: St James.

Roberts, E. (1984) *A Woman's Place: An Oral History of Working-Class Women, 1890–1940*, Oxford: Blackwell.

Robertson, A. J. (1991) 'Lancashire and the rise of Japan, 1910–1937', in M. B. Rose (ed.) *International Competition and Strategic Response in the Textile Industries since 1870*, London: Frank Cass.

Robison, R. (1986) *Indonesia: The Rise of Capital*, Sydney: Allen & Unwin.

Robson, R. (1957) *The Cotton Industry in Britain*, London: Macmillan.

—— (1958) *The Man-Made Fibres Industry*, London: Macmillan.

Roche, J. (1994) *The International Cotton Trade*, Cambridge: Woodhead.

Rodan, G. (1989) *The Political Economy of Singapore's Industrialization*, Basingstoke: Macmillan.

Rose, M. B. (1986) *The Gregs of Quarry Bank Mill: The Rise and Decline of a Family Firm 1750–1914*, Cambridge: Cambridge University Press.

—— (1989) 'Social policy and business: parish apprenticeship and the early factory system, 1750–1834', *Business History* 31, 4: 5–32.

—— (1991) 'International competition and strategic response in the textile industries since 1870', in M. B. Rose (ed.) *International Competition and Strategic Response in the Textile Industries since 1870*, London: Frank Cass.

Rosenberg, N. (1976) *Perspectives on Technology*, Cambridge: Cambridge University Press.

Rostow, W. W. (1978) *The World Economy: History and Prospect*, London: Macmillan.

Rothwell, R. (1980) 'Innovations in textile machinery', in K. Pavitt (ed.) *Technical Innovation and British Economic Performance*, London: Macmillan.

Rouland, R. W. (1991) 'Toyoda Automatic Loom Works, Ltd.', in A. Hast (ed.) *International Directory of Company Histories*, vol. 3, London: St James.

Rourke, E. (1992) 'Levi Strauss & Co.', in A. Hast (ed.) *International Directory of Company Histories*, vol. 5, London: St James.

Roy, T. (1993) *Artisans and Industrialization: Indian Weaving in the Twentieth Century*, Delhi: Oxford University Press.

Rudie, R. (1993) 'Guilford turns the tide', *Bobbin* 34, 8: 18–20.

Rullani, E. and Zanfei, A. (1988a) 'Networks between manufacturing and demand – cases from textile and clothing industries', in C. Antonelli (ed.) *New Information Technology and Industrial Change*, Dordrecht: Kluwer.

——— (1988b) 'Area networks: telematic connections in a traditional textile district', in C. Antonelli (ed.) *New Information Technology and Industrial Change*, Dordrecht: Kluwer.

Rumelt, R. P. (1974) *Strategy, Structure, and Economic Performance*, Boston, Mass.: Division of Research, Graduate School of Business Administration, Harvard University.

Rumelt, R., Schendel, D. E. and Teece, D. J. (eds) (1994) *Fundamental Issues in Strategy*, Cambridge, Mass.: Harvard Business School Press.

Sabel, C. F., Herrigel, G. B., Deeg, R. and Kazis, R. (1989) 'Regional prosperities compared: Massachusetts and Baden-Württemberg in the 1980s', *Economy and Society* 18, 4: 374–404.

Sabin, L. (1992) 'The Qinghe Woollen Textile Mill', in W. A. Byrd (ed.) *Chinese Industrial Firms Under Reform*, Oxford: Oxford University Press.

Safrai, Z. (1994) *The Economy of Roman Palestine*, London: Routledge.

Salaff, J. W. (1981) *Working Daughters of Hong Kong*, Cambridge: Cambridge University Press.

Salome, B. and Charmes, B. (1988) *In-Service Training: Five Asian Experiences*, Paris: OECD Development Centre.

Sandberg, L. G. (1974) *Lancashire in Decline*, Columbus: Ohio State University Press.

—— (1981) 'The entrepreneur and technological change', in R. Floud and D. N. McCloskey (eds) *The Economic History of Britain since 1700*, vol. 2, Cambridge: Cambridge University Press.

Saunders, C. (1978) *Engineering in Britain, West Germany and France*, Brighton: Sussex European Research Centre.

Saxonhouse, G. R. (1977) 'Productivity change and labor absorption in Japanese cotton spinning 1891–1935', *Quarterly Journal of Economics* 91, 2: 195–219.

Saxonhouse, G. R. and Wright, G. (1984a) 'New evidence on the stubborn English mule and the cotton industry, 1878–1920', *Economic History Review* 37, 4: 507–19.

———— (1984b) 'Rings and mules around the world: a comparative study in techno-logical choice', in G. R. Saxonhouse and G. Wright (eds) *Technique, Spirit, and Form in the Making of Modern Economies*, Greenwich, Conn.: JAI Press.

Schatz, K. W. and Wolter, F. (1987) *Structural Adjustment in the Federal Republic of Germany*, Geneva: ILO.

Scherer, F. M. and Ross, D. (1990) *Industrial Market Structure and Economic Performance*, 3rd edn, Boston, Mass., Houghton Mifflin.

Schieppati, C. and Viesti, G. (1988) 'Profiles of major Italian multinationals', in F. Onida and G. Viesti (eds) *The Italian Multinationals*, London: Croom Helm.

Schmid, G. and Phillips, O. (1980) 'Textile trade and the pattern of economic growth', *Weltwirtschaftliches Archiv* 116: 294–305.

Schmitz, C. (1995) 'The world's largest industrial companies of 1912', *Business History* 37, 4: 85–96.

Schmookler, J. (1966) *Invention and Economic Growth*, Cambridge, Mass.: Harvard University Press.

Schröter, H. G. (1993) 'Swiss multinational enterprise in historical perspective', in G. Jones and H. G. Schröter (eds) *The Rise of Multinationals in Continental Europe*, Aldershot: Edward Elgar.

Schumpeter, J. A. (1950) *Capitalism, Socialism and Democracy*, New York: Harper & Row.

—— (1961) *The Theory of Economic Development*, New York: Oxford University Press.

Schusteff, S. (1992a) 'Burlington Industries, Inc.', in A. Hast (ed.) *International Directory of Company Histories*, vol. 5, London: St James.

—— (1992b) 'VF Corporation', in A. Hast (ed.) *International Directory of Company Histories*, vol. 5, London: St James.

Scranton, P. (1983) *Proprietary Capitalism: The Textile Manufacture at Philadelphia, 1800–1885*, Cambridge: Cambridge University Press.

—— (1989) *Figured Tapestry: Production, Markets, and Power in Philadelphia Textiles, 1885–1941*, Cambridge: Cambridge University Press.

—— (1993) 'Build a firm, start another: the Bromleys and family firm entrepreneur-ship in the Philadelphia region', *Business History* 35, 4: 115–51.

—— (1994) 'The transition from custom to ready-to-wear clothing in Philadelphia 1890–1930', *Textile History* 25, 2: 243–73.

Seki, K. (1956) *The Cotton Industry of Japan*, Tokyo: Japan Society for the Promotion of Science.

Selwyn, M. (1993) 'Indorama Synthetics: spinning a profitable yarn', *Asian Business* July: 18–19.

Sengupta, N. K. (1974) *Corporate Management in India*, New Delhi: Vikas.

Shapiro, S. (1967) *Capital and the Cotton Industry in the Industrial Revolution*, Ithaca, N.Y.: Cornell University Press.

Shaw, R. W. and Shaw, S. A. (1983) 'Excess capacity and rationalisation in the west European synthetic fibres industry', *Journal of Industrial Economics* 32, 2: 149–66.

Shaw, R. W. and Simpson, P. (1988) 'Synthetic fibres', in P. Johnson (ed.) *The Structure of British Industry*, 2nd edn, London: Unwin Hyman.

Shepherd, G. (1981) *Textile Industry Adjustment in Developed Countries*, London: Trade Policy Research Centre.

—— (1983) 'Textiles: new ways of surviving in an old industry', in G. Shepherd, F. Duchene and C. T. Saunders (eds) *Europe's Industries: Public and Private Strategies for Change*, London: Pinter.

Shimizu, H. (1986) *Anglo-Japanese Trade Rivalry in the Middle East in the Interwar Period*, London: Athlone.

Shiraishi, T. (1989) *Japan's Trade Policies 1945 to the Present Day*, London: Athlone.

Shirley Institute (1988) *The Story of Shirley: A History of the Shirley Institute, Manchester, 1919–1988*, Manchester: Shirley Institute.

Shulman, S. (1994) 'A new king cotton?', *Technology Review* 97, 5: 16–17.

Silin, R. H. (1976) *Leadership and Values: The Organization of Large-Scale Taiwanese Enterprises*, Cambridge, Mass.: Harvard University Press.

Singleton, J. (1991) *Lancashire on the Scrapheap: The Cotton Industry, 1945–1970*, Oxford: Oxford University Press.

—— (1994) 'The cotton industry and the British war effort, 1914–1918', *Economic History Review* 47, 3: 601–18.

—— (1995) 'Debating the nationalisation of the cotton industry, 1918–50', in R. Millward and J. Singleton (eds) *The Political Economy of Nationalisation in Britain 1920–50*, Cambridge: Cambridge University Press.

Sit, V. F. S. and Wong, S. L. (1989) *Small and Medium Industries in an Export-Oriented Economy: The Case of Hong Kong*, Hong Kong: Centre for Asian Studies, University of Hong Kong.

Smith, B. (1991) 'Market development, industrial development: the case of the American corset trade, 1860–1920', *Business History Review* 65, 1: 91–129.

Smith, T. C. (1955) *Political Change and Industrial Development in Japan: Government Enterprise, 1868–1880*, Stanford, Calif.: Stanford University Press.

Smith, W. C. (1993) '25 years of industrial textiles', *Textile World* 143, 9: 79–89.

Spinanger, D. (1994) 'Profiting from protection in an open economy – Hong Kong's supply response to EU's MFA restrictions' (Kiel Working Paper, no. 653).

—— (1995) 'Prosperity for all? Real adjustment in the MFA complex after Marrakech' (Kiel Working Paper, no. 681).

Spinanger, D. and Piatti, L. (1994) 'Germany's textile complex under the MFA – making it under protection and going international' (Kiel Working Paper, no. 651).

Standing, G. (1992) 'Identifying the "human resource enterprise": a South-east Asian example', *International Labour Review* 131, 3: 281–95.

Steedman, S. and Wagner, K. (1989) 'Productivity, machinery and skills: clothing manufacture in Britain and Germany', *National Institute Economic Review* 128: 40–57.

Steele, P. J. B. (1987) 'Profile of Jamaica's export clothing industry', *Textile Outlook International* May: 20–34.

Steven, R. (1990) *Japan's New Imperialism*, Armonk, N.Y.: M. E. Sharpe.

Stewart, P. J. (1975) *Patterns on the Plain: A Centennial History of Mosgiel Woolens Ltd*, Dunedin: The Company.

Stifel, L. D. (1963) *The Textile Industry – A Case Study of Industrial Development in the Philippines*, Ithaca, N.Y.: Cornell University.

Stogdon, R. (1993) 'Retailing of clothing and home textiles in the European Community', *Textile Outlook International* 48: 137–51.

Stopford, J. M. and Dunning, J. H. (1983) *Multinational Company Performance and Global Trends*, London: Macmillan.

Sugiyama, S. (1988a) *Japan's Industrialization in the World Economy, 1859–1899*, London: Athlone.

—— (1988b) 'Textile marketing in east Asia', *Textile History* 19, 2: 279–98.

Sun, I. S. (1969) 'Trade policies and economic development in Taiwan', in T. Morgan and N. Spoelstra (eds) *Economic Interdependence in Southeast Asia*, Madison: University of Wisconsin Press.

Sung, Y.-W. (1991) *The China–Hong Kong Connection*, Cambridge: Cambridge University Press.

Sunley, P. (1992) 'Marshallian industrial districts: the case of the Lancashire cotton industry in the inter-war years', *Transactions of the Institute of British Geographers* 17: 306–20.

Suphachalasai, S. (1992) 'Thailand's growth in textile and clothing exports', in K. Anderson (ed.) *New Silk Roads: East Asia and World Trade*, Cambridge: Cambridge University Press.

Suzuki, Y. (1985) 'The formation of management structure in Japanese industrials 1920–40', *Business History* 27, 2: 257–82.

—— (1991) *Japanese Management Structures, 1920–80*, Basingstoke: Macmillan.

—— (1994) 'The competitive advantage of Japanese industries: developments, dimensions and directions', in R. Fitzgerald (ed.) *The Competitive Advantages of Far Eastern Business*, London: Frank Cass.

Swainson, N. (1980) *The Development of Corporate Capitalism in Kenya*, London: Heinemann.

Sweezy, A. R. (1938) 'The Amoskeag Manufacturing Company', *Quarterly Journal of Economics* 52, 2: 473–512.

Tamura, S. and Urata, S. (1990) 'Technology policy in Japan', in H. Soesastro and M. Pangestu (eds) *Technological Challenge in the Asia-Pacific Economy*, Sydney: Allen & Unwin.

Tanner, D. (1992) 'Matsuzakaya Company', in A. Hast (ed.) *International Directory of Company Histories*, vol. 5, London: St James.

Taplin, I. M. (1994) 'Strategic reorientations of U.S. apparel firms', in G. Gereffi and M. Korzeniewicz (eds) *Commodity Chains and Global Capitalism*, Westport, Conn.: Praeger.

Taplin, I. M. and Winterton, J. (1995) 'New clothes from old technologies: restructuring and flexibility in the US and UK clothing industries', *Industrial and Corporate Change* 4, 3: 615–38.

Tatsuki, M. (1995) 'The rise of the mass market and modern retailers in Japan', *Business History* 37, 2: 70–88.

Tattum, L. (1990) 'Akzo emphasizes industrial fibers in a slow market', *Chemicalweek* June 13: 32.

Taub, S. (1993) 'Burlington's house is back in order', *Financial World* 30 March: 12.

Taussig, F. W. (1931) *The Tariff History of the United States* 8th edn, New York: Capricorn.

Taylor, M. (1986) 'The product-cycle model: a critique', *Environment and Planning A* 18: 751–61.

Tedlow, R. S. (1990) *New and Improved: The Story of Mass Marketing in America*, New York: Basic Books.

Temin, P. (1971) 'Steam and waterpower in the early 19th century', in R. W. Fogel and S. L. Engerman (eds) *The Reinterpretation of American Economic History*, New York: Harper & Row.

—— (1988) 'Product quality and vertical integration in the early cotton textile industry', *Journal of Economic History* 48, 4: 891–907.

Textile Institute (1969) *Management in the Textile Industry*, London: Longman.

Thayer, A. (1994) 'Transgenic cotton highlights patent issues', *Chemical & Engineering News* 72, 11: 18.

Thompson, E. P. (1991) *Customs in Common*, Harmondsworth: Penguin.

Thomson, R. (1987) 'Learning by selling and invention: the case of the sewing machine', *Journal of Economic History* 47, 2: 433–45.

Tiano, S. (1990) 'Maquiladora women: a new category of workers', in K. Wood (ed.) *Women Workers and Global Restructuring*, Ithaca, N.Y.: ILR Press.

Tidrick, G. (1986) 'Productivity growth and technological change in Chinese industry' (World Bank Staff Working Paper, no. 761).

Ting, W. L. and Schive, C. (1981) 'Direct investment and technology transfer from Taiwan', in K. Kumar and M. G. McLeod (eds) *Multinationals from Developing Countries*, Lexington, Ill.: Lexington Books.

Tomlin, E. W. F. (1978) *Arnold Toynbee: A Selection from his Works*, Oxford: Oxford University Press.

Tomlinson, B. R. (1993) *The Economy of Modern India, 1860–1970*, Cambridge: Cambridge University Press.

Toyne, B., Arpan, J. S., Ricks, D. A., Shimp, T. A. and Barnett, A. (1984) *The Global Textile Industry*, London: Allen & Unwin.

Tran, V. T. (1988) 'Foreign capital and technology in the process of catching up by the developing countries: the experience of the synthetic fiber industry in the Republic of Korea', *The Developing Economies* 26, 4: 386–502.

Trela, I. and Whalley, J. (1990) 'Unravelling the threads of the MFA', in C. B. Hamilton (ed.) *Textiles Trade and the Developing Countries*, Washington, D.C.: World Bank.

Truelove, C. (1987) 'The informal sector revisited: the case of the Talleres Rurales mini-maquilas in Colombia', in R. Tardanico (ed.) *Crises in the Caribbean Basin*, Newbury Park: Sage.

Tse, K. K. (1985) *Marks & Spencer*, Oxford: Pergamon.

Tsokhas, K. (1990) *Markets, Money and Empire: The Political Economy of the Australian Wool Industry*, Melbourne: Melbourne University Press.

Tsuru, S. (1993) *Japan's Capitalism*, Cambridge: Cambridge University Press.

Tsurumi, E. P. (1984) 'Female textile workers and the failure of early trade unionism in Japan', *History Workshop Journal* 18: 3–27.

Tsurumi, Y. (1976) *The Japanese Are Coming: A Multinational Interaction of Firms and Politics*, Cambridge, Mass.: Ballengarra.

Tucker, B. M. (1981) 'The merchant, the manufacturer, and the factory manager: the case of Samuel Slater', *Business History Review* 55, 3: 297–313.

UNCTAD, Division on Transnational Corporations and Investment (1994) *World Investment Directory*, vol. 4, *Latin America and the Caribbean, 1994*, New York: United Nations.

UNIDO (1986) *International Comparative Advantage*, Vienna: UNIDO.

—— (1993) *Handbook of Industrial Statistics 1992*, Aldershot: Edward Elgar.

United Kingdom, Central Statistical Office (1990) *Annual Abstract of Statistics, 1990*, London: HMSO.

——— (1993) *Size Analysis of United Kingdom Businesses 1993, Business Monitor PA1003*, London: HMSO.

United Nations, Department of Economic and Social Affairs (1975) *Yearbook of International Trade Statistics 1974*, vol. II, New York: United Nations.

—— Department for Economic and Social Information and Policy Analysis (1995) *1993 International Trade Statistics Yearbook*, vol. II, New York: United Nations.

United States, Department of Commerce (1992) *Census of Manufactures 1987, Subject Series, Concentration Ratios in Manufacturing, MC87-S-6*.

—— Office of Technology Assessment (1987) *The U.S. Textile and Apparel Industry: A Revolution in Progress – Special Report, OTA-TET-332*.

Utterback, J. M. (1994) *Mastering the Dynamics of Innovation*, Boston, Mass.: Harvard Business School Press.

Veblen, T. (1922) *The Theory of the Leisure Class*, New York: Random House.

Velasco, E. T. (1990) 'The textile industry', in H. Soesastro and M. Pangestu (eds) *Technological Challenge in the Asia-Pacific Economy*, Sydney: Allen & Unwin.

Vernon, R. (1966) 'International investment and international trade in the product cycle', *Quarterly Journal of Economics* 80, 2: 190–207.

—— (1979) 'The product cycle hypothesis in a new international environment', *Oxford Bulletin of Economics and Statistics* 41, 3: 255–67.

Vibert, F. (1966) 'Economic problems of the cotton industry', *Oxford Economic Papers* 18, 3: 313–43.

von Tunzelmann, G. N. (1978) *Steam Power and British Industrialization to 1860*, Oxford: Clarendon Press.

—— (1995) 'Time-saving technical change: the cotton industry in the English industrial revolution', *Explorations in Economic History* 32, 1: 1–27.

Wadsworth, A. P. and Mann, J. de L. (1931) *The Cotton Trade and Industrial Lancashire, 1600–1780*, Manchester: Manchester University Press.

Wakasugi, R. (1989) 'Technological innovation in the Asian-Pacific region: facts and economic interpretations', in M. Shinohara and F.-C. Lo (eds) *Global Adjustment and the Future of the Asian-Pacific Economy*, Tokyo: Institute of Developing Economies.

Waldinger, R. (1984) 'Immigrant enterprise in the New York garment industry', *Social Problems* 32, 1: 60–71.

Walkley, C. (1981) *The Ghost in the Looking Glass: The Victorian Seamstress*, London: P. Owen.

Webster, A. (1990) 'The political economy of trade liberalization: the East India Company Charter Act of 1813', *Economic History Review* 43, 3: 404–19.

Weiner, E. and Green, H. (1984) 'A stitch in our time: New York's Hispanic garment workers in the 1980s', in J. M. Jenson and S. Davidson (eds) *A Needle, a Bobbin, a Strike*, Philadelphia: Temple University Press.

Weiss, L. (1988) *Creating Capitalism*, Oxford: Blackwell.

Wells, F. A. (1972) *The British Hosiery and Knitwear Industry*, Newton Abbot: David & Charles.

Wells, L. T. (1978) 'Foreign investment from the Third World: the experience of Chinese firms from Hong Kong', *Colombia Journal of World Business*, 13, Spring: 39–49.

Wells, S. J. (1964) *British Export Performance*, Cambridge: Cambridge University Press.

Westphal, L. E., Rhee, Y. W., Kim, L. and Amsden, A. (1984) 'Exports of capital goods and related services from the Republic of Korea' (World Bank Staff Working Paper, no. 629).

White, G. S. (1967) *Memoir of Samuel Slater*, New York: Augustus M. Kelley.

Wilkins, M. (1974) *The Maturing of Multinational Enterprise: American Business Abroad from 1914 to 1970*, Cambridge, Mass.: Harvard University Press.

—— (1987) 'Efficiency and management: a comment on Gregory Clark's "Why isn't the whole world developed?"', *Journal of Economic History* 47, 2: 981–3.

Willoughby, L. (1993) *Fair to Middlin': The Antebellum Cotton Trade of the Apalachicola/Chattahoochee River Valley*, Tuscaloosa: University of Alabama Press.

Wilson, J. (1992) *The Manchester Experiment: A History of Manchester Business School 1965–1990*, London: Paul Chapman.

Wolcott, S. (1992) 'British myopia and the collapse of Indian textile demand', *Journal of Economic History* 52, 2: 367–84.

—— (1994) 'The perils of lifetime employment systems: productivity advance in the Indian and Japanese textile industries, 1920–1938', *Journal of Economic History* 54, 2: 307–24.

Wolf, G. (1992) 'Kmart Corporation', in A. Hast (ed.) *International Directory of Company Histories*, vol. 5, London: St James.

Wong, S. L. (1988) *Emigrant Entrepreneurs: Shanghai Industrialists in Hong Kong*, Hong Kong: Oxford University Press.

Woo, J. (1992) 'The Nanning Silk and Ramie Textile Mill', in W. A. Byrd (ed.) *Chinese Industrial Firms Under Reform*, Oxford: Oxford University Press.

Woo, K. D. (1978) 'Wages and productivity in the cotton spinning industries of Japan, Korea and Taiwan', *The Developing Economies* 16, 2: 182–98.

World Bank (1993) *The East Asian Miracle*, New York: Oxford University Press.

Wright, A. C. (1995) 'Strategy and structure in the textile industry: Spencer Love and Burlington Mills, 1923–1962', *Business History Review* 69, 1: 42–79.

Wright, G. (1986) *Old South, New South: Revolutions in the Southern Economy since the Civil War*, New York: Basic Books.

Wu, Y. (1993) 'One industry, two regimes: the Chinese textile sector: growth, reforms and efficiency' (Chinese Economy Research Unit, University of Adelaide, Discussion Paper, no. 93/2).

Wurm, C. (1993) *Business, Politics and International Relations: Steel, Cotton and International Cartels in British Politics 1924–1939*, Cambridge: Cambridge University Press.

Yamamura, K. (1978) 'Entrepreneurship, ownership, and management in Japan', in P. Mathias and M. M. Postan (eds) *The Cambridge Economic History of Europe*, vol. 7, part 2, Cambridge: Cambridge University Press.

Yamazaki, H. (1992a) 'Teijin Limited', in A. Hast (ed.) *International Directory of Company Histories*, vol. 5, London: St James.

—— (1992b) 'Toray Industries, Inc.', in A. Hast (ed.) *International Directory of Company Histories*, vol. 5, London: St James.

Yamazawa, I. (1980) 'Increasing imports and structural adjustment of the Japanese textile industry', *The Developing Economies* 18, 4: 441–62.

—— (1988) 'The textile industry', in R. Komiya, M. Okuno and K. Suzumura (eds) *Industrial Policy of Japan*, Tokyo: Academic Press.

—— (1990) *Economic Development and International Trade: The Japanese Model*, Honolulu: East–West Center.

Yang, Y. (1994) 'The impact of MFA phasing out on world clothing and textile markets', *Journal of Development Studies* 30, 4: 892–915.

Yasumuro, K. (1993) 'Engineers as functional alternatives to entrepreneurs in Japanese industrialisation', in J. Brown and M. B. Rose (eds) *Entrepreneurship, Networks, and Modern Business*, Manchester: Manchester University Press.

Yonekawa, S.-I. (1984) 'University graduates in Japanese enterprises before the Second World War', *Business History* 26, 2: 193–218.

—— (1987) 'Flotation booms in the cotton spinning industry, 1870–1890: a comparative study', *Business History Review* 61, 4: 551–81.

Yoshihara, K. (1978) *Japanese Investment in Southeast Asia*, Honolulu: University of Hawaii Press.

—— (1982) *Sogo Shosha: The Vanguard of the Japanese Economy*, Tokyo: Oxford University Press.

—— (1988) *The Rise of Ersatz Capitalism in South-East Asia*, Singapore: Oxford University Press.

Young, A. K. (1979) *The Sogo Shosha: Japan's Multinational Trading Companies*, Boulder, Colo.: Westview.

Zahedieh, N. (1994) 'London and the colonial consumer in the late seventeenth century', *Economic History Review* 47, 2: 239–61.

Zeitlin, J. (1988) 'The clothing industry in transition: international trends and British response', *Textile History* 19, 2: 211–38.

Zeitlin, J. and Totterdill, P. (1989) 'Markets, technology, and local intervention: the case of clothing', in P. Hirst and J. Zeitlin (eds) *Reversing Industrial Decline?*, Oxford: Berg.

Zevin, R. B. (1971) 'The growth of cotton textile production after 1815', in R. W. Fogel and S. L. Engerman (eds) *The Reinterpretation of American Economic History*, New York: Harper & Row.

INDEX